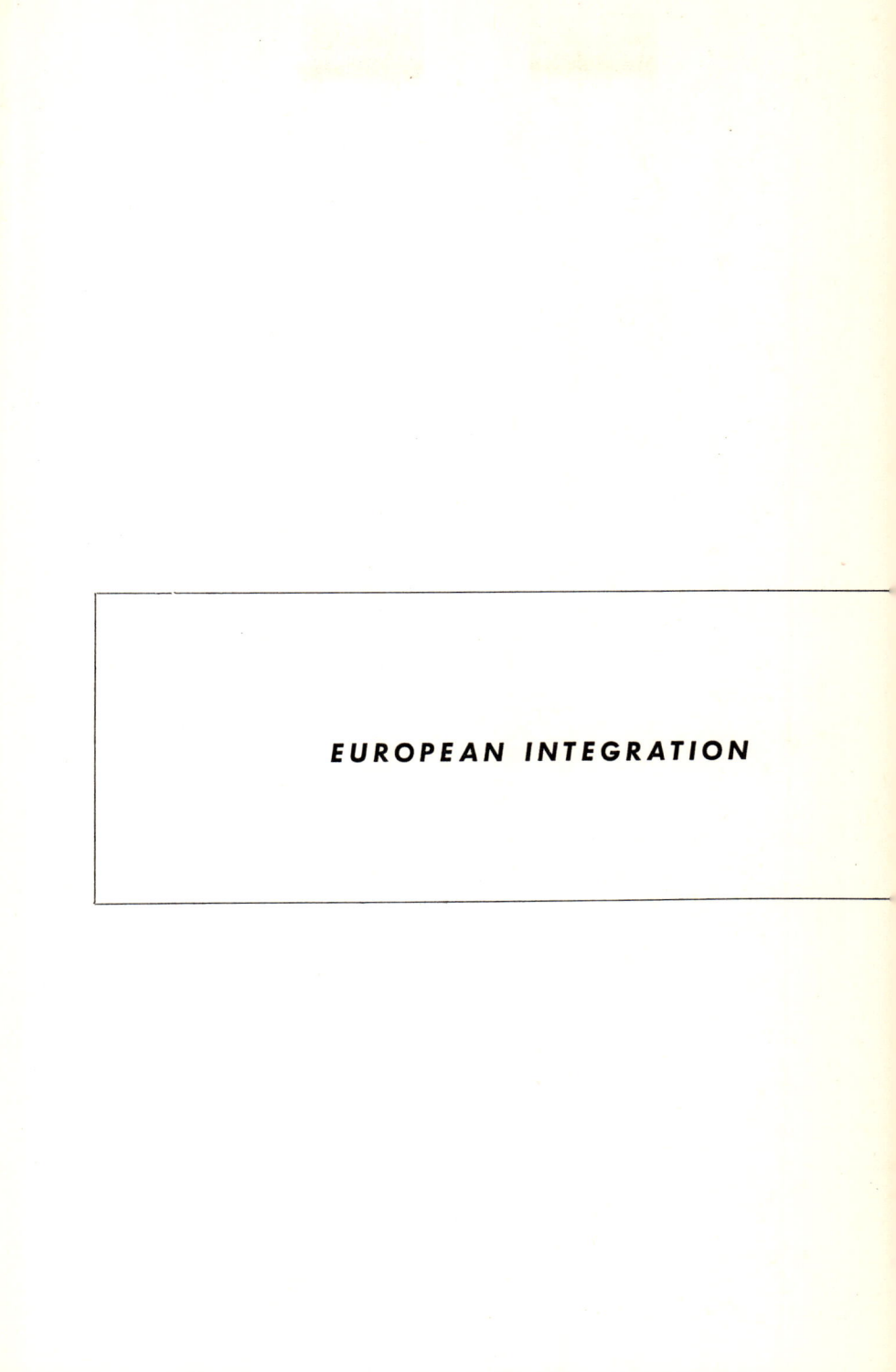

EUROPEAN INTEGRATION

European Integration

Edited by **C. GROVE HAINES**

with an Introduction by
PAUL VAN ZEELAND

THE JOHNS HOPKINS PRESS / *Baltimore*

© 1957 by The Johns Hopkins Press, Baltimore 18, Md.

Distributed in Great Britain by
Oxford University Press, London

Printed in U.S.A. by The William Byrd Press
Richmond, Va.

Library of Congress Catalog Card Number 57-9515

Foreword

THIS VOLUME is the product of a conference on "The Status of European Integration" which was convoked in Bologna during May-June, 1956 under the sponsorship of the Bologna Center of The Johns Hopkins University. The articles which appear here were originally presented as papers at the conference, where they were debated and discussed by a distinguished group of participants coming from all parts of Europe, the Middle East, and the United States. Some will be found to be highly critical of the integration movement, even pessimistic about future prospects; others are more hopeful that the obstacles which are strewn in the path of European "unification," whether economic or political, functional or sectoral, can be successfully overcome. It was not the purpose of the Bologna Center to propagate any of the differing points of view which were expressed, but to provide a platform for their presentation and critical, objective examination.

During the interval between the convoking of the conference and the publication of this volume, the integration movement acquired fresh impetus. It will be helpful to review very briefly what has happened, for there has been clarification of some of the issues which have been examined by a number of contributors.

While the conference was meeting late in May, 1956, another conference was meeting in Venice, a conference of the foreign ministers of Italy, France, the West German Republic, and the Benelux Countries, to examine a very important report which the Belgian Foreign Minister, Paul-Henri Spaak, had been requested to draft on the common market and Euratom. This report, which had been published some weeks previously, was the result of decisions taken by the foreign ministers of these six countries at a meeting held in Messina, Sicily, just one year previously, when it was resolved to "re-launch" Europe, that is to take a fresh initiative after the disillusioning failure of the European Defense Community in August, 1954.

The "Spaak Report" examined the main issues involved in the establishment of a common market and a European Atomic Community, suggested the broad outlines of the treaties which might be drafted, and recommended procedures to follow in drafting them. It was accepted by the Council of Foreign Ministers and during the succeeding months an intergovernmental conference of the Six assembled at Brussels for the purpose of drafting the treaties. This was a painful and difficult task, since there were many divergent national interests to reconcile, but it was brought to completion and on March 25, 1957 at Rome the common-market and Euratom treaties were signed by the governments of the Six. The several parliaments must still approve and there will surely be many difficult obstacles to surmount, should ratification be assured, but whatever the future may hold in store in this regard, the mere fact of succeeding in drafting acceptable treaties is a historic event.

The Suez and Hungarian crises of October-November, 1956 accentuated the sense of urgency among responsible European political leaders, not least of all because the complications arising over Suez threw into high relief fundamental divergencies between the international policies of the United States and the European nations in extra-European areas where European interests have long been established and, at the same time, dramatically exposed the relative weaknesses of the greater European states in a situation of power struggle. On the Continent, the attractions of "integration" certainly increased, and Great Britain, while standing aloof from Euratom and the common market, was persuaded to take a fresh look at its ties with the Continent and to encourage negotiations which were already in process for the establishment of a free-trade area embracing much of Europe and the Commonwealth.

The present volume, perforce, does not deal with these events, but rather with the historical setting and the main issues which have been and many long continue to be the subject of debate wherever the subject of European integration is discussed.

I cannot conclude this foreword without expressing my personal gratitude to all of the distinguished men who contributed to this book, and to those who participated in the conference, as well as to all of the members of the Bologna Center staff, past and present, who bore so large a part of the burdens involved in bringing it to

FOREWORD   vii

successful issue. Our indebtedness to the University of Bologna, especially to its Rector in those days, Professor Felice Battaglia, and to Professor Walter Bigiavi, President of the Facultà di Economia e Commercio, who made the facilities of his school available to our use for the conference, is a particularly heavy one. It would be impossible to conceive of co-operation more generous or more complete.

Bologna, Italy   *C. Grove Haines*
April 17, 1957   DIRECTOR OF THE BOLOGNA CENTER

Preface

PAUL VAN ZEELAND / *Minister of State, Belgium*

EUROPE WILL BE. It will be because it has to be. Indeed, it is already coming about. But will the forces leading to its creation be powerful enough to succeed before it is too late? Which are the most effective, the most certain methods for achieving this goal? Should one proceed by stages—or should one pass them by and go immediately to a comprehensive solution?

Scores of questions and difficulties appear immediately, and they seem to multiply the more one reflects. Yet, satisfactory answers must be found. It is impossible to ignore them, to place our faith in luck or in blind destiny to resolve them, for good or ill. A thought comes to mind. I could not find the citation, but I think it was Machiavelli who said that "When men of wisdom abandon the leadership of human affairs, human passions begin to rule. . . ." Fortunately, "men of wisdom" have not abandoned Europe to the whims of fate. Certainly, blind, violent, stubborn passions abound in Western civilization. We should have to shut our eyes and stop our ears if we wished neither to see nor to hear them. But men of good will are on guard, more alert than ever. Europeans and Americans amongst them have had the wisdom to come together under the auspices of a common intellectual center and to attack in its manifold aspects the problem of European integration.

Whoever reads the studies which compose this work will be struck by the mastery with which the debate is begun, developed, expanded, and deepened. It covers, as it should, the analysis of facts, the search for solutions, and the criticism of points of view. History is called upon to testify to the unity in diversity which is the very nature of Europe. Reason is invoked in favor of European integration, as much in economic as in political affairs, at least to the extent that it is necessary. The authors strive, one after the other, to define the conditions and the limits of an undertaking as ambitious as the integration of Europe. The study ends with a consideration of the reactions which this integration will provoke in the relations of Europe with other parts of the free world.

Thus composed and realized, the work of this conference impresses one with its unity and its sincerity. Several of the studies which compose it develop strikingly original points of view. Indeed, no educated person will be able to accept, as a whole and without reservations, all the arguments and all the suggestions with which this work abounds. But, once the work is read, a concise and powerful conclusion comes forth from the whole. Europe is a task at once magnificent and necessary. The difficulties which lie on the way are in proportion to the magnitude of the goal to be achieved. If the problems are numerous and on occasion unprecedented, there is no one of them which is not susceptible to a practical and reasonable solution. The building of Europe is now a question of will!

It is impossible to imagine a more favorable moment for the session of such a conference, nor could there be a more propitious moment for publishing the results. The defeat of the European Defense Community had given a mortal blow to the European idea. Its opponents—defenders of vested interests, the timid and the uneasy—all believed Europe to be buried. Yet the masses, in whom an enduring political sense produces sometimes a sort of deep intuition, had lost neither faith nor hope. They remained deeply convinced of the need to recreate, in one form or another, a united Europe, which would be adapted to the needs of our time.

Unfortunately, too many Europeans were dreaming of the memories of a splendid past, hoping that, despite all, everything would work out, Heaven knows how. Events of the last months, however, proved a cruel awakening for many. Complications and dangers in the Middle East on the one hand and the Hungarian tragedy on the other opened many eyes. The loss of prestige and the material and moral weakness of Europe revealed themselves beyond all doubt. It was necessary to recognize that if Europe remained in the state of division with which it had been satisfied, its role in the world would not cease to shrink. Europe would indeed soon lose control over its own destiny!

PREFACE   xi

Today, as a result, it seems that the climate of opinion is more favorable than it has ever been to the reconstruction of a united Europe. The lesson of these last defeats has not been completely lost. The political approach, that of military defense, has failed? So be it. Let us not persist. We must then change our tactics and redirect our efforts. A simple reasoning follows. Politics and economics are closely related. Let us try, then, for progress in economic matters. Let us suppress those obstacles of an economic nature which divide and compartmentalize the nations of Europe.

Thus the decision was reached to establish a common market in the countries of Europe. Without delay, the six nations of Little Europe affixed their signatures in a solemn ceremony to a treaty establishing the European Economic Community, that is, the common market. Is the text of this treaty perfect? Does it fulfill completely the hopes of its partisans, or the definitions and rules proposed by the defenders of the common market? No one claims this, for it falls far short. Politics is the art of the possible. It was better to sign an imperfect treaty than to do nothing. Truly, a great step forward has been achieved in uniting the economic futures of six countries of Europe.

But how long indeed is the road to be followed before arriving at our goal! Europe is not six countries only. The means must be found—and soon—which will enable co-operation with the true, the traditional Europe—the Europe of the Fifteen, for example. Yet, the Six did well to go ahead. At least a wedge will have been driven into the inertia in which some were drowsing. We may think that it will be followed by another—it matters little whether it will be sooner or later, in one form or another.

It would be a serious mistake to delude oneself as to the function of the treaty of the European Economic Community. Actually, the common market is not a panacea. It brings nothing, in itself, to the solution of the problems which face Europe. After its application begins, the real problems will be neither fewer nor lighter. On the other hand, the common market will add a certain number of new ones; it obviously will not come about without exacting heavy sacrifices on the part of a whole series of industries which have been protected artificially up to now.

And yet the introduction of the common market into the life of Europe is an event of major significance. Indeed, so long as the common market does not function, insoluble obstacles will oppose the assumption, in Europe, of true solutions, of the essential measures of health and progress. In other words, if the common market does not itself bring the solution, it does permit the ultimate application of those solutions without which Europe cannot rediscover a real impulse of economic expansion. Once these obstacles have disappeared, all dreams are permitted, all hopes are realizable. Let no one doubt this: if the common market, despite the imperfections of the treaty, is realized during the next few years, if it brings to its member nations a strengthening of their economic positions, it is almost certain that no steps will be taken backwards and that the necessary modification will be made, as needs develop.

I would have liked to cite a few of the original ideas or considerations which struck me while I was reading the various chapters. But there would have been too many of them; I have had to deny myself the pleasure. Still, those who took part in this worthy intellectual undertaking deserve thanks for the eminent service they have rendered the cause of Europe. Their studies, their advice, their analyses will all find fruition or synthesis in the new political construction which, I hope, will bring back to Europe its greatness, its strength, and its prestige.

The day when Europe resumes the position amongst the Great Powers which belongs to it by virtue of the role it has played for thousands of years, peace will again have a chance in a balanced world. We know that nothing great and permanent can be built without difficulty, effort, and time. But there are moments in history when time must be saved by courage and effort. This moment has come for Europe. May Europeans remember this and act accordingly!

It would be unfair not to take this occasion to give their due to the two universities who have sponsored this undertaking, the University of Bologna and The Johns Hopkins University. They have seen far and clearly, on a broad horizon, as is appropriate to intellectual leaders. I may be permitted to say briefly that in acting thus they have followed an old European tradition.

In 1650, Jean Jacobs, a goldsmith of Brussels, had the same vision. He founded a scholarship to enable young Belgians to train themselves at the cultural center which Bologna already was at that time. Since then, the path thus marked out has been followed by many young persons seeking knowledge and culture. Let us hope that, three centuries hence, the same terms of praise and gratitude will be used in speaking of the Bologna Center and of the School of Advanced International Studies of The Johns Hopkins University.

Contents

Foreword, v
C. GROVE HAINES

Preface, ix
PAUL VAN ZEELAND

Introduction, 1
FELICE BATTAGLIA

1. EUROPE: UNITY IN DIVERSITY

Europe as a Historical Concept, 11
J. B. DUROSELLE

Nationalism and the Integration of Europe, 21
HANS KOHN

2. THE RATIONALE OF EUROPEAN INTEGRATION

The Growth of the European Movement since World War II, 37
ALTIERO SPINELLI

The Case for European Integration: Economic Considerations, 64
UGO LA MALFA

The Case for European Integration: Political Considerations, 80
E. N. VAN KLEFFENS

An Inquiry into Feasible Forms of European Integration, 97
JOHN A. LOFTUS

3. ECONOMIC INTEGRATION

Economic Integration: Problems and Possibilities, 114
PAUL DELOUVRIER

European Integration: Commercial and Financial Postulates, 125
MICHAEL A. HEILPERIN

The Coal and Steel Community as a Case Study in Integration, 137
GIUSEPPE PELLA

European Integration and the World Economy, 150
GIOVANNI DEMARIA

4. POLITICAL ASPECTS OF THE QUESTION OF EUROPEAN INTEGRATION

The Dynamics of European Integration, 161
HENRI BRUGMANS

Germany and Europe, 177
ALFRED GROSSER

Neutralism, 196
ALDO GAROSCI

In Search of a Political Framework for an Integrated Europe, 215
HANS NORD

5. EUROPEAN INTEGRATION AND THE NON-COMMUNIST WORLD

Asian Views of an Integrated Europe, 231
CHARLES MALIK

The North Atlantic Community and Western Europe, 250
L. D. WILGRESS

The United States and the Integration of Europe, 262
HENRY STEELE COMMAGER

The British Commonwealth and Western Europe, 279
CHARLES E. CARRINGTON

Index, 293

Introduction

FELICE BATTAGLIA / *Rector, University of Bologna*

THERE IS no doubt that Europe constitutes a reality, a reality which may be perceived in several dimensions, such as the geographical, the ethnological, and especially the historical. The latter is characterized by a diversity of cultural profiles, the economic, the religious, the juridical, and the ethical. In the geographical sense, Europe may be defined as that part of the Euro-Asiatic Continent which extends from the Caucasus and Ural Mountains west to the Atlantic Ocean, and from the northern polar cap and the North and Baltic seas south to the Mediterranean. Ethnically, Europe is that area populated by Aryan, Indo-Germanic groups and by other indigenous and non-indigenous races like the Celts, the Iberians, the Latins, the Germans, and the Slavs, which collectively, in spite of internal differences, are still clearly distinguishable from other races, such as those of Asia and Africa. But all of this is secondary to the concept of Europe as a historical reality, fashioned historically, created in its own historical process.

Europe is the heir to a double legacy, that of law and philosophy inherited from Greece and Rome, and that of religion inherited from the Orient. As Hegel observed, Greece, Rome, and Israel contributed to Europe's formative philosophy, law, and religion; the formation of Europe was eminently cultural, rather than political, and consequently Europe's unity, developed in this tradition, is a cultural one.

It would be difficult to fix the time when this cultural unity emerged, but I would associate it with the dissolution of the Roman Empire and the combined pressures of Christianity and the barbarians. As the political framework provided by Rome disintegrated, and with it its ancient materialistic civilization, a new world came into being, a world which, while retaining some of the philosophical and juridical values of the old, made spiritual values the cornerstones of its life and embraced an otherworldly perspective. From the deposition of Romulus Augustulus by the hand of Odoacer in 476, through years of trouble and the ravages of warfare, through the upheavals of revolutions and involutions, Europe, as the heir to Greece, Rome, and Israel, has remained a historical reality and a cultural entity, exerting a powerful influence on history and still influencing men today as they struggle to resolve the problems of their time.

Europe, then, is a historical concept, emerging from the crucible of the past fifteen centuries and unfolding itself through cultural manifestations into a unique civilization. From this point of view, Europe is and has been a unity. It is important to note that the cultural values of European civilization have shown a marked tendency to reproduce themselves, as in the case of the Americas and Australia. They have left a profound imprint also on Asia and Africa, and these continents owe to European influence their final awakening from a millenarian lethargy and their active participation in the community of nations. But in spite of this cultural unity and the interaction of its many forces through the centuries, Europe has failed to achieve a political and economic unity, to give life to a common political structure which would duplicate, in these other important fields, the synthesis achieved in the cultural field. In fact, it may be said that while the cultural synthesis has been in the making, giving birth to an extraordinary and homogeneous civilization based on historical reality and with an otherworldly orientation, the political differences have been increasing steadily, and all efforts to reconcile them have failed.

Europe did enjoy, during the Middle Ages under the Holy Roman Empire, a certain degree of political unity, but this disappeared within the course of a few centuries as the Renaissance period, with its consolidation of monarchies and national states, made its appearance. The onset of this new cycle of European history was accompanied by a rejection of the old co-ordinates of life and of the concept of a temporal and spiritual power. The *coordinatio ad unum* of life through the temporal and spiritual unities of law, reason, religion, and faith as steps leading to the unity of heaven and of God, Three

Persons in One, came to be replaced by political pluralisms and juridical particularisms. The breakdown of the *Respublica Christiana,* the political unity of which stemmed from the unity of law, knowledge, and religion, brought about the emergence of independent powers struggling for supremacy in Europe, first among these France, and of a number of territorial states and national monarchies, each sovereign in its own right, each prepared to reject the assertion of a superior power. Sovereignty, once the inalienable prerogative of the emperor, became the mark of exclusive power, self-sufficiency, and independence of a great number of political entities.

It was inevitable that this fracturing of the common political bond by creating a vacuum would keep alive in many minds the hope that some day a political union might be restored, especially since the political, juridical, philosophical, and religious unity—whether Catholic or Protestant, still Christian—had persisted. But all such hopes have so far remained unfulfilled. The reason for such failure, all the more remarkable in the presence of other unifying factors, may perhaps be due to two basic tendencies in European politics, the endeavor to restore political unity by conquest, or the attempt to create an equilibrium among the various sovereignties. The first approach has a long list of paladins, Barbarossa, Frederick II, and at a later period Charles V and Napoleon. Hitler's and Mussolini's efforts to create a Europe which, though divided into two spheres of influence, would be united in a common ideology may be placed in this classification. Even small nations such as Sweden, Portugal, Prussia, and Hungary in the hour of their historical greatness entertained dreams of conquering all of Europe.

Since the Peace of Westphalia, however, a new force has been present as a counterpoise to that of conquest, the balance of power concept, which recognized the plurality of sovereignties, and attempted to supplement the cultural unity of the Continent with a political relationship based on the position of the respective states. The fateful results of this attempt to balance sovereign powers are known to all; small states have been forced to fall into one or another orbit, divisions have been increased, and wars have plagued Europe. The concept of equilibrium, which should have meant a balance of each component part in accordance to its weight in relation to the whole, was reduced to an arbitrary situation in which only the big powers counted and the equilibrium of the whole was replaced by the balance of blocs, creating a semblance of coexistence, but of such a precarious nature that disaster was always in the air.

This great hiatus between the cultural unity and the political fragmentation of Europe has been critically highlighted by the international developments of the past fifty years, revealing a situation which can be solved only by a concentration of all efforts toward the achievement of total integration. The time is past when states could hope to retrench behind their own Chinese Walls in the hope of shutting off the perils of war. The interplay of political, economic, and other forces is so important and so basic to modern society that it is no longer possible for European states to exist in isolation or autarchy, as it is no longer possible for Europe as a whole to remain aloof from the rest of the world. The need for integration has turned into an imperative. The task for all sincere and serious-minded Europeans is to study in depth the problems involved, with an eye to all possible ways of resolving them, and to utilize all measures and techniques so that the forces of integration may be put in motion.

Europe for the first time stands threatened by a non-European civilization with a view of life which is the negation of its own and by the teeming and awakened Asiatic and African worlds as well. Even the great struggle with Islam, reaching its climax in the crusading expeditions, was basically a clash between two spiritual civilizations, two similarly oriented and otherworldly eschatologies, two universalistic religions seeking temporal expansion. With the containment of Islam, the danger was removed. On other occasions when Europe has come in contact with other non-European civilizations it has overwhelmed them completely. The Aztecs and the Incas now remain as a footnote to world history, or at best as a specialized field of research for archaeologists, ethnologists, and philologists. But today Europe is face to face with an entirely different challenge. Pitted against an adversary championing an antithetical view of life and intent on destroying the deeply religious values of its civilization, Europe must measure up to the challenge, rally all its forces, reconcile the multitude of political and economic particularisms, and unite, lest this life-and-death struggle be concluded with the obliteration of its civilization.

There is a tendency to reduce today's problems to terms of a struggle between East and West, between the countries on this side of the Iron Curtain, forming an area homogeneously European with a common humanistic and religious tradition, and those beyond the Iron Curtain, an area not entirely European and with a common ideology of dialectical materialism. For us it is not a question of discussing the validity of these assertions, but of going beyond mere generalizations and getting at the heart of the problem. If, for instance, one attempts to explain this geographical dichotomy in terms of a different historical development in the two areas, then one is treading on weak ground. Surely all agree that Christianity, through the Orthodox faith and the Neo-Platonic and messianic aspirations issuing from Byzantium, has been a powerful force conditioning the development of the Russian and other Slavic nations. Russia, in fact, due to this and other influences, such as that of the Italian Renaissance, the German Romantic movement, the thinking of Schelling and Hegel, the general cultural exchange of the nineteenth century, and the indigenous flowering of liberalism and populism, must be considered as a European nation, at least until the time of the Bolshevik revolution. If, on the other hand, the dichotomy is to be explained in terms of the historical situation of our own times, then it must be remembered that it cannot be formulated in geographical terms, because the ideological battle is not contained within any geographic lines, but is rampant also in all Western nations, as well as in the hearts of many individuals. The two ideological camps are striving, moreover, each according to the philosophical postulates of its civilization, to resolve the crisis of our times through the integration process.

The integration of Europe responds to a variety of needs felt by the European nations, and the most strongly felt need at this time is seen as that of the defense of the West as a cultural and spiritual whole against the first real threat, both from outside and from within, to its traditional values. But here it becomes necessary not to confuse the means with the end result, and not to become satisfied only with a defensive integration, forgetting all the positive goals. In this case nothing new would be accomplished, nothing constructive, but there would be simply a return to the old policy of balance of powers. Of course one's civilization must be defended, and it is possible that where other factors have failed, fear of aggression or a common enemy might crystallize an otherwise elusive political union. Spain facing the Moors, Italy facing the Germanic peoples, and

Poland between Prussia and Russia are historical examples of such crystallization. But those who, in today's ideological struggle, tend to view European integration only in terms of military needs fall into grave error. It should be much more than that; it should represent a common effort to solve common problems by the utilization of all techniques and all experiences. It should be an open integration process in which the needs and peculiarities of all involved are carefully considered. And if the integrating process should be set in motion by the necessity of military defense, then it should be stated clearly from the outset that it is not a question of political and military defense per se, but that this common military bloc exists specifically for the defense of the high values and principles of European civilization. Failing this, such an integration could not be justified and, moreover, it could rightly give rise to the accusation that the integration process is nothing but a camouflage for a variation in the old game of power politics.

Perhaps there is too great a tendency to visualize the situation in terms of the possible outbreak of war, while in reality the greater danger lies in the ideological struggle. Arms and weapons are of no use in settling this conflict; here the solution must come from the dictates of moral law and the moral strength of those genuinely interested in solving the problem. Victory will surely be with those who show more courageously the strength of their convictions and believe strongly in the moral values of life. It is to be hoped that, together with the safeguarding of these values and the resolving of the political relations of European states, the integration process will also help solve the many problems inherent in modern civilization.

I must admit, however, that I have strong misgivings on the various integration formulas so far proposed or initiated; there is the constant fear that the old concept of equilibrium is still very much in the minds of statesmen. Only recently a British cabinet member stated flatly that his country was opposed to the creation of a third force in Europe, which would act as a buffer between the two contending blocs.

It would be desirable that the integration process be kept open to the eventual inclusion of Russia, especially if we are to take as genuine her recent political orientation. If this were possible, then the whole concept of a balance of power could be jettisoned. Here it is not a question of proposing goals which cannot be achieved. On the contrary, due to the difficulties which characterize this great operation and to the persistence of national egoisms, the concept of sovereignty, and the principle of domestic jurisdiction, it is a duty for all Europeans to be open to all contacts and to try to unite now what can be united, so that integration may get under way, by the system of trial and error, if necessary. We must refrain from isolating ourselves and isolating others from us. There is a need for a realistic approach, but also of a great deal of imagination in the spirit of Dante, Erasmus, Mazzini, and Mickiewicz, as has been shown by the best statesmen of our tormented generation, Churchill, De Gasperi, Adenauer, Schuman, Spaak, Van Zeeland. It is also necessary to renounce national egoisms, political and economic particularisms. It will then be realized that Europe is not standing alone in this crucial moment, but that all countries which have drunk from the fountainhead of European civilization will be ready to help, because they realize that the loss of Europe would imply the loss of the best part of themselves. And inevitably the innate good sense of peoples, much more than the efforts of diplomats and politicians, will lead in the right direction.

1
Europe: Unity in Diversity

Europe as a Historical Concept

J. B. DUROSELLE / *Professor, University of the Saar and Institut d'Études Politiques, Paris*

THE WORD *Europe*, inexistent for Homer, appears in line 357 of Hesiod's *Theogony*. Europe is a sea nymph, one of the three thousand daughters of Ocean and Thetis. By the time of Herodotus, in the middle of the fifth century B.C., the word already had acquired a geographical connotation:

As for Europe, just as no one knows whether or not it is surrounded by water, so no light has been shed on the origins of its name or on him who imposed it; unless one says that the country received the name from the Tyrian Europé; in that event it would previously have been anonymous like the other parts of the world. But it is certain that this Europé was of Asiatic origin and that she never came to this country now called Europe by the Greeks.[1]

The etymology of the word is uncertain. Does it derive from the Semitic *oreb* or *éreb*, which means 'western,' or from the Homeric epithet for Zeus, *the far-seeing* (*eurus*, 'wide,' and *ops*, 'eye')? The interesting point is to know that, for the Greeks, Europe was distinct from Asia and Africa.

But antiquity did not make much use of the word *Europe*. The political overlordships, the empire of Alexander, and above all the Roman Empire, took no account of continents. The Roman Empire in particular had as its unit the Mediterranean. The barbarian invaders sometimes crossed it. The Vandals, in the fifth century A.D.,

[1] Herodotus *History*, IV, 45. Quoted by Bernard Voyenne, *Petite Histoire de l'Idée Européenne* (Paris: Éditions de la Campagne Européenne de la Jeunesse, 1952), p. 11.

founded an empire in Africa. The Arabs, starting out from Asia, destroyed what was left of Justinian's Western Empire, and in 711 Tarik crossed the straits which were to preserve his name, Gibraltar. Spain came under Arab rule, which might have been extended over a great part of France, had not Charles Martel been victorious at Poitiers in 732. It is hardly possible to speak of Europe, after these events and up to the end of the fifteenth century, as a political concept. The Arabs had been established for a long time in Africa and in Sicily. The disappearance of the Western Roman Empire in 476 had made room for a number of monarchies, for the most part Germanic, in western Europe. The Eastern Roman Empire, separated as far as religion was concerned from the West at the time of the schism of Michael Cerularius at the end of the eleventh century, led the fight against the Turks in the East and against the invaders from the northeast, the Bulgarians, the Avars, and others. The only classifying factor available is thus the religious one—Moslems to the south, Roman Catholics in the western and the central regions, Orthodox Christians to the east, and to the north pagan races converted to Christianity through conquest with varying degrees of lateness. For western Europe, the spiritual and intellectual center of present-day Europe, the idea which predominated was thus that of Christianity.

The situation changed at the end of the fifteenth century. The Byzantine Empire disappeared in 1453, and the Ottoman domination was manifestly of an Asiatic character. The stemming of the Ottoman invasion enabled the "Europeans" to take stock of themselves. The second half of the fifteenth century was the period of the great discoveries—those of the Portuguese prince, Henry the Navigator, along the coasts of Africa, and of Vasco da Gama, who reached the Indian Ocean at the very end of the century. Furthermore, there was the discovery of America in 1492. In this period there appeared the earliest forms of the modern state in France, in England, and even in Spain, where Ferdinand of Aragon and Isabella of Castile drove out the last of the Moslem rulers. Permanent taxation, standing armies, royal administration in an embryo state, but firmly constituted—all these helped form the substratum upon which the notion of a political Europe was to be built.

In this account we shall examine first the historical conception of a Europe divided into states and second the idea of European unity.

The Europe of States and European Balance of Power

One of the essential elements in the development of modern Europe was the crumbling of the idea of Christianity as a political phenomenon—crumbling, not violent destruction. In fact, for a long time there were still to be alliances and wars directed against the Turks, especially in Central Europe. But when the French king François I, in order to combat the moral danger in which his realm was being placed through encirclement by the empire of Charles V, allied himself with the German Protestant princes and with the Moslem Turks, modern Europe was born. Two factors remained to be determined: one was the establishment, at least summarily, of eastern European limits, which were extremely indefinite; the other was the realization of some balance which would enable the various powers to fix their policies. Until the time of Peter the Great (1685-1725), Europe extended no farther than the kingdom of Poland. Peter the Great exerted an immense effort to Europeanize Russia, and this effort produced results so rapid that there exists only one other comparable example in history, that of the Westernization of Japan in the Meiji era. Westernization, perhaps, affected only the higher levels of the Russian aristocracy. But the essential phenomenon was that Russian literature, partly in French in the eighteenth century (Catherine II), but mainly in Russian, while possessed of an originality of its own, was nevertheless imbued infinitely more with Western than with Asiatic influences.

It should be noted, moreover, that Russia extended to the Arctic Ocean by the end of the fifteenth century and to Kamchatka by the seventeenth century. In the sparsely populated immensities of Siberia, the colonization which was being slowly carried out was a Russian colonization. From the seventeenth century onward, Omsk and Tomsk were Russian towns. An arbitrary limit, therefore had to be set between Asiatic Russia and European Russia, and as a frontier the chain of the Urals was chosen completely arbitrarily.

To the southeast of Europe, in spite of the Ottoman hold, there was a consciousness that the limits were constituted by the Black Sea, the Turkish straits, and the Aegean Sea. The progressive driving back of the Turks reached its climax when, in 1912, only the town of Constantinople was left to them. They were to regain in 1913, and again by the Treaty of Lausanne in 1923, a part of eastern Thrace.

As to the northern limits, the North Sea and the Arctic Ocean defined them perfectly.

Thus the only problem was that of the eastern boundaries. To us it would seem that knowing whether Soviet Russia is Asiatic or European is a purely academic question, or, if one prefers, a propaganda argument, the effectiveness of which is, to say the least, doubtful.

The idea of the European balance of power seems to be at once more complex and more interesting. The problem arose in western Europe and then spread to eastern Europe, including Russia. At first it was a question of knowing whether Charles V, who, because he was the sole heir of his four grandparents, possessed Spain, the Low Countries, the Duchy of Burgundy, lands in Italy, and the domains of the House of Austria, could absorb France. The whole policy of François I and of his son Henri II consisted in fighting this unbalance. France's victory was complete when Charles V, disheartened, abdicated in 1555 and divided up his vast empire between his son Philip II and his brother Ferdinand. It was confirmed by the revolt of the Protestant Low Countries in 1578, by the conquest of Alsace (1648) and the Franche-Comté (1678), and above all by the will of the King of Spain, Charles II of Hapsburg, who in November, 1700, bequeathed his crown to the grandson of Louis XIV, hence a Bourbon.

In the reign of Louis XIV, the question of the balance of power already was of interest to new states. England and the United Provinces, rivals of long standing, united in 1688 in a coalition against France to stop her from annexing the Spanish Low Countries, which would have made her too powerful. Denmark, Poland, and Russia united in a coalition against Sweden, which possessed all the lands surrounding the Baltic Sea. On the other hand, Louis XIV was almost always hesitant when an appeal was made to his feeling of Christian solidarity in an endeavor to enlist him in the fight against the Turks. This was because every victory over the latter was a success for the Austrian Hapsburgs and consequently upset the balance of power.

But let us open the *Memoirs* of Louis XIV. We shall find there many allusions to the greatness of his dynasty and to the dignity of kingship, but the expression *balance of power in Europe* cannot be discovered.

In the eighteenth century the term was not yet in common use. But the practice it covered was becoming general. At the risk of oversimplification, it can be said that this practice derived from the four following principles:

1. No European power, and there was a fixed number of these (France, Spain, the House of Hapsburg, England, Prussia, and Russia), might achieve hegemony over a vast region of the European Continent.

2. When one of the powers acquired any new territory, the others, or at any rate the neighboring powers, were entitled to compensation. When in 1738 Louis XV's father-in-law, Stanislas Leczinski, received Lorraine, which was thus destined for annexation by France, the Duke of Lorraine, François, husband of the Hapsburg heiress, was given Tuscany. When Russia had designs on Poland, Austria and Prussia also obtained a share, and this constituted the first partition of Poland in 1772. More or less the same thing happened regarding the second and third partitions of Poland.

3. When one coalition was formed, it was certain that another coalition would be set up to oppose it. In 1755, the famous Diplomatic Revolution (Reversal of Alliances) brought Austria and Russia to France's side and Prussia to England's side. Spain, which had remained neutral, entered the French camp in 1761. Almost immediately, upon Elizabeth's death in 1762, Russia went over to the Prussian camp.

4. A practice which became increasingly general was that by which the great powers made the decisions concerning territorial or other changes to which the smaller powers had to submit.

We should note that this idea of European "balance of power" did not in any way form part of the principles of international law. It was a practical method, but a method to which the powers progressively accustomed themselves, to the extent that all infractions of the system appeared immoral (witness the conquest of Silesia by Fredrick II in 1741). It seems to be beyond doubt that in the eighteenth century all the powers, however imperialistic, whatever their desire for prestige and expansion, were not really in search of hegemony. It took the French Revolution to disturb this system. And, in the final issue, what the 1815 treaties amounted to was precisely a reestablishment of the European balance of power.

In clearly proclaiming the right of peoples to self-determination as the new foundation of international law, the French revolutionaries implicitly rejected European balance of power. At the beginning of the Directory, that is at the moment when Bonaparte was winning the amazing victories of his first Italian campaign, the only one of the directors wise enough to want to maintain the balance of power was Carnot, who proposed that France return to her 1791 frontiers. The Alsatian Reudel, on the contrary, upheld a theory which was making great progress at that period, that of natural frontiers, which presupposed the annexation of the whole of the left bank of the Rhine. Going still further, Larevellière-Lépeaux advocated revolutionary expansion, that is, some sort of missionary activity on the part of France, to procure for other peoples through the use of French armies the principles of liberty.[2] This ambition coincided perfectly with Bonaparte's views of conquest, and it doubtless led to the suppression of feudalism and to the granting of internal liberty in numerous countries of western Europe. But at the same time it destroyed their independence. The famous Sister Republics of the Directory, as much as the future kingdoms of the empire, were purely and simply vassal states.

When at the beginning of 1815 Talleyrand, at the Vienna Congress, tried to expound a doctrine for the reconstruction of Europe, he based his argument on two principles. First, he said, as far as possible "legitimate" sovereignties should be restored everywhere, but for all the "vacant" territories the balance of power should be applied to the best advantage. The legitimacy principle, for example, resulted in the maintenance of an independent Saxony. But Prussia, which had coveted the whole of Saxony, received as compensation a large part of the Rhineland, the part which before 1793 had constituted the Ecclesiastic Electorates. Because Prussia had expanded to the west, Russia's share of Poland was increased and, in particular, she received Warsaw.

In the nineteenth century, the four characteristics we described above reappeared, but this time with what might be called increased rigidity. The practice of the great powers imposing their will on the smaller ones took on great importance. While in the seventeenth century monarchs and even foreign ministers had never met, leaving the full responsibility for negotiations to the ambassadors, now

[2] "Bring fraternity and assistance to all peoples desiring to regain their liberty" (decree issued by the Convention Nationale, November 9, 1793).

meetings of high-level personalities became increasingly more frequent. There were meetings of two or three people, such as the numerous encounters between 1791 and 1874 which constituted the Entente of the Three Emperors. Above all, there were meetings of five or six people; congresses and conferences, mostly ambassadors' conferences; foreign ministers' conferences such as the Paris Congress of 1856; prime ministers' conferences; and gatherings attended by a number of monarchs. The system of compensating a great power when her neighbor had expanded still persisted. Napoleon III took advantage of the formation of the kingdom of Italy to annex Nice and Savoy. He wanted to do the same thing in 1866 when Bismarck created the Confederation of Northern Germany, but the skill of the German Minister-President was enough to prevent him from succeeding. Bismarck ridiculed compensation by dubbing it the "tipping policy."

Between 1850 and 1870, the principle of nationality, as Renouvin demonstrated in his recent *History of International Relations,* played a greater part than economic considerations. The psychological pressure exerted on rulers was such that in March, 1862, for the first time, Napoleon III, in a note to the other great powers, invoked the nationality principle and no longer either international law or European balance of power. The government of Vienna replied immediately that this principle could not possibly form the basis of European diplomacy, for in that event the Austrian Empire would disappear, which was inconceivable. As to the balance between two blocs of alliances, this was to come about after Bismarck's disappearance, and whether or not it contributed to the outbreak of World War I, it was to afford tragic proof of its reality. For more than three years, two groups of armies, of about equal strength, were evenly balanced along lines of trenches.

The fact that the intervention of a powerful non-European army, that of the United States, was needed to upset this balance, made a profound impression on President Wilson. He came to Europe with the idea that it was absolutely necessary to give up the old balance of power system, which he saw as the principal cause of the war. He therefore propounded a system in which, without excluding other considerations, the principle of nationality played a fundamental part. Thus there developed a Europe completely out of balance with, among other things, a strategically indefensible Czechoslovakia, and with the disappearance of the formidable counterpoise to Germany of Austria-Hungary, friend or foe. Momentarily weakening Germany from the military point of view, while her economic reserves were left intact, the Treaty of Versailles strengthened her to a formidable degree as far as the European balance of power was concerned. From 1933 onward, the world witnessed an attempt at hegemony which, though infinitely more inhumane than that of Napoleon I, nevertheless had some of the same characteristics. Germany corresponded to the great empire which stretched from the delta of the Elbe to the delta of the Tiber. The protectorates, or governments-general, strangely resembled the kingdom of Italy of which Napoleon himself was king. The satellites of the Axis evoked the kingdoms of the lesser Bonapartes. And, finally, the countries allied by force corresponded to Austria, Prussia, even Russia at the time of the First Empire. The radically new phenomenon was that, after the war, the bipolar orientation of the world, the concentration of power between one country which was extra-European and another which was at any rate on the periphery, rendered obsolete all ideas of European balance of power and consequently gave diplomats an entirely new field of action.

The Idea of European Unity

The idea of unifying Europe came relatively late. It only appeared in the writings of certain intellectuals and even their ideas were frequently confused in the extreme. Bernard Voyenne, in his *Petite Histoire de l'Idée Européenne,* has drawn up a careful list. At the beginning of the fourteenth century, Pierre Dubois wrote a treatise entitled *De recuperatione Terre Sancte,* which contained a plan for a European federation depending on neither the pope nor the emperor, but on a council, a representative assembly of "the Most Christian Republic." In 1464, a French adventurer, Antoine Marigny, suggested to George of Podebrad, King of Bohemia, "the emancipation of peoples and kings by the organization of a new Europe." "The exigence of universality," as Voyenne says, led a growing number of intellectuals or statesmen to envisage unification plans which were varied in coherence and in scope—Sully's Most Christian Republic, the celebrated English Quaker William Penn's establishment "of a European Diet, Parliament or State," the plans of Leibnitz, the

Projet de Paix Perpétuelle by l'Abbé de Saint-Pierre (1713). This latter is undoubtedly the most interesting, for it proposed a perpetual alliance between the sovereigns, the submission of the sovereigns to a European senate, a financial contribution by all states to the expenses of the alliance, and collective intervention against those infringing the pact.

In the nineteenth century, there was a curious contradiction between the existence of violent nationalistic movements, occasionally of romantic inspiration, and of a romanticizing of peace which foreshadowed the European idea. This represented a second stage, for the theorists of the preceding centuries had expressed individual ideas, while in the nineteenth century there were actual movements of opinion which, without reaching very wide circles, were nonetheless collective manifestations. For example, regarding the 1848 crisis, Renouvin has written a study on the idea of the United States of Europe, *Actes du Congrès Historique du Centenaire de la Révolution de 1848,* on pages 31–45 of which he states: "It was 1848 which introduced into political thought the formula of the United States of Europe, through the voices of Carlo Cattaneo and of Victor Hugo." Renouvin demonstrated its origins, which were essentially of a religious, republican, or socialist character. It was in 1834 that Mazzini published the statutes of his "Young Europe." It was in 1837 that the German jurist Johannes Sartorius, in his book *Organe des Vollkommenen Friedens,* proposed a federation of European states based on the covenant of the Germanic confederation. Cobden, Michel Chevalier, and the free-traders in general were thinking of a European federation. Chevalier said in 1843:

> Formerly under the name of the Holy Alliance, today under that of the Concert of Europe, Europe seems to be on the march towards the final goal of unity, a unity perfectly compatible nonetheless with separate nationalities. Everything urges us to it, commerce and the improvement of communications, the full appreciation of the benefits of peace, the softening of manners and customs and the feeling of universal brotherhood which was sown by religion and has taken so long to germinate.[3]

But to some extent 1848 brought about a momentary crystallization

---

[3] Michel Chevalier, *Essais de Politique Industrielle, Souvenirs de Voyage* (Paris: Librairie de Charles Gosselin, 1843), p. 328.

of this tendency in circles which were sometimes identified with the general public. Cattaneo synthesized the two contradictory ideas outlined above by saying that the day when the principle of nationalities and the republican idea triumph, the European peoples, constituted in a federation of free peoples, "will form the 'United States of Europe.'" "We shall have peace," he said, "when we have the United States of Europe." And in 1849 Mazzini published an article under the heading "La santa alleanza dei popoli." A Scottish journalist, Charles MacKay, also spoke of the United States of Europe in two articles in the *London Telegraph* of March 28 and April 1, 1848. The celebrated American blacksmith Elihu Burritt, who had come to Europe to organize peace congresses, proposed a United States of Europe which would have a much looser organization than the United States of America and which would be an intermediate step toward a league of nations.

Nationalism and the Integration of Europe

HANS KOHN / *Professor of History,*
The City College of New York

THE UNITY of Europe, in a geographic sense, is as difficult to understand as that of Asia or of Africa. The concept with which we wish to deal, however, is not a spatial one. Europe will be considered here as a cultural concept, as a civilization and a way of life. In this sense, European unity more closely approached reality in the eighteenth century than at any previous time. Formerly confined to what Leopold von Ranke called the community of the Latin and Teutonic peoples, Europe expanded to include Russia and the Near East. Michael Lemonosov and Nikolai Novikov in Russia, Josef Dobrovský among the Czechs, Adamantios Coray among the Greeks, and Dimitrije Obradović among the Serbs, all were conscious outposts of that spirit of Enlightenment, of that *république des lettres* which had its origin in late seventeenth-century northwestern Europe and which, during the following one hundred years, united the whole Continent in a spirit of optimistic benevolence and in a new respect for the dignity of the individual.

Although, nations existed, there was hardly any nationalism. The educated classes all over Europe felt as one. French was the recognized universal language for all official and private intercourse as, in the more limited space of Western Christendom, Latin had been in the Middle Ages. Wars were fought in Europe, but they were fought without arousing nationalist passions or hatreds. The word *fatherland* or *patrie* came into use, but it did not mean country against country, national culture against national culture. It meant a government based on individual liberty, securing the happiness of its citizens through all the new forms of freedom, in which the newly awakened individual self-confidence found its expression. This human or universal, but in no way national or ethnic, concept of liberty became the foundation of the eighteenth-century fatherland. Fatherland, all writers agree, existed only where individual liberty and human dignity were secure. *"Qu'est-ce en effet que d'être libres?"* Voltaire wrote, *"c'est raisonner juste, c'est connaître les droits de l'homme; et quand on les connaît bien, on les défend de même."*

This feeling of European unity ended with the Napoleonic wars. The French Revolution had aroused in France a revolutionary and missionary nationalism which still carried the universalist heritage of its eighteenth-century origins, but which was full of a burning and self-centered faith, which opened the age of nationalism. At the end of the first decade of the nineteenth century the Napoleonic wars aroused a similar self-centered and burning nationalism in other European lands, from Spain to Russia, from Italy to Norway, but this time devoid of that spirit of enlightened universalism characteristic of the preceding age. Herder and the new historicism stressed the uniqueness of each nationality, its special God-ordained mission, its manifest destiny, which easily conflicted with similar destinies of other nationalities. The differences between nations and their cultures were emphasized and regarded as praiseworthy. The Bible, in the story of the tower of Babel, regarded the multiplicity of languages as a curse imposed upon a sinful mankind. The new nationalism glorified the diversity of tongues and tried to increase it. Liberty began to mean national independence and participation in national greatness and power rather than individual freedom and human dignity within a common civilization based upon participation in the blessings of a free constitution and of security of rights.

The unity of Europe still survived in great eighteenth-century figures who remained aloof from the new nationalism. After the war against Napoleon, which is often called the war of liberation, although it did not enhance liberty at all, but inflamed national hatreds, Goethe remarked:

> How could I, to whom culture and barbarism alone are of importance, hate a nation which is among the most cultivated of the earth, and to which I owe so great a part of my own cultivation?[1]

[1] Goethe's conversations with Johann Peter Eckermann, March 14, 1830.

Turning to national hatred in general, Goethe continued:

> You will always find it strongest and most violent where there is the lowest degree of culture. But there exists a degree of culture where national antagonism vanishes altogether, and where one stands, so to speak, above nations, and feels the weal or woe of a neighboring people as if it had happened to one's own. This degree of culture was conformable to my nature.[2]

Little did Goethe foresee that in the new age dawning all over Europe, men of culture would assume the task, not of combating national hatreds, but of finding semirational and semimystical justification for regarding the weal or woe of a neighboring people differently from that befalling their own people.

Goethe's French contemporary, twenty years younger than the great poet, was the French social thinker, Saint-Simon. His fertile mind anticipated the future forms not only of social organization, but also of European society. Together with his young disciple, Augustin Thierry, he submitted at the end of the Napoleonic wars a proposal for "The Reorganization of European Society." The industrial society of which he became the prophet demanded the preservation of peace and the security of liberty. To that end, the peoples of Europe had to enter into a federation. As a cornerstone of such a free Europe, Saint-Simon suggested the closest collaboration between Britain and France. As these two nations were then the leading liberal and parliamentary states of Europe, they seemed destined to form the nucleus of a liberal European federation. Saint-Simon went further. He believed that such a Franco-British union alone could end the turmoil of French society and guide it in the ways of ordered liberty. Britain had behind her long experience in parliamentary government, upon which the French were then only embarking. In Britain alone could the constitutional French parties find support against the domestic threats both of despotism and of extravagant liberty. Saint-Simon and Thierry demanded the formation of an Anglo-French parliament, composed two-thirds of English and one-third of French deputies, and explained this disproportion by the French need for guidance by the more experienced Englishmen and by the greater gain in stability and liberty which the union would bestow upon France.

[2] *Ibid.*

Such a subordination of national vanity to the interests of Europe and to considerations of liberty soon became unthinkable in the nineteenth century. Midway in the century Europe was stirred by two mighty currents, sometimes uniting and sometimes competing—the liberal urge for constitutional government, respectful of the freedom of individuals and the rights of minorities, and the nationalist urge for the creation of states which would powerfully express the distinctive character and the collective might of a nationality. Many Europeans entered the critical year 1848 with the hope of being able to fuse the two currents into one living reality. The events of 1848 and of the following three decades disillusioned them. Nationalism on the whole proved stronger than liberalism. Collective power and passion triumphed over both individual considerations and European interests. The problem of federative solution, which would respect the historical individualities of countries and peoples and yet unite them for common progress in liberty and prosperity, was posited all over Europe, in Italy and in Germany, in the Hapsburg monarchy, in Scandinavia and in the Balkans, even in the vastness of the Russian Empire, and in the last resort for the whole of Europe.

In only one case was a true federative solution found, and that was in Switzerland, where the constitution of 1848, conceived after the model of the Constitution of the United States of America, made it possible for people of very different ethnic origin, historical tradition, and linguistic culture, to live together on a footing of equality and mutual consideration, irrespective of numbers or power, on the basis of democratic liberty and tolerance. This achievement was all the more remarkable because elsewhere in Europe people speaking the languages spoken in Switzerland were involved in wars against each other, and democracy, a robust and deeply rooted plant in Switzerland, lacked that stability and vitality among Switzerland's neighbors who shared linguistic and ethnic backgrounds with the peoples of Switzerland.[3]

European nationalists moved by the spirit of idealism and illusionism characteristic of the 1830's and the 1840's had hoped that the rise and triumph of nationalism in Europe would usher in a period of firm constitutional liberty, of lasting peace, and of fraternal association of the "liberated" people. The European age, however, which

[3] See Hans Kohn, *Nationalism and Liberty. The Swiss Example* (New York: Macmillan, 1956).

began with the wars of Italian and German unification and which culminated in the great European war which became known in history as World War I turned out to be of an entirely different character than Mazzini, Michelet, and Mickiewicz had expected. It was an era of self-centered nationalism and of growing nationalist conflicts. The admirable spirit of compromise and rational solution which the North Atlantic Community had inherited from the Glorious Revolution, the concept of an open society which had characterized early Western liberalism, and the insistence on humanitarian values which the Enlightenment had fostered gave way more and more to a narrow faith in one's own kind and its overriding rights and to a belief in political, economic, and even cultural self-sufficiency. What was called "original" or "organic" was accepted as superior to interchange and intercourse with "alien" elements. Although the causes of all wars, like the causes of all important events, are most complex and composite and often even contradictory, and although the unforeseen and unforeseeable, and the accidental, play a great role in the course of history, nevertheless it can be said that the main cause of the outbreak of World War I, and the reason for which so many peoples were drawn into it, was nationalism. In that sense the war of 1914 marked the outcome and the climax of the European age of nationalism. It did not mean its end.

It meant, however, the end of the European age of world history. The war left the European victor nations, France, Britain, and Italy, exhausted. The entry of the United States had decided its outcome. This event confirmed what many observers in the eighteenth and nineteenth centuries had foreseen, what had become clearly discernible from 1898 on, and what the British were perhaps the first fully to understand, though the Americans were the last to realize or willingly accept it. In 1917 the United States, which had originated as a nation in the late eighteenth century and as the frontier land of English liberty and of the eighteenth-century Enlightenment, had became the leading power of the liberal Western world and had come to the rescue of liberal Europe. The United States was qualified for its new position because it was deeply rooted in the English tradition of individual liberty and in the heritage of the two English revolutions of the seventeenth century, above all the Glorious Revolution. In separating from the mother country, the United States had broken new ground. Through the federal principle it became a republic of many republics, which set the example for future developments throughout the British Commonwealth and (in Europe) in Switzerland. By transforming the English historical right of liberty into a universal principle, it gained the strength for the unique venture of welcoming many millions of immigrants from the most varied ethnic stocks and religious faiths. Thus the United States became a nation of many nations, assimilating them into an ideological, not a racial, melting pot, changing them into Americans through the ideas of individual liberty and tolerance, and organizing them through unity in a free interplay of diversity.[4] The example of the United States could have pointed the way for the European nations which had based their lives on the common traditions of modern Western civilization. The spirit of self-centered nationalism, however, not only remained dominant in Europe after World War I, but the war, originating in nationalist conflicts and ambitions, raised it to feverish heat. Nationalism grew to that malignancy which became known as fascism and which sacrificed the gains of the Enlightenment—individual liberty and regard for the interests of mankind and of "alien" nations—to an exclusive national self-glorification and self-interest.

This intensification of nationalism in Europe happened at the very same time when Europe as a whole was suffering from a deep malaise. This malaise was caused not only by the war, but also by the preceding emphasis on nationalism which undermined the faith in the common values of the free European tradition. Europe was in no way prepared for the new situation with which it was faced after the war. The war had brought to the fore forces which challenged Europe's free civilization and its validity. Fascism itself was such a challenge; it denied the very foundations of the modern civilization of liberty. But an even more powerful challenge—more powerful perhaps for the very reason that at least in its initial stage it rejected the narrowness of nationalism—had arisen under Lenin's leadership in Russia. Traditional Russian autocracy, economic backwardness, uncritical orthodoxy, together with the chaos and disorganization caused by the war, had prepared the ground in Russia for Lenin's daring attempt to end the two-century-old rapprochement of Russia with Europe and Russia's progressive and fruitful integration with

[4] See Hans Kohn, *American Nationalism, an Interpretative Essay* (New York: Macmillan, 1957).

the West. With the transfer of the capital from St. Petersburg back to Moscow, the period of Russia as one of the European powers came to an end.

The rulers of the Kremlin not only rejected modern Western civilization; they rebuilt the wall which had separated Russia from Europe for many centuries and into which Peter the Great had broken an ever widening window. Under the leadership of Lenin and Stalin, Russia again became a closed society, anxiously guarded from contact with the Western world. Lenin and his successors held out the prospect of fulfilling hopes of some extreme Russian nationalists of the nineteenth century like Danilevsky, who had maintained that Russia was more than one of the European powers, that she was the leading world power of the future, the center of a world-wide system of social justice, peace, and regeneration. But on one point, Lenin went beyond the earlier Russian nationalists—from the beginning he turned Russia's face away from Europe toward Asia. He saw in the Asian revolutions, which were partly inspired by the Russian Revolution of 1905, the proof that the revolutionary fire, extinguished in the reformism of the West and in the indubitable consolidation of capitalism and middle-class sentiments among the workers of the economically advanced countries, was rapidly growing in Asia. He proclaimed the united front of Russia and Asia in order to overthrow the position of Europe and to destroy modern Western civilization.

All these unexpected developments—the weakening of Europe, not only politically and economically but in its moral fibers; the challenge of communism and fascism; the rising tide of Asian and African nationalism—found Europe unprepared. Nationalism continued to disunite and disintegrate it. The conditions of the years following 1918 accelerated this development. The victorious Western nations of World War I were prevented by their nationalist jealousy and self-centeredness from standing together and preserving the fruit of their hard won victory in a collectively maintained system of peaceful order. Thus it was that World War I, which so many thought was to be the last war in their generation, was resumed only twenty years later. The former victors, the Western democracies, had to fight again, even more bitterly, for their lives and for the Western civilization of which they should have been the responsible heirs and guardians. Their disunity had tempted the Germans to resume the war and to try a second time to establish their hegemony over Europe. This time they believed themselves to be better prepared for the struggle against the West by having eradicated in Germany those foundations of free Western civilization which the Fascists, wrongly and to their own undoing, regarded as a weakness of modern society instead of recognizing them as its essential strength. Whereas the Napoleonic bid for European hegemony had left the French exhausted, the Versailles Treaty, so wrongly judged by many contemporaries, had in no way sapped German strength. In their second bid for European hegemony the Germans came nearer their goal than they had a quarter of a century before.

Therein they were helped by the abuse of the principle of national self-determination. Woodrow Wilson in his Fourteen Points had demanded the reorganization of the Hapsburg monarchy on a federal basis, giving free development to its various nationalities while preserving their economic prosperity and military security by maintaining a common bond. A solution of this kind had been proposed as far back as 1849. To the misfortune of the monarchy, of its component peoples, of European peace, and of Western civilization, the proposal had not been followed. The Czech historian František Palacký stressed in 1848 that the existence of Austria was a necessity, because it provided for its peoples a protective bulwark, not only against Prussian-German expansion, but also against another threat to their liberty and civilization, which he called the Russian urge for establishing a universal monarchy. His fears were fully substantiated a century later. In 1918 the dissolution of the Hapsburg monarchy opened the way for German and Russian expansion whenever Germany or Russia recovered from the effects of their defeat in World War I.

Against the expectation of many early nationalists, the "liberation" of nationalities in the twentieth century and the creation of new nation-states did not strengthen the trend to peace and liberty. Nationalities which had demanded release from oppression often became oppressors themselves. Innumerable disputes about historical and natural frontiers sprang up. Nationalist bitterness about the disposal of often minor territories helped the rise of fascism, fostered an excessive militarism, and undermined the respect for civilized processes of law and for human rights. All over Central Europe and eastern Europe the nationalities, often in spite of close racial or linguistic affinity, felt profoundly hostile to each other. Their mutual animosities and jealousies hindered their political and economic co-operation. Their nationalism and disunion facilitated the conquest of Central Europe and central-eastern Europe, first by National Socialist Germany, then by Communist Russia. So it came about that by the early 1940's the cause of individual liberty and civilized peace —the proud and beneficent heritage of modern Europe—seemed defeated for any foreseeable time over almost the whole of Europe. National independence and sovereignty, multiplied and sanctified in the twentieth century, have not turned out to be reliable formulas for greater individual freedom or for more secure international peace.

In the early part of 1941, Continental Europe, except for two small enclaves, suffered under forms of tyranny which Europeans around 1900 would have believed impossible in their lands. The Continent was ruled by Hitler, Stalin, Mussolini, and Franco. Each one appealed to the nationalism and the unmeasured national dreams of glory of his people. At the moment the Germans were the leading dynamic force. By the treaty of August, 1939, they had opened the way to the West for the Russians. By destroying Poland and abandoning the Baltic republics to Russia, the Germans destroyed the barrier which protected them and Europe from Russia. The hubris characteristic of German national socialism drove Hitler, two years after having made common cause with communism against the West, to break his pact of friendship with Stalin and to invade the vastness of the Russian Empire. This German aggression brought the Russian armies to the Elbe and the Adriatic Sea, where they replaced the anti-Western tyranny of national socialism with a similar anti-Western tyranny of their own. But they did not take over Europe as many people feared in 1945. In 1940 the *Völkische Beobachter* had triumphantly proclaimed that democracy had been obliged to take refuge in the little island where it had originated. Four years later Anglo-American forces set out from this little island to liberate much of Europe, even the larger part of Germany, from Fascist rule and to restore these ancient seats of European civilization to the community of the West and its liberty under law.

The free Europe which emerged from World War II found itself greatly diminished not only in power and prestige, but also in territory. It would be unjust, however, to forget that this free Europe was much more than many people had dared to hope for in 1941.

Free Europe in the late spring of 1945 had grown surprisingly compared with the sad state of the spring of 1941. At that time it had seemed that at least the first part of Mussolini's famous boast about the coming world leadership of fascism and Italy might become true. On October 25, 1932, the Italian leader had assured his Milan audience with a fully tranquil conscience, that "the twentieth century will be the century of fascism, the century of Italian power, the century when it will become for the third time the leader of mankind." Only six years later it was quite clear that Mussolini was wrong about Italy; his nationalism had not raised, but debased Italy. Yet fascism, though not in its Italian garb, seemed triumphant and highly confident in 1941. In 1945, that era of a Fascist century definitely collapsed.

But not the whole of Europe could be freed. Through the misdeeds of fascism, the grip of communism, the older form of totalitarianism, clamped down over the lands east of the Elbe and east of the Alps. Thus the area in which the values of free Europe were recognized as valid was tragically reduced compared with the free Europe at the outbreak of World War I. This war has been revealed more and more as the greatest calamity of modern European history—a calamity without which the rise of totalitarianism and the burden which it imposed upon the liberty and dignity of European man would have been unthinkable. Europe has not recovered from its consequences.

But what remained of Europe after 1945,—Britain and France, Germany west of the Elbe and Italy, the Low Countries and Scandinavia, that immense wealth of great cultural traditions and cultural vitality, of political wisdom and inventive skill?—was it ready for a new beginning? Europe had lived through a harrowing experience. Certainly it could not go on in the old way. On one hand, the old nineteenth-century confidence in the permanence and untrammeled progress of a civilization of liberty was gone. On the other hand, its values, which had been accepted in the nineteenth century as obvious in a matter-of-fact way, had become dearer and understood better for the very reason that their fragility and vulnerability were revealed so painfully. Europe's position as mistress of the world was undisputed in the nineteenth century. Now she found herself not only outdistanced by Russia and the United States, but facing entirely new and unprecedented situations in Asia and Africa which would have been unpredictable at the beginning of the century.

The economic distress which was so manifest at the end of the war was overcome with astonishing speed, partly with the help of the United States, but to a large extent through the abilities of Europeans and the potentialities of the Western economic system. It is too easily forgotten in our time that the destructive powers revealed in the recent wars are matched, if not outshone, by the recuperative powers of free economy and human resourcefulness. Europe now surprises the visitor with vigorous prosperity and great advances in all fields such as no visitor in 1946 would have anticipated. But economic prosperity is not enough. New political foundations must be found to reinvigorate the moral and spiritual traditions common to the modern West. To me, as a long-time student of nationalism, the foremost question seems to be whether Europe can outgrow the nationalism which led it into two devastating wars and which not only brought to it immeasurable suffering, but also sapped its moral and spiritual strength. In the present predicament neither Europe nor the Western world, divided, can revive the West's vitality enough to face new challenges unknown to the nineteenth century. This can be accomplished only by their common efforts.

Can Europe or the West be reorganized in such a way that peoples of different historical background and tradition, while preserving their cultural personality, can live in a common political and economic order? Hopeful steps in that direction have been taken. The United States has pioneered with federal solutions. In the United Kingdom and in Canada peoples with sharply defined individuality—English, Welsh, and Scottish in one case, British and French in the other—have learned to live together in varying degrees of harmony. As Reginald Coupland has pointed out:

> Britain was once a Balkan. The age-long strife between the stronger nation and its weaker neighbors was a constant factor in British history—wars of conquest and wars of liberation, rebellions and repressions, a stubborn tradition of border fighting, and from generation to generation a legacy of hate as bitter as any that vexed the peace of continental Europe.[5]

In the United Kingdom, Scottish and Welsh nationalities have

---

[5] Reginald Coupland, *Welsh and Scottish Nationalism: A Study* (London: Collins Sons and Co., 1954), p. xv.

survived. The price of unity, peace, and common progress has not been uniformity. On the European continent Switzerland and Belgium also have shown a remarkable ability for satisfying the legitimate aspirations of diversity within the strength and the stability of a state which does not identify itself with any one nationality or language, but gives to all of them a broad scope on the basis of individual liberty and mutual tolerance.

There are many very complex technical problems to be solved before such an integration of several or all the nationalities of the Western world can be achieved, but in spite of their importance and difficulty, these problems are secondary to the primary issue, on the solution of which all future progress depends. Will it be possible to de-emphasize nationalism, to disintensify its emotional appeal, and to reduce it to proportions compatible with a supranational order, in which the decisive unit of history no longer would be the nation, a relatively late growth in historical development, but the civilization, in this case modern Western civilization? Will it be possible to bring nationalism in the West back to those attitudes which characterized it at the time of its rise in the eighteenth century? Can nationalism be imbued with the spirit of compromise and co-operation, instead of fanatical insistence on one's own full rights? These seem to me to be the fundamental questions for the future of Europe and of modern Western civilization.

No one can answer these questions. There are hopeful signs. The initiative taken by French governments after 1945 which resulted in the coal and steel union; the existence of the German Federal Republic instead of the Deutsches Reich of the later nineteenth century and the first half of the twentieth century; the leadership shown by Netherlandish and Belgian statesmen in their emphasis on the need for closer Western integration, demonstrating the importance to the West's vitality of the small and democratically consolidated nations; the settlement of the troublesome dispute over Trieste in a spirit of compromise and mutual concessions—these are some of the signposts on the road to a promising future. But recently there have been some worrisome indications of undue emphasis on nationalism. It might be useful to point out two of them, not because they are the only ones, but because they show clearly the disruptive force of nationalistic claims directed against incipient integration. Since the nineteenth century, national self-determination has become a recognized right, but it is neither an absolute nor an overriding right, nor always conducive to good results. There are higher considerations to be taken into account—concerns of individual liberty and human rights, of international peace and Western solidarity, strategic and economic necessities.

One of the few achievements of constructive statesmanship in the period between the two world wars was the rapprochement between Turkey and Greece, which Mustapha Kemal achieved. A determined nationalist, Kemal could nevertheless cut loose from all hankering after past greatness. He energetically discarded any aspiration to recreate the Ottoman empire or to revive Pan-Islamic or Pan-Turanian expansionism. Greeks and Turks had been hereditary enemies. During the nineteenth century, Greece grew steadily at the expense of Turkey, and as late as 1919 Greek armies invaded Anatolia. After 1930, however, it seemed that the age-old hostility and bitterness between the two peoples might be allowed to fade. Such a transformation takes a long time and during the transition period demands utmost caution and restraint. Cyprus, distant from other Greek-inhabited lands, but strategically situated as a guardian of the approach to southern Anatolia, lately has been the scene of violent nationalistic agitation. In 1878 Cyprus was ceded by Turkey to Britain for the very purpose of defending Asian Turkey against Russian advance.

Today the strategic need is greater than ever. Individual liberty and due process of law are as well safeguarded in Cyprus today as is possible. Greece became an outright Fascist country when General Metaxas became dictator in August, 1936. His regime was overthrown by another Fascist regime, that of Germany. After its collapse, it was only British help which prevented Communist forces from taking over Greece, thereby putting Turkey into a strategically indefensible position. The Greek nationalist demands upon Cyprus, in which many Turks see the revival of Pan-Hellenism, not only have darkened and perhaps destroyed the recently bright outlook for a Greco-Turkish rapprochement, but also have impeded the integrating forces of the Balkan Pact and of the North Atlantic Treaty Organization.

Whereas Cypriot nationalism threatens the growth of integration in a border region of Europe, recent events in the Saar have had a similar effect in the very heart of Europe. The Saar is a typical frontier area which ethnically is linked with Germany and economically with France. It could have become a cornerstone for Franco-German co-operation and partnership. The Saar once demonstrated a vote in which national self-determination meant the abandonment or rejection of individual liberty, of the civilized process of law, and of the concern for international peace. In January, 1935, the population of the Saar—in its large majority, Socialist workers of the Roman Catholic faith—voted in the full knowledge of the character of Hitler's Reich for nationalism against liberty. The vote in the same region in October, 1955, was a warning again, above all, of the slogans and methods employed by the German nationalist parties, especially by the Democratic party. It is very strange how in the last years democracy has been abused in eastern and Central Europe and in Asia. In view of the experiences suffered in the twentieth century, the much-needed Franco-German co-operation will require assurances given to France that she will be entering into this co-operation in not too glaring a position of inferiority. With a little less nationalism the Saarlanders could have made a lasting contribution to the welfare of Germany and France alike and to the integration of Europe.

But the integration of Europe may not be enough today. In the security of the nineteenth century, Europe and North America could go their separate ways. Both stood ultimately for the same values of a free civilization. As de Tocqueville had seen, the Anglo-Americans were able, under uniquely favorable circumstances, to expand western European inheritance into a democracy and thereby set the example for what de Tocqueville believed to be an inevitable trend in western Europe. When he wrote, a hierarchical social order still seemed firmly entrenched in Europe, in sharp contrast with American equalitarianism. Since then, though in each case in an individual form determined by economic and geographic factors as well as by local traditions, the democratic countries of Europe and of North America have all approached a balance between the liberal insistence on the rights of the individual and the social needs of a modern mass society. Their common civilization faces similar challenges and tensions in all the countries of the free West. Only by the co-operation and integration of its individual states can the West hope to see its modern civilization, in unity respectful of diversity, not only survive, but strengthen its moral and spiritual foundations.

2

**The Rationale
of European Integration**

The Growth of the European Movement since World War II

ALTIERO SPINELLI / *Secretary General,*
European Federalist Movement

The Forerunners

The question of European unity has been recurring for a number of centuries in the political literature of the Continent. It was not until the nineteenth century, however, in the midst of the struggle for the creation of national democratic states, that this idea of unity was made more precise and, utilizing the American experience, there was talk of a European federation or, better yet, of a United States of Europe. But even then men like Mazzini, Cattaneo, Proudhon, Victor Hugo, and others who advocated European union were regarded as prophetical or visionary. They did not think in terms of practical realizations of political action or understand that problems might be solved by pooling the respective forces of the various nation-states.

In a certain sense, one may include among the forerunners of this movement Luigi Einaudi, who between the end of 1918 and the beginning of 1919 wrote articles arguing against the erroneous concept of the League of Nations and advocating a federalistic solution for the European situation. Because of the clarity with which Einaudi defined the problem, these pages represent federalist thinking of the highest caliber. Unfortunately, these views were published as personal opinion, and no political movement developed from them.

The First Attempts

Pan-Europe. The first of these proposals for the unification of Europe was that of Count Coudenhove-Kalergi, which had the advantage of arousing some unrest in public opinion. Coming from the Austrian aristocracy, and thus used to the plurinational idea, Coudenhove-Kalergi became, after the end of World War I, the self-appointed paladin of a federated Europe. A movement called Pan-Europe came into being, but it lacked mass following and appealed mostly to diplomats and intellectuals of old Europe, most of whom have since disappeared from the political scene. Its greatest hour came when Briand and Stresemann tried to reconcile the profound differences between their two countries. Coudenhove-Kalergi, backed by his followers, many of whom were men of authority, suggested to Briand that he propose a European federation. Actually Coudenhove-Kalergi himself did not have a very clear idea of what a European federation should mean, since he did not think it at all objectionable to include in such a democratic federation even Fascist Italy, where there was no elected parliament and no political freedom. To add confusion to this already fuzzy program, Briand suggested a project for a European constitution which would set up a little league of nations for Europe. This league provided just as palliative a solution as the big League, since here again member states retained all their sovereign powers.

The Briand project died stillborn, mainly because of British and Italian opposition. With the failure of Franco-German rapprochement and of the Briand-Stresemann policies with it, and with the triumph of national socialism in Germany a few years later, the Pan-Europe movement withered away. Coudenhove-Kalergi is still active today, and still considers himself the leader of Pan-Europe, but his project is no more than a name without any content. Respected as a pioneer of the Pan-Europe movement after World War II, he nevertheless has failed to establish an effective collaboration with the present-day federalist movement.

A second and more coherent surge of federalist thinking and activities is represented by the Federal Union movement, which came into being in Great Britain during the years immediately preceding World War II. We are used to thinking of the British as completely averse to any idea of federation, and they, themselves, seem to strengthen this impression by often repeating that this is a strictly Latin or a Cartesian idea, very foreign to their method of thinking. The Latin people are supposed to think always in terms of well spelled-out, written constitutions, while the British, whose political system is based on an unwritten constitution, are supposed to apply the empirical approach also in the field of international co-operation. This is not actually so, however. The Latin supranational idea is not an idea of federation, but of empire, of the violent conquest of as many people as possible, bringing them under the law of the strongest. The idea that it is possible to bring about a supranational government by means other than conquest, i.e., through free consent of states, and that it is possible to divide sovereignty, assigning portions of it to different organs of the government, is a typically Anglo-Saxon conception.

The first example of two states uniting by a free decision and without war was the union between England and Scotland, which took place at the beginning of the eighteenth century, and it may be considered as an incipient step to federation. The first real federal constitution was that of the United States, which was written by Englishmen, rebels to their king, of course, but men who had benefited from a British political education. It was this group of people who invented the new constitutional formula, on the basis of which the states keep part of their sovereignty while transferring another part to a higher authority. The British Parliament is, moreover, the only parliament in the world which has created a priori federal constitutions for both Canada and Australia, constitutions which have worked very well. It also took the first steps toward a study from which the federal constitution of India emerged later. The only real example of federation outside the Anglo-Saxon countries is Switzerland. But it is also known that the Swiss, passing in 1847 from the confederate to the federal structure, based their action a great deal upon the experience of the United States Constitution. From this brief résumé, we must conclude that the federal experience is very close to the British political spirit, and also that the British can easily understand the federal concept and its logical political and economic implications. Another proof of this understanding is seen in the federalist literature of the Federal Union, which is of first quality and even today superior to the average Continental literature on the subject, because of the coherence with which problems are presented, obstacles examined, and solutions proposed. It is interesting to note here that the most coherent federalist movement today is the Italian, which has absorbed a great deal from the study of this English federalist literature.

The flowering of the English federalist movement during the 1930's and the sudden abandonment of federalist activities during the following decade must be studied a little more carefully. Many English people at that time had realized that the era in which Great Britain was the political and economic center of the world had definitely come to an end. Following the great economic crisis of 1929, the British Empire had ceased to be the great free market, open to everyone, and it also came to close itself behind protective barriers and preferential tariffs. The economic unity of the world was thus definitely brought to an end. At the same time, the revival of German nationalism showed that England was no longer capable of being, in Europe itself, the decisive element of political equilibrium. It appeared that World War I and the British victory had been in vain. In Europe there were now two powerful states, too powerful to be either controlled or guided by Great Britain. Country after country set up totalitarian regimes and prepared for war. England, still following its traditional policy, risked being eliminated as a factor in European politics.

Many Britishers, therefore, came to the conclusion that England, in order to put a stop to the economic and political decomposition of the free world, should change its political course and promote a European federal union. This European federation would have created an area of peace and equilibrium around England. Initially, the federation was to be formed by Great Britain, the Low Countries, Belgium, France, and the Scandinavian countries, but eventually it was hoped that the Fascist countries might be absorbed after the overthrow of the dictatorships.

Side by side with these proposers of a European federation there were, although less influential, those who favored an Atlantic federation, which looked toward union with the United States, and even those who favored transforming the Commonwealth into a federation. The high mark of British federalism was reached when Churchill proposed to France, crumbling under the onslaught of German military might, a union between the two countries with one parliament and a common citizenship. Churchill's proposal, of course, was dictated by the urgent needs of the situation, which meant that the British government was trying to find a formula which would permit France to continue the war. But it is important to note that if this proposal was a federal proposal, it was due to a great extent to the action and the influence of the Federal Union, which counted among its backers eminent political and cultural personalities, as well as the man in the street. The idea of federation was, so to speak, in the air, and Churchill only had to reach for it.

Among the men who at the time were close to Churchill and who contributed to the inspiration of this proposal, there was a Frenchman whom we shall see later among the fighters for European unity. He was Jean Monnet, who since then has become convinced of the necessity for abandoning the system of national states in favor of a higher, supranational organization. Churchill's proposal, however, caught the French completely unprepared, and, because of its novelty, they considered it absurd. It was also very difficult for the French political mind to admit that there could be a power stronger than France. For this reason, the British proposal for a federal union was unsuccessful, and France accepted capitulation as a vassal state of Germany.

With this French refusal, it can be said that the active cycle of the British federal movement came to an end, although the Federal Union, as a small and insignificant movement, is still in existence. After the fall of France, England found herself alone, facing a Europe conquered by Hitler, in the gravest moment of her national history. In this period we note the consolidation in the British public conscience of two attitudes destined to weigh heavily in the following years. First, there was reappraisal of the value of the British nation as able to hold fast in the moment of greatest danger and to organize the life of the whole nation, counting on the full loyalty of all citizens, thus becoming the absolute center and surest bulwark for the safety of the whole British people. Second, there was a complete loss of faith in Europe, and the old sentiment for unification with Europe was replaced by the firm conviction that no confidence could be placed in the European states.

The entire course of the war strengthened the British in these attitudes. And in order to understand properly the meaning of the Labour party's postwar experience, we must look at it as the result of the rallying of the British nation during the war. The same state which had been capable of mobilizing and organizing all the energies of the country to lead it to victory could also be mobilized to attain higher levels of social justice.

All this meant, too, a strengthening of nationalism—British nationalism to be sure, better-mannered than that of other countries, alien to exaggeration, but nationalism nonetheless, strengthening the persuasion that outside of national unity there is nothing that has the right to interfere with it. It is clear why, in a situation like this, British federalism has withered away, no longer finding political forces to support it.

The Situation following World War II

The problem of European unity became acute and pressing following World War II, which created an entirely new situation in Europe. To understand the meaning of the movement for European unification and the forces which moved toward this unification, its achievements, its failures, and its present prospects, it is advisable to stop for a minute and analyze the situation from which it emerged.

THE DOWNFALL OF THE IDOL OF THE SOVEREIGN NATIONAL STATE

A generation ago, during the war of 1914, the Continental European nations went through an experience analogous to that of the British during World War II. Some states won and others lost the war, but all, with the exception of the Hapsburg Empire, which had collapsed, managed to maintain their positions as sovereign communities, demonstrating the capacity to survive, to face a perilous political situation, and to organize national life and guide it with a firm hand. The citizens of the various countries were convinced of the value and worth of the national state as the best expression of political life. Even Russia, where the archaic political and economic order had collapsed as a result of the war, succeeded, through a terrible revolution, in emerging as a more dynamic and cohesive political entity, capable of asserting her national unity and defending her independence.

A consequence of these experiences was the rapid spreading of ideals which tended to emphasize and strengthen the power of the state, and to restore to it, even in time of peace, that ascendancy over the population which it had had during the war, and to render it even more detached from the community of nations. Loud voices calling for the continuation and the enhancement of the power of the state were those of Rathenau, Lenin, Mussolini, and Hitler, and crowds came to listen. The war had given birth to two new powerful ideologies which glorified the state, communism and fascism.

The experience of World War II has had the opposite effect for Continental Europe. With the advance of Germany, all other states involved in the war, whether opponents or allies of Hitler, collapsed and showed they could no longer guarantee a minimum of security and independence to their people; they were turned, voluntarily or reluctantly, into dependencies of the Nazi Empire. Then the German state, which had absorbed the others, was crushed violently, her military power annihilated and her political organization destroyed. Germany became a territory swamped by the victors, and when a few years later the victors attempted to give back to the people some form of political organization, it was discovered that they were not able to reconstruct one state, but had to create two.

All European people had experienced military defeat, but this time there were different results; the idol of the national state, which had been respected up to then, aroused disgust and fell to pieces. Hundreds of thousands of Europeans had ignored national loyalties, often fighting against their own countrymen side by side with those who were officially enemies of their country.

After the war, the European states regained formal sovereignty at some point, but the national institutions were unstable, lacked force, and were not capable of facing the problems of reconstructing a normal national life without the protection and pressure of the great victor powers. That the national state was an idol which did not merit that absolute respect which the pressure of political propaganda had enforced had already been pointed out by nonconformist thinkers. To this now had to be added the obvious and irrefutable evidence of the facts.

This elementary experience penetrated the minds of all, even though not all were fully conscious of it, and it brought about a situation which has made possible the spreading of the movement for European unity, that is, the attainment of order which could replace the discredited and obsolete formula of national states.[1]

[1] From this basic experience one must exclude Great Britain, for reasons which we have seen already, and the neutral countries such as Switzerland

THE LEADING ROLE OF CATHOLIC POLITICAL PARTIES

After the war there was a tendency for political parties inspired by the Catholic religion to become predominant in all countries of western Europe. This is not the place to examine the reasons for this predominance, which was further evidence of the declining power of the state and of the increased prestige of its secular antagonist, the Catholic church. What matters here is to note that of all the democratic forces which appeared during the immediate postwar period, the Catholics were the least imbued with a nationalistic point of view.

The forces of nationalism had been swept away by the catastrophe, and the democratic currents which prevailed were inspired more or less consistently by liberalism, socialism, and the idea of Christian democracy. Men sympathetic to the problem of European unity were to be found in all three, but their respective influence within each of these groups varied because of their differing political traditions, although all three were built on antinationalistic and universalistic ideological foundations.

The liberals who had been the builders of, or at least the inspiration for, the modern European states tended to believe, quite naturally, in the conservation of these states as creatures they loved dearly.

The Socialists had been from the outset strongly antinationalistic, even if only sentimentally so. Their manifesto had stated clearly that "the proletarians have no fatherland." But the manifesto had also stated a clear indication of how the Socialist program could evolve: "In so far as the proletariat of every country ought, above all, gather all the political power to itself, to raise itself to a national class and to constitute itself as a nation, so it still is and remains national." The Socialists had, in fact, exerted their political action by inserting the working classes into the national picture. Their political aims increasingly took the form of an ever-growing and consistent program of national planning. A shrewd Socialist like Ignazio Silone said that

---

and Sweden. English and Swedish influence has also contributed to keeping Denmark and Norway outside the European movement. Spain and Portugal have stayed outside the movement because of their Fascist type of dictatorships, as have countries of eastern Europe which, transformed into satellites of the USSR, cannot hope to follow roads other than those prescribed by the Kremlin.

of all the nationalizations advanced by socialism, the one which has succeeded best has been the nationalization of socialism itself. When, after World War II, the democratic states were restored, the Socialists consistently advocated that these states follow a national, socialistic policy, aware perhaps of the fact that abandonment of national sovereignty would weaken their position. The experience of the English Labourites, which seemed to be the great model, made the Socialists deaf to the problem created by the crises of national states.

The hands of the Catholic parties were not quite so tied with respect to their universalistic doctrine, although the church had intrigued to some extent with Fascist regimes. Catholic political forces had kept aloof for a long time from politics in the three most important states of western Continental Europe. The Third French Republic had been a secular state; the German Reich was Protestant at its beginning and pagan by the end; the kingdom of Italy had a struggle with the Vatican. The Catholics, indeed, had not remained immune from the spread of nationalism, but still remained outside its influence, and it cannot be said that they had much sympathy for the European national states. This explains why, following the war, when the Catholic parties assumed control of various European countries, they did not prove themselves to be jealous custodians of national sovereignties, but were open-minded enough to admit the possibility of unification at the supranational level, even though they had no clear ideas how this should be brought about. It is worth while to note that among the least European-minded Catholics have been the Belgian Social Democrats, and this because, unlike their French, German, and Italian counterparts, they had identified themselves for several generations with the forces of their national state.

To this general predisposition to a European union on the part of the Catholic parties must be added another factor which, although accidental, is not without significance. The three men destined to direct French, German, and Italian foreign policy after the war, Schuman, Adenauer, and De Gasperi, came from borderlands. Two of them in their time had belonged to two different states; the third, Adenauer, had been involved in the separatist movement in the Rhineland after World War I. All three were fundamentally conservative, but national sovereignty was not one of the values that they were anxious to protect.

DECLINE OF THE TRADITIONAL FORCES OF NATIONALISM

If the respect of the public and of rulers for national sovereignty has fallen, this is also true for administrative, social, and economic bodies. Such bodies, which are normally profoundly interested in the maintenance of sovereignty and to whom the system of national states usually gives a strong voice in the conduct of the political life of the state, found themselves in full decline at the end of the war.

The bureaucracies which had represented the backbone of the states and had become to a great extent the organizers of national life were in a position at the end of the war in which they were not even able to satisfy the most elementary needs of the state. The general staffs had either been dissolved or, if still existing, were left without troops to command and certainly were not in a position to claim to be the tutors of national security. The great coalitions of sectional interests, whether representing capitalists or labor, that had obtained from the state a monopoly or had been given a free hand to exploit the national market, were no longer in a position to assure even a reduced movement of the most needed consumer goods and, of course, could not still expect the state to guarantee them the privileged position formerly enjoyed.

In Continental Europe at this time public administration bodies, armed forces, and the economic system existed, as it were, disemboweled and incapable of action. That unnoticed force which is continuously generated by the administrative bodies of the national state, and which more often than ideologies and the will of politicians determines the development of national life, had suddenly been found missing. Not until the old mold had been recast could these forces effectively impede the various political tendencies moving toward a reconstruction of Europe along supranational lines.

THE GREAT FORCE OF SOVIET IMPERIALISM

After World War II Europe had ceased to be the center of world politics and had been replaced by the USSR and the United States as the leaders in world affairs, with England, still important, definitely confined to play a secondary role. An inescapable result of this shift in the power system has been the large influence that the policies of the United States and the USSR have had on European politics.

The USSR through its policy of expansion has contributed indirectly, but nonetheless effectively, to the development of the ideas of European unity. All of eastern Europe has fallen under its domination, and progressively, but inevitably, the earlier democratic experiments have suffocated wherever Communist governments, satellites of the Soviet Union, were formed. The Soviet Union never actually concealed the intention of reaching beyond the Trieste-Stettin line. The developments of this policy have been varied, and are known too well to need further discussion here. The power differentials between the European democratic states and the Soviet Union were extremely great, and the fear of affecting the fate of the Russian and eastern European people was felt very deeply by the majority of western Europeans. The fear factor, always present in political situations, played a very important role in the development of the European idea after World War II. Men and political forces who might have been hostile or indifferent to the idea of European unity understood clearly that this was the only way of giving Europe the necessary strength to preserve its independence. The traditional rivalries among European states, and especially between France and Germany, seemed now anachronistic. The idea of European unity had come up as a means to prevent wars among the people of Europe, but such wars were now pointless, and the real problem was the threatening march of Soviet imperialism. In a certain sense the influence of this great fear on the development of a united European action has been excessive, and we shall see that, after Stalin's death and the subsiding of war jitters, it has had adverse consequences on the European movement.

THE AMERICAN INFLUENCE

The countries of western Europe found themselves, thanks to the decisions reached at Yalta, in the zone of Anglo-American influence or, to be more realistic, in the American sphere of influence. Had the United States chosen to follow an imperialistic policy, like the USSR, there would have been no serious resistance to it in western Europe. Moreover, the Americans disposed of the military power necessary to command obedience and the economic power with which to aid and to corrupt the European populations.

This did not take place, nor indeed was the United States equipped to carry out a policy of imperial conquest, for the American mind, like the Russian, is basically Jacobin, irrespectful of the past, and convinced that the political organization in its own country should serve as a model for the rest of the world. Fortunately, the Americans were enemies of dictatorship under any guise, and the ideas which they brought along were those of federal democracy. They wanted to see Europe forget all its petty nationalism and unite itself in liberty as the American states had done.

American influence has been applied continually and with increasing momentum in favor of a unification of Europe. This was made possible by the great prestige of the United States, which had given ample evidence of its military strength and so much economic aid—so much more than could ever have been expected—to European populations reduced almost to desperation. In fact, it may be said that the American attitude toward the unification of Europe has been a decisive factor in whatever initiatives have been taken by European statesmen in this direction. Indeed, it should be remembered that initiatives of this type were taken by these statesmen not so much in a spirit of loyal dedication to European unity, as through a desire to please the Americans. This duplicity on the part of the European ruling class is another example of the moral degeneration of Europe, and it also explains the many shortcomings of their efforts in bringing about unification. Unfortunately for Europe, the Americans very often have been deceived by the promises and words of European statesmen, trusting that the words were followed by deeds, which in many instances was not the case.

THE GERMAN PROBLEM

The solution of the German problem immediately after the end of the war was a military one and obviously could not last long. A people of seventy million, intelligent and highly developed economically, occupying the heart of Europe, and with such a strong national tradition as to constitute a threat to all Europeans, could not be permanently subjugated. But, on the other hand, it was not advisable to give back to them full sovereignty, as had been done light-heartedly after World War I. Soviet expansion, moreover, had swallowed part of Germany, while the problem of coexistence had not come any closer to being resolved. The only solution which appeared possible to the average individual called for a restoration of governmental functions to West Germany, minus some of the sovereign attributes, especially those pertaining to the conduct of foreign policy, military matters, and economic life in general. But it was to be expected that if these attributes remained in the hands of the visitors for a while, eventually they would of necessity fall back into German hands. For some time German officials and the public in general have been so sincerely disgusted with their past political experience that it would seem they would never again desire to be the possessors of the fatal sovereign power. The idea of European unity, therefore, has been more and more put forth as a solution to the question of what to do with Germany, of how to establish a coexistence with her, recognizing her right to be free while still denying her full sovereignty.

THE NEW FORCE-IDEA

All the data that we have so far examined constituted at the end of the war the sum of the circumstances which made the problem of European unity so urgent and actual without, however, providing a solution. The solution might, of course, take the form of integration with either the Soviet Union or the United States, or of a restoration of the old national state system, or of a free union of existing European states under a new supranational body superior to that of the national states.

This last possibility has been taken up and has manifested itself in two currents of European political thought, both of which today are striving to gain the support of all who are interested in European unity—federalism and functionalism.

Both of these currents had formulated their programs before the end of the war, when any action was still in the realm of possibility. In the very heart of anti-Fascist conspiracy, during the Resistance, in the prisons, concentration camps, and in underground groups, some individuals had come to the conclusion that a pure and simple restoration of sovereign national states would be an absurdity. The two world wars had been the direct consequence of a Europe divided into national states. To restore these states even with a democratic form of government, and leave them in possession of sovereign prerogatives, would mean an inevitable rebirth of political and economic nationalism, thus perpetuating the cause of international conflicts.

The political originality of these first thinkers did not lay in their method for realizing a European federation, for they reverted to the already existing models in the American and Swiss experiences. Their originality was in the proposals to promote a political action which, by demonstrating the impotence of the national sovereign states and the critical conditions in which European states would find themselves after the war, would pave the road for a movement which would create European federal institutions.

When the first such groups began to gather and to elaborate their ideas in illegal underground meetings, no one knew whether in other European countries there would be other people like themselves thinking the same thoughts or whether the idea of a federal movement existed only in their minds and had no factual relation with reality. Only during the last years of the war, when direct contact among men of the Resistance from various countries was established through Switzerland, did it become evident that under different circumstances and starting from different political premises men from different nations, unknown to one another, had elaborated the same thoughts and reached the same conclusions. At a meeting held clandestinely in Geneva in May, 1944, and in the first public meeting in Paris of March, 1945, the first stones were laid of what was to become the federalist movement in all democratic countries and eventually their common association in June, 1947, at Montreux in the Union Européenne des Fédéralistes.

In juxtaposition to the advocates of federalism stood what has been called the functional approach. Public officials, politicians, and experts in the various European states were not accustomed to thinking of solving European problems along federalist lines. The only supranational experience in their memory was that of the two great world wars, in which the partners in the fight had deemed it opportune to establish some specialized integrated authorities of a military and economic character (unified commands, boards for common procurement and allocation of war material, monetary pools, etc.). The execution of these tasks was entrusted to a supranational authority, while the power of political decisions remained in the hands of national governments. It was natural enough to transfer this line of thinking to the field of European reconstruction, and it was a Rumanian, Mitrany, who became the theoretician of functionalism.

Jean Monnet during the war years had elaborated the idea of applying the functional approach first to the coal and steel industries, and it was from this that there emerged the European Coal and Steel Community, the first and until now the only example of a functional supranational authority.

Functionalism, born in the minds of high public officials, seemed to be a much more practical approach than that of political federalism. It did not attack directly the problem of the limitation of national sovereignty. It was based on experiences known to European politicians. It was hoped that by increasing the number of specialized institutions a point would be reached when the setting up of a European supranational power would become natural and effortless.

In contrast to the federalists, the functionalists have never organized themselves, but their ideas have spread everywhere. When European statesmen were faced with the problem of European unification, they espoused the functionalist approach, adopting federalist points of view with hesitation and halfheartedly only when forced by necessity and discarding them when the pressure diminished.

From the End of the War to the Marshall Plan

As the various European countries were being liberated and the end of the war was in sight, and the democratic forces were coming back to life, many political parties in the process of reorganizing themselves made declarations, more or less vague, in favor of European union. In reality these were empty declarations, since the European states were not in a position to influence European policies, the power of which was in the hands of the victors who, at Yalta and at Potsdam, had decided to divide the Continent into two spheres of influence.

The Russians and Anglo-Americans alone made decisions regarding boundaries, political institutions, economic life, and relations with neighboring countries. Germany ceased to control its own affairs. Russians and Anglo-Americans made solemn promises to reestablish liberty, democracy, and independence in Europe and even to reunite Germany, but actually theirs was an attempt to set up a new kind of Holy Alliance of great world powers with the task of maintaining order in the world and particularly in Europe. The Europeans were in such a state of weakness and desperation as to applaud, with a few rare exceptions, the magniloquent declarations of the great powers, and to hope that among them there would prevail the same co-operation that had existed during the war.

If it had been possible for the United States and the Soviet Union to remain good friends, European history would have ended in 1945. The old Continent would have been divided between the two powers, as had happened in Africa in the preceding century, when that continent was parceled out into spheres of influence of the European powers.

As long as the Americans and Russians attempted, in spite of the growing rivalry, to maintain the basic agreements of Yalta, there was no real European policy. The ideals of European unity remained vague utopias without any following and federalist movements remained small and limited in scope.

Fortunately for Europe a real agreement between Russia and America was not possible. The USSR looked at the Yalta agreements as a transitional phase in the development of its own imperialism. While on one hand increasing its control over eastern Europe and taking the first steps to transform these weak democracies into Communist dictatorships and Soviet satellites, Russia on the other hand was unfolding a complex policy which had as its aim the final conquest of the rest of Europe.

The Americans realized that by continuing the Yalta policy they would be playing straight into Soviet hands and sanctioning the expansion of Soviet imperialism. Western European states were in such complete political and economic confusion that it was relatively easy for the Communists, who represented the only totalitarian force to survive the war, to rout the democratic forces and set up police-states.

In order to remedy this ill-fated and dangerous situation, the United States decided, after much hesitation, to put an end to this new Holy Alliance policy and to consider the Soviet Union as a dangerous enemy whose expansionistic aims had to be stopped. Consequently, the Americans began to view democratic Europe as a political whole, to be aided as such and to be helped to unite, so that it could become an effective force able to resist by itself the advance of Soviet imperialism.

The problem was not yet viewed in military terms. It was a matter of reorganizing European economies so as to provide solid ground for the reborn democracies. With the announcement of the Marshall Plan there was a profound change in the European situation. The Russians stepped up their control of eastern Europe, cutting out for these countries any hope for autonomous action. In western Europe the Russo-American impasse was the determining factor in foreign policy. It was obvious that western Europe had to choose siding with the Americans and welcoming their protection. But since America offered them economic aid and asked them to devise the best way to utilize it, the Europeans were suddenly confronted with a problem of international policy, since it was up to them to elaborate a common way to share this aid. Here was a purely European situation which could be resolved only through a union of the interested states. Churchill, in his famous speeches at Zurich and at Fulton, was the first statesman to proclaim that European states should reciprocate the new American policy by showing a desire to unite, and he thus gave the first impulse to the creation of the European movement.

Churchill's initiative had been conditioned by English policy. Great Britain had abandoned every prospect of taking part in some kind of European union, and in fact was in the midst of the great Socialist experience inaugurated by the Labour Party. The British, by tradition, opposed any kind of political consolidation of Europe, since it could mean the creation of a great Continental power. But the presence of Russian imperialistic policy prevented Great Britain from taking a position openly against European integration, which would have meant against the United States and indirectly in favor of Russia.

To get out of this diplomatic entanglement, Churchill came up with an idea both clever and cynical. The British would take over the role of guardian of the European movement, which they would guide so as to make sure that a real union never would be achieved. There was no talk of federation, transfer of sovereignty, supranational institutions, or for that matter of creating a real European political framework, but instead an abundance of platitudes and generalities concerning a generic "union," the heritage of a common civilization, solidarity against communism, a permanent resolution of the Franco-German question, and so on.

It was thus at a moment when the problem of European unity had become alive that there began also the erosive action of the various national conservatisms. This was exemplified by the fact that the most prominent European statesman, Churchill, and the most powerful European state, England, were sabotaging the process of unification which was about to take the first steps.

Unfortunately, the prestige of the man was so great that the still young and poorly organized federalist movements which had been formed between 1945 and 1947 were completely deceived by the Churchillian rhetoric and became founding members of the European movement. Important people gave their support, and a great European congress gathered at The Hague in 1948. There were only a few federalists who, unheeded, denounced the falsity of this propaganda.

Parallel to the propaganda activities of Churchill and of the European movement came the British government's official sponsorship of leadership in European action. To the Marshall Plan the British government responded, backed by European governments, with the Organization for European Economic Co-operation and, somewhat later, with the Council of Europe, that is, with the creation of international institutions which, while giving the impression of unity, were only consultative organs, and thus by-passed completely the problem of national sovereignty.

The Marshall Plan represented the one chance for Europe to unite. If the American government had seen through the false European spirit of the British and had granted the aids contingent on the creation of political federal institutions on the Continent, we would now have European union, since no serious opposition could have been given by the forces favoring maintenance of sovereignty, except, of course, by Great Britain. It is to be regretted that the Americans, on this score, were duped by Great Britain in one of the greatest deceptions in modern European history, and so instead of a political union we have witnessed the maintenance and the strengthening of the national particularisms, vaguely disguised in European terms, which for some time have deceived both American and European public opinion.

The money which the Americans thought they were giving to help the Europeans to overcome economic nationalism served only to reconstitute the old national economies, instead of creating one market and one European economy.

From the Schuman Plan to the Korean War

The uproar raised by the birth of the OEEC and the Council of Europe among those who favored European integration did overshadow for a while the real issues at hand, but it could not obliterate them completely.

With the advent of the Marshall Plan there reappeared also the German problem. West Germany, included in the project of economic rehabilitation, could no longer be treated as an occupied country deprived of political rights. The United States, Great Britain, and France had to take a hand in the reorganization of the country by restoring its currency and economy, and by setting it up as a political entity. Little by little the conquerors were giving back to Germany some attributes of its sovereignty. If this came relatively easy for America and England, the same was not true for France, where it seemed obvious that this procedure would once again make possible the resurrection of a powerful German state on the Rhine frontier.

The apparent pro-European attitudes of the English succeeded in part in deceiving French public opinion and political leaders, creating the impression that the British, deeply involved in the reconstruction of Europe, would never again leave them alone to face the Germans. This British attitude, however, did raise some doubts in the minds of Frenchmen, since it did not answer any of the questions which, for them, had been raised by the rebirth of a German state.

France's weak position was rendered more precarious by an economy in a state of disorder and a political life in decay. Attacked by Communists and by the supporters of De Gaulle, the democratic elements in France sought a way out in the European idea. Frenchmen did not know for sure what the making of Europe meant; they had a vague notion that it would imply a union with yesterday's enemies, the Germans and the Italians. It was not a situation which aroused emotions and enthusiasm, and thus the policy issuing from it had of necessity to be methodical, cold, rational, and calculated. The politicians who occupied policy-making positions in the Fourth Republic were considerably devoid of any of these qualities. Federalist thinking and the federalist movement were weaker and less influential in France than elsewhere. At a moment when French politicians were forced to tackle the problem of a European political community, the best that French federalists could offer, out of their confused perspective, was a rhetorical exposition of what a perfect federal society should be at the municipal, regional, French, European, and world level.

It so happened that the first concrete suggestion made in France on the problem was along functional lines. For France, the central problem was still that of the sovereignty of Germany, but the aspects of this problem which were of importance at that moment were neither political nor military, but stemmed from the rebirth of the heavy industry in the Ruhr. Jean Monnet pulled out of his drawer the project which he had elaborated during the war years of a Franco-German coal and steel pool, and prevailed upon Schuman, then Foreign Minister, to promote it. Schuman showed a great deal of courage in taking up the project, which aimed at setting up a common market for coal and steel under the control of a supranational authority, because he knew that Great Britain would never accede to it; he even declared that France was ready to proceed alone with Germany on this road.

With the conference on the Schuman Plan, composed of representatives from six countries, there began a real attempt at a policy of European unity. With willfulness and clarity, Monnet, presiding over the conference, persuaded the six participating states to accept the creation of a specialized community with a supranational High Authority which, rather than the individual states, would control the common coal and steel market.

The limitations of the European Coal and Steel Community were serious. The common market for these two important raw materials could not be completely divorced from the various economies of the member states, which continued as national economies subject to the control of their respective governments and parliaments. The executive functions of the High Authority were strongly restricted by the ministers of member states, who sat in a special council and alone were empowered to pass on those measures involving the various national economic policies without which the Coal and Steel Community would remain but a pious hope. The Common Assembly of the European Coal and Steel Community, moreover, had no legislative power whatever; this was retained by the respective national parliaments. The birth of this first functional-type community was made possible partly by the French desire not to give back to Germany full control over the Ruhr, and partly by the German maneuver to escape, as much as possible, the limitations which the victors had forced upon her. At the time of ratification by the six parliaments, the founders of the community, Monnet, Schuman, and the delegates from the other states, declared publicly that the European Coal and Steel Community would be long-lived only if European unification proceeded along other roads. The European Coal and Steel Community was only a breach in the walls of sovereignty to let Europe pass through, and unless it grew wider, there was the danger of its being closed again.

The elaboration of the Schuman Plan gave important impetus to the federalist movements, which at that time were beginning to rebel against the false position of the European movement and to assume definite political aspects. Starting from the premise that European unification implied essentially integration of the six countries which made up the Schuman Plan, during the period from 1949 to 1951, the federalists, in opposition to the functional thesis then accepted by the governments, championed the idea that the six countries, instead of proceeding toward the formulation of additional pools and markets, should bind themselves with a federal union pact and with a common constitution and political organs. As a procedure to be followed for the drafting and approval of such a pact, the federalists suggested that instead of proceeding through normal diplomatic channels, the parliaments of the member states elect representatives to a European constituent assembly, which in turn would submit to the national parliaments for ratification the constitution that had been elaborated.

These suggestions made no impression on the European governments at a time when the Marshall Plan and the Schuman Plan seemed to indicate the right road to European reconstruction.

Actually the Marshall Plan was restoring the national economies to a normal state, but it was not creating a European economy. The first visible results of the Marshall Plan were the halting of the Communist menace and the reappearance of big sectional monopolistic business concerns intent on preserving and defending the national economic systems with the privileges inherent in them.

On its part the Schuman Plan had instilled a conviction that the functional approach was the answer to European integration and that what was needed were more attempts along this road.

While Europe and America were emphasizing economic reconstruction, the Korean War broke out in 1950, underlining the fact that western Europe, the most important industrial force in the world besides America, would not be capable of defending itself in the event of a Russian invasion.

From the Korean War to the Ad Hoc Assembly

The Korean War highlighted in a dramatic fashion the problem of the defense of western Europe. Under the Atlantic pact the United States was bound to help Europe in case of aggression. It was American military protection, following economic assistance, which saved western Europe, and the prospect of American intervention served as a deterrent to Soviet encroachment. But in spite of this protection, the fact remained that Germany was still disarmed and the other countries were poorly armed, which meant that Europe could not be defended.

Now the Americans began to supply military aid and to contribute to European rearmament. In the same spirit with which they had backed German economic rebirth within the framework of the Marshall Plan, they now called for the rebirth of German military power, without which the defense of Europe would have been impossible.

The reaction to this in Europe was similar to that which had characterized the formulation of the Marshall Plan. Churchill spoke of a European army, which, of course, would not include Great Britain; the French government, shocked by the prospect of a resurrected German army, proposed also the formation of a European army, but following the functional approach in vogue. When the conference for a European army opened, the only states present were the members of the European Coal and Steel Community.

But to apply the functional approach to the problem of military organization bordered on the absurd. For months and months the delegates of the six countries tried to come up with some sensible scheme for the multinational army, but were constantly rebuffed by insurmountable obstacles of a political nature. To whom would the European army have belonged? Certainly neither to the national states nor to a central European political power, which did not exist. Could it have been made dependent on SHAPE? But SHAPE was only a military command of the Atlantic Council within which the guiding principle was that of a coalition of sovereign states. The European army was a necessity, but it was impossible to create it.

The criticism of the federalists, which at the time of the Marshall and Schuman Plans had been dismissed, began now to take hold on the minds of the politicians. It was inescapable any longer that a unification of the armed forces implied the relinquishing of some sovereign attributes on the part of national states. It was absolutely necessary to create a European political entity to which the individual states would relinquish their sovereignty in military matters.

The first government to give consideration to this request of the federalists was that of Italy, whose delegation at the conference for a European army requested from the beginning that the community be given its own parliament and fiscal powers. When it became evident that the other delegations were not disposed to intepret their mandate so broadly as to mean the preparation of a real constitution, the Italians proposed that at least the assembly which was envisaged as the organ of the EDC be charged with the formulation of a political constitution for the whole community.

This request was accepted and incorporated, in complicated and unsatisfactory language, in article 38 of the proposed EDC Treaty, and with a limitation so serious that it would have caused the failure of the whole effort. The assembly of the EDC was, in fact, not charged with the preparation of a constitution to be ratified by the respective parliaments, but of a preliminary study to be sent to the member governments, which in turn, would have convened an intergovernmental conference to discuss it. What the diplomats granted with one hand, they retrieved with the other.

The federalist campaign, in spite of this, was scoring other successes in the course of 1951. In July, General Eisenhower acknowledged the fact that without a federation of Europe, the Atlantic Pact could not function properly. In November, Spaak, who up to this time had remained on the unsteady ground of the European movement, of which he was President, recognized the necessity of making a formal request for a supranational constitution. He dramatically resigned as President of the Consultative Assembly of the Council of Europe and allied himself with the federalist movements setting up an Action Committee for a European Constituent Assembly. The problem was now coming into focus. Even the governments represented at the conference for the European army had realized that the EDC could at best be a provisional arrangement, and were inclined to agree that the EDC Assembly should prepare the final statute for the defense community. Since this assembly would be the same as that of the European Coal and Steel Community with the addition of nine members, there was no need to await the ratification of the EDC in order to start working on it. The European Coal and Steel Community Assembly was convened on September 10, 1952, for the first time, since the treaty had now been ratified. The situation was clear-cut; all there was to do was to take article 38 of the projected EDC Treaty as a basis upon which to elaborate the first outline of a political constitution.

The absurd manner in which the problem of a European army had been approached highlighted serious difficulties of a constitutional and political nature, and finally induced the ministers of the six countries to abandon the functional in favor of the constitutional approach. The request of the action committee was accepted. On September 10, at its inaugural session, the Assembly of the European Coal and Steel Community was charged by the six ministers with the mission of organizing itself as the assembly of the EDC as well, and of drawing up within six months a constitutional project for the European political community.

The assembly modestly turned itself into an ad hoc assembly under the leadership of Spaak, and on March 10, 1954, with conscientious punctuality, presented a constitutional project. It was still a rather weak step, since after calling for a European government and a freely elected parliament endowed with fiscal powers, the organs of which were also given the tasks of assimilating the Coal and Steel Community and the proposed EDC, and of legislating on matters pertaining to the common market, it placed at the side of these institutions a council of ministers from the member states who had to approve unanimously every act of the community. This free federal construction, restricted at every move by the ministers of national state, was the best that the parliamentarians of the ad hoc assembly could do.

When the proposed plan was sent to the six ministers, that phase of European and world politics favorable to European action was coming to an end.

The Failure

The train of events which had forced the leaders of six countries to attempt a policy of supranational integration began to slow down with the death of Stalin. From the very beginning it became evident that his successors did not wish to continue the hard policy of the Cold War and, perhaps, lacked the ability to do so. Facing a difficult period of internal readjustments, they inaugurated the policy of distension. And with the lessening of the danger of war, the enthusiasm of many for European unification also diminished. American military and economic aid, if it had failed to bring about European unification, had helped European states to strengthen their administrations, their armed forces, and their national economies. Those forces interested in the preservation of national sovereignty were strong again and made their weight felt. In addition, the general economic situation was rather good, and this contributed to the spread of a general feeling favorable to the maintenance of the status quo in Europe.

These circumstances explain why attempts at a European unification on the part of the six nations failed.

The project of the ad hoc assembly was passed by the ministers to a committee of experts and diplomats and, within a few months, nothing more was heard of it.

Four parliaments wearily ratified the EDC Treaty. The Italian Parliament, now incapable of following them, awaited leisurely the decision of France. The French National Assembly, in a sudden surge of national pride for its own army, declared the treaty unconstitutional, while a few months later it approved the rebirth of a German national army. With this act another important factor in European politics was eliminated; Germany was again a fully sovereign state. Here ended in failure the attempts of European governments to create a new level of sovereignty and to abandon the road of particularism and nationalism.

The relaxation in international relations, together with the economic boom, and the revival in all countries of conservative forces interested in the maintenance of national sovereignty, carried in its wake a new equilibrium in world and especially European politics. Europe had not solved any of its problems, but was able to keep alive by accepting this state of affairs. With the passing of the great fear of war, single countries gained greater freedom in the conduct of foreign affairs, even permitting themselves the luxury of acting with more independence with respect to American policy. This new freedom of action did not generate any greater sense of responsibility with regard to the establishment and maintenance of world peace; in fact, because of their division, the European states constituted an element of imbalance. They had become the new Balkans in the world politics and seemed pleased with their accomplishments.

Germany had long believed that she had to choose between national unity and a European community. Now it was obvious that both prospects had vanished. Similarly, France had thought the choice for her lay between French union and European unity. But here again events were taking care of the situation, making no choice necessary.

European Revival and the New Federalist Approach

In spite of all this, the governments of the six countries had not completely lost sight of the question of European unity, although the force of events had confused the problem. And so, partly because of the general listlessness and partly in order to hang on to a political formula that might be useful some day, on June 2, 1955, at Messina, the six countries decided to set up a commission of experts, under the leadership of Spaak, in order to carry out the so-called European Revival and, more precisely, in order to promote the creation of a common European market and of an atomic pool.

Monnet, who by then had resigned from the presidency of the High Authority, together with the secretaries of democratic parties and of the non-Communist unions of the six countries, formed an Action Committee for the United States of Europe. This committee, in spite of its ambitious name, is concerned only with the rapid promotion of an atomic pool. The functional approach is riding high again. Toward the end of last April the experts of the Spaak Commission presented to the interested governments a long report which tries to resolve the impossible. They propose a merging of the various national economies into a common market without, however, touching national sovereignty.

It is probable that the government will discuss at length this report and its proposals, but it is certain that, with the present lack of interest in the problem of European unification, a river of words will flow, but no action will be taken.

The defeat of the efforts for European union has had profound repercussions in the ranks of the supporters of the federalist idea. Many of them insist on believing that the governments are genuinely interested in formulating a realistic European policy; and in order not to embarrass them the federalists refrain from criticizing the erroneous steps which are being taken. Others have come to the conclusion, based on past experience, that nothing can be expected from national governments and from national political forces and that the problem of European integration will be seriously taken up again only if and when a new crisis faces Europe. They plan to form small nuclei of nonconformists seeking to point out that the national states have lost their proper rights, since they cannot guarantee the political and economic safety of their citizens.

They also insist that European union should be brought about by the European populations, and not by diplomats, by directly electing a European constituent assembly, and by the approval, through a referendum, of the constitution that this assembly would prepare.

This is the point now reached by the movement for European integration which grew out of the last war. Whether this is the passing of an experience or the beginning of a new cycle, in the words of Socrates, "is known to no one but God."

The Case for European Integration: Economic Considerations

UGO LA MALFA / *Former Italian Minister of Foreign Trade*

WHEN SPEAKING of European integration, it is difficult to separate economic from political considerations. A distinction between the two may be made at the risk of falling into abstraction, but even then it must be admitted that economic and political factors are always intermingled, that any differentiation between the two is arbitrary, and that the only purpose it may serve is to facilitate discussion.

It is generally conceded that Europe for the past fifty years has been in a state of continuing decadence and that the Continent, which at one time was the center of world power, has been reduced to the position of a border area or, perhaps, to that of a no man's land between two great powers. The dilemma that faces European leaders today is either to accept this situation or to attempt to reverse the process and try to change the status quo. In 1913, Europe west of the Oder produced 45 per cent of the world's industrial goods. By 1937 the percentage had gone down to 34, and in 1955 it was producing only one-fourth of the total world industrial output. During this same period, when the world's industrial production had increased three times, production in Europe had barely doubled. Europeans must now decide either that it is possible to put an end to this backsliding or that the old Continent is beyond all hope of being saved.

In western Europe at present the per capita consumption of

energy per year in its various forms equals two tons of coal, while in the United States such consumption equals eight tons. No less indicative is the per capita consumption of steel, which in the countries of the Coal and Steel Community is 230 kilograms, in Great Britain 310 kilograms, in the United States 610 kilograms, and in the Soviet Union between 160 and 180 kilograms per year. Per capita income in the United States is $1,575 per year, while in the six countries forming the Coal and Steel Community it ranges from $250 to $500. It should be noted that these figures, far from reflecting a situation of economic stagnation or decline, represent an all-time high and reflect an unprecedented economic growth and general well-being. Actually it is this upswing of the economic situation which Europe is experiencing today that permits us to see clearly the inferior structural characteristics of the individual European countries in comparison with the United States and the Soviet Union. In fact, taking 1938 as the index year for industrial production at 100, we find that in 1955 the countries of the Coal and Steel Community reached an index of 155, while the Soviet Union and the United States increased theirs to 250 and 260 respectively. This indicates clearly that, in spite of the great efforts of individual European countries even at a time of increasing economic development like the present, the rhythm of our economic progress is decidedly slower than that of the great powers.

The figures cited above, moreover, do not tell the whole story of Europe's inferiority, because, while up to now we have been able to assimilate all the technical improvements developed in other countries, we cannot expect to be able to continue to do so in the future, in spite of all efforts and good will, simply because the rhythm of world technological progress and expansion is too rapid. On this point Spaak, in the report in which he summarized the findings of the Brussels Committee, pointed out three specific cases which illustrate the enormous difficulties with which the European countries will have to cope in the near future, namely, that there is no single automotive industry in Europe which can utilize economically the most powerful American machinery, that no European country is in a position to build large transport airplanes by itself, and that the knowledge and know-how in the atomic field which have been gained by Europe, after enormous expenditures, represent only a small fraction of the knowledge that the United States is now turning over free of cost to American industries and to those of other countries as well. It has been announced recently that the United States is putting at the disposal of private industry and the world in general forty tons of enriched uranium; it would take Europe several years to produce a few thousand kilograms.

No European country is in a position to support the huge efforts and financial investment for research which are basic to the technological revolution promised by the atomic age. In addition the increase in production which is made possible by the use of atomic energy would be suffocated within the narrow limits of separate European markets. The atomic revolution, more than anything else, will demonstrate plainly within a few years the antiquated character of our economic structures. If the atomic revolution has the same consequences as did the Industrial Revolution in the eighteenth and nineteenth centuries, it can be expected that countries remaining outside the orbit of this revolution will be fated for fast decadence. It is common belief among the advocates of European integration that, should their efforts fail, Europe will be relegated, with respect to the United States, to the position occupied at present by the Balkan, or indeed by the Asiatic, countries with respect to Europe. In order to halt, correct, and reverse the spiral of impoverishment and decadence, the European countries must put an end to the era of divisions and wars and create a common market, a vast zone of common economic policy which will thus constitute a powerful productive unity.

Up to now, countries have based their economic policies upon a fundamental differentiation between their production and consumption and the production and consumption of other countries. In this process each country, in an effort to gain advantage at the expense of others, ends up by weakening its own position with regard to foreign competition. This, in fact, is the end result of customs which increase the price of imported goods so that they cannot compete with national production. This is also the meaning of import quotas which, by restricting the quantities of imports, place a limit on competition. Low production and high prices are the natural consequences of restricted markets with a consumer population of ten to fifty million people. External discriminatory practices and restricted production within are the two typical faces of economic nationalism. Occupied with their mutual struggles, European countries have not been able to dedicate to research and to investments the large budgets which, for example, American business has earmarked for these ends. Expansion of plants, division of labor, specialization of production, which have prospered greatly in the large American market, have been suffocated by rivalry and internecine strife on the Continent.

The postwar period with its devastations and miseries finally drove part of the European ruling class to the realization that Europe could survive only by uniting. But the hard work which up to now has been directed toward the realization of this goal has shown how difficult it is to overcome the obstacles and how long and hard is the road yet to be traveled.

From the time of the launching of the Marshall Plan, Europeans have sought to unite through various methods. But today, almost ten years later, although the national structures have been repaired, the fortress of national sovereignty has remained untouched, with a few sporadic exceptions. The mere fact that national structures have been rebuilt does not signify that they are strong. States which are incapable of guaranteeing the protection of their citizens from military aggression, which are not in a position to insure the stability of democratic institutions nor an adequate level of economic well-being, are weak and precarious. They continue in a fixed state opposed to change. This is quite apparent now, especially if we look at the efforts directed toward a European federal state, the creation of which implies a revolutionary alteration of present structures. This was not quite so obvious shortly after the war and at the inception of the Marshall Plan. Since there was so much to rebuild, it seemed that European countries might decide to pool their resources to lay the foundations for a common future and make a break once and for all with the old habit of selfish nationalism.

But the supporters of European unity both in Europe and in America deluded themselves; the time was not ripe for federation. Europeans preferred to concentrate their efforts on national reconstruction, made possible by American aid, while paying lip service to the eventual necessity of creating a larger area of co-operation. So it happened that the European countries pulled themselves out of the ruins and miseries into which the war had plunged them, while Europe stood waiting to be united.

Some concessions to the prevailing feelings of co-operation were made, however, and so we had the first forms of political and economic collaboration among national governments in the shape of the OEEC and the Council of Europe. These two institutions have demonstrated that it is impossible to take positive steps toward European unification without effectively delegating sovereignty or without establishing federal or supranational institutions. Leaving aside the Council of Europe, which lies outside the confines of my discussion and which as far back as the summer of 1949 was labeled by an English newspaper as a "talking shop," the OEEC, in whose activities I personally have taken part, suffered from the great limitations intrinsic to its juridical structure, mainly the lack of real power to have its decisions respected by the member countries. For instance, within the framework of the OEEC, Italy has almost completely liberalized its import policy, while at the same time France has failed to do so, and there is nothing that the OEEC can do to induce France to follow the same line. These liberalization measures, however, are not final, which means that the governments which adopt them can revoke them when they deem it opportune. There is no guarantee within the OEEC that the process of liberalization, once begun, will inevitably grow, or at least lead to a situation of common economic stabilization.

At last we come to the Schuman Plan, which represents the first real attempt at federal integration. In order to give an organic treatment to my topic, I must make some general observations on the European Coal and Steel Community, which, I believe, remains the fundamental example to be studied by those interested in the economic integration of Europe. The Coal and Steel Community is not only the fundamental pattern to be studied for a realistic approach to the problems of economic integration, but it is the one experiment which, at certain points, has proved itself to be the shortest and only feasible means of integrating Europe at a supranational level.

The very high concentration of coal and iron ore respectively in the Ruhr and Lorraine areas furnished a unique example of the necessity for some sort of economic collaboration between France and Germany. At the same time it provided an opening through which the forces of federalism began to operate persistently, making it unnecessary to start with a frontal attack, doomed to failure, against the forces opposing the unification of Europe. The integration of the coal and steel industries would imply a union of sorts between France and Germany, and by throwing this bridge across the Rhine the opportunity was finally presented of resolving in the only way possible the centuries-old antagonism between the two countries. Here we have a clear example of the interrelation between economic and political factors and of how one cannot be divorced from the other. In fact, since political factors are the more pressing, and since the *porro unum* of any long-lasting European integration is the elimination of the Franco-German antagonism, no reasonable economic integration of Europe can be conceived unless it includes France and Germany.

The Schuman Plan has served also to clarify another fundamental question, the position of Great Britain. Before any integration initiative is taken, the basic political question to be resolved is that of knowing how far participating countries are willing to go, what resources they are willing to pool, which sovereign rights they are willing to relinquish. During the uncertain first steps of the integration initiative following the war, the marching order was that of a convoy in which the speed was set by the slowest unit. The Schuman Plan, however, forced the governments to make a clear choice—to renounce their sovereign powers in matters relating to coal and steel industries and to transfer this sovereignty to a European community endowed with supranational powers in these sectors. The British government refused to make the choice, and this refusal, far from being considered a hostile act, actually proved to be the most positive incentive to European integration that could come from the British Isles. The Foreign Office could have assumed a different attitude; for instance, it could have participated in the negotiations with a view to cutting away the federative character from the treaty as much as possible, and backing the creation of a new community of the OEEC type. Instead, Great Britain preferred to recognize the fact that Continental European countries wanted to move along the road to integration at a more rapid pace than she was ready to do and so excluded herself. This was indeed a revolutionary gesture on the part of a power which, by tradition, has followed a policy of inserting itself in the European equilibrium.

From this moment on, the basic problems of European integration became clear-cut, and as a consequence the European Coal and Steel Community came into being as the first practical example of European federal organization. Once this was accomplished there ensued a struggle within the governments and parliaments of the six member countries to extend the supranational integration to other sectors of the entire common market. The great advantages of the European Coal and Steel Community lie in the fact that all problems and polemics pertinent to the economic integration of Europe are taken up by the community. As a result, from its day-by-day activities in the coal and steel sector a wealth of practical experience is derived in matters of integration in general. There are at present two projects under consideration at the ministerial level in the six countries, the common market and Euratom. The common market is the most long-range objective, while Euratom is an objective which must be achieved immediately and urgently.

 The debates and struggles which are underway in the parliaments, the executive and foreign offices, and the presses of the various countries revolve mainly around the question of the powers which must be delegated to the new supranational institutions. The backers of a united Europe argue that it is impossible to create an effective common market and an atomic community unless federal powers are delegated to the new institutions. We assert that without such delegation of federal or constitutional powers there can be no real economic integration. This assertion is not based primarily on any personal principles or abstract logic, but on the concrete experience gained from the European Coal and Steel Community and on the fact that there are no objective reasons to prevent the creation of supranational institutions. The European Coal and Steel Community proves that a supranational parliament and executive can operate without creating havoc with the national institutions of the member countries. It proves that the creation of a common market is possible and that it does not represent a dangerous adventure nor an economic jump in the dark for the countries involved, the weaker partners included. It proves that the common European market is neither a utopia nor is it economic suicide, as long as some steps are taken to guarantee gradual development and clauses are provided, including some measures of safeguard for the industries involved, to regulate the period of transition.

 Before leaving the High Authority, Jean Monnet, who is one of the most tireless and gifted advocates of European unity, summed up very clearly the experiences of the European Coal and Steel Community. The synthesis is not only applicable to the experience of the community, but it is also a valuable measuring stick for the other feasible goals of integration. In fact, a reading of the "Spaak Report" will show that the general reasoning of the Brussels Committee is based on the same principles.

"In the system of national economies, producers pressure governments in order to protect their markets and maintain their profits, consequently passing the burden of higher costs to the consumers through higher prices. The common market would give all entrepreneurs greater possibility for expansion, so that industries could defend their interests only by a constant effort to better their productive facilities and their costs. This would act as a stimulus to better management, modernization of capital goods, more rational production, and would be of great benefit to all consumers. Naturally it is important that the creation of the common market be lasting, that the elimination of trade barriers and discriminations never be abandoned —in other words, that the common market be stable and permanent, and not have the characteristics of a transitory experiment. The entrepreneurs must be certain that all the efforts and sacrifices necessary to adapt themselves to the common market will be justified by the lasting character of the new economic situation. In substance, the fundamental fault with so-called functional integration lies in the fact that there is no assurance that such integration will be lasting, since there is always the possibility that the agreements reached may be broken, and since there are no common institutions endowed with sovereign powers to guide and preside over the process of functional integration.

"It must be added that the common market will make it possible to continue the fight against monopolies, and keep alive a system of industrial competition, while at the same time allowing maximum development to industries so that they will be in a position to utilize the most recent technological improvements. This has already been accomplished in the coal-steel market through a merging of industries. Here something which had been advocated for many years, but which had always seemed impractical within the narrow limits of national markets, has taken place without any difficulty within the larger bounds of a common market such as that of the European Coal and Steel Community, in which steel production is above fifty million tons per year. Together with making possible the optimum plant expansion, a larger market in which the producer finds himself in competition with a greater number and diverse types of industries, and in which the consumer has a choice of products, also modifies the relationship and attitudes between producers and consumers during the fluctuations of the economic cycle. Once again the Coal and Steel Community furnishes a practical example of great importance. Since the establishment of the common market there have been, in fact, two distinct periods of business fluctuation. During the low phase of the cycle, and contrary to what usually occurs, there has been no letdown in the rhythm of investment. In fact, there was a decided increase in investments to lower the production costs. The widening of the market has made the adoption of restrictive practices unnecessary during periods of recession and also has forced industries of the common market to search for new consumers in those areas where they previously could not expand because of discriminations existing in favor of this or that producer.

"On the other hand, in the present high phase of the cycle, the producers' competition within a large market limits the effects of rising prices due to a greater demand. Consumers do not need to worry about the scarcity of goods and therefore do not resort to hoarding during the period of high demand, nor are they forced to bear the monopolistic tyranny of a single producer. Greater production coupled with a greater demand have, in spite of the upswing of the business cycle, created imperceptible variations in the price scale. In countries such as France and Germany, in which most of the production is absorbed by the home market, in order to guarantee economic stability in the past, the governments had to resort to measures of allocation and price-fixing. Holland and Italy, countries which counted heavily on imports for a great part of their needs, saw, at the time of the Korean boom, steel prices skyrocket from $50 to $150 per ton. The common market has been able to absorb a suddenly increased volume without showing noticeable variations in the price scale."[1]

The benefits of the common market may be said to consist chiefly in the expansion of plants and facilities, increased production, improvement of competition, and containment of prices. But which

---

[1] European Coal and Steel Community, Debates of the Common Assembly, Regular Session, May, 1955.

are the measures needed in order to create these conditions? What does the setting up of a common market really mean?

First of all, the creation of a common market does not mean only the elimination of customs tariffs and quotas. As has been stated clearly by the experts of the Brussels Committee, "the object of a European common market must mean the creation of a vast common political and economic zone, which will make possible a strong productive unity."

Speaking of the OEEC a short while ago, I said that the elimination of quotas would mean practically nothing, since this elimination could be replaced either by new customs duties or by an increase of the old ones. At the same time elimination of quotas, and duties as well, would serve no purpose unless at the same time an elimination of discriminatory transport tariffs took place. Similarly, elimination of all these barriers and discriminations would be useless unless an end also was put to a repartition of markets on the part of cartels and to governments still being allowed to subsidize this industry or that sector of industrial production, all measures which would falsify the normal market competition.

This is not all. We must also consider the indirect effect of national legislation upon competition. A government's action determines different levels of economic activities and prices, and these differences actually are the chief causes of disequilibrium in the balance of payments. A common market is not compatible with the existence of such disequilibria. The co-ordination of economic policies, made possible by the common market, makes it possible to overcome the obstacles which such disequilibria impose upon the balance of payments. In addition, the adoption of a common economic policy necessarily must make provisions to insure economic expansion. The first of these provisions consists in facilitating the movement of the labor force left unemployed by the modernization and rational reorganization of industries. As Monnet stated in a speech to the Assembly of the Coal and Steel Community, the fundamental problem of modern economy lies in a reconciliation between job security of labor and the necessity for industrial, technological, and economic improvement. Here we see clearly the importance of the measures of reapportioning the labor force, measures which protect labor from the risks and uncertainties inherent in the process of transformation. In this field, too, the Coal and Steel Community stands out as a unique example. In fact, various cases of reapportionment of labor have already been carried out by it. At present, Italy, in conjunction with the High Authority, is studying the best way to resolve the problem of about 8,000 steel workers left jobless as a result of the rational readjustment of our steel industry within the framework of the community.

The second condition is to facilitate, for the industries, the process of reorientation, that is, of the reconversion of their plants. This necessitates the common market being presided over by an institution which has at its disposal sufficient means to assign to this important function.

There is also a third condition. We have learned from experience (and particularly from the history of Italian unification) that a union of several regions at differing levels of economic development does not mean necessarily that the more backward areas will catch up with the more developed. It is necessary here to follow a policy which will foster, in the underdeveloped areas, the creation and progress of those structures necessary to economic development, so that there can be a full utilization of the differences of labor cost or of greater possibilities for profits. There is need here for measures to stimulate regional development and to utilize labor locally. Only these conditions will eventually close the gap between production and the standard of living of the various regions.

All in all, co-ordination of economic policies, productive investments in underdeveloped areas, the reabsorption of the labor force left jobless by technological improvements, will in the end insure conditions for a free circulation, not only of products and services, but also eventually of the essential elements of production, capital and manpower. In this way the unemployed labor force, which is still a burden for some countries, will become a new resource for a united Europe.

These general conclusions are not my own, but a synthesis of those expressed by the Brussels Committee, based on the experiences of the Coal and Steel Community, and it should be mentioned here that officials of the Coal and Steel Community have made important contributions to the deliberations of the Brussels commission.

At this point it seems worth while to express my opinion on the proposals made by the Brussels experts to the various governments in order to arrive at a common market, proposals which the respective governments will be discussing shortly. The experts have done an excellent job, and I am in substantial agreement with their general conclusions. Some decisions, however, are of a political nature and can be made only by ministers and parliaments, and the experts must learn to adjust their suggestions to the dominant political climate of the time. As we have seen, the common market can be achieved through two fundamental types of measures: those which can be clearly defined in a charter, because their development can be foreseen, and those which take the form of day-by-day action to be handled by the institutions entrusted with the creation of the common market. The abolition of customs and quotas falls, for instance, within the first type of measure; the charter of the common market will decide that tariffs be scaled down by, say, 30 per cent every four years for the first eight years, and by 40 per cent for the following four years, so that at the end of a twelve-year period the customs barriers will be eliminated completely. It is quite clear that, regardless of what criterion is used to decide the lowering of tariffs with regard to different merchandise, the tariffs will fall automatically. The institution presiding over the development of the common market, with the exception of the safeguard clause which I will mention later, will only have to make sure that the terms of the agreement are respected.

Let us now examine other measures, such as the fight against monopolies, the stabilizing influence of the balance of payments, the policies of earmarking funds for investment, and redeployment of labor—measures which have to be taken in order to eliminate or reduce wherever possible the inequalities in social and fiscal legislation. It is obvious that with respect to these and similar measures the articles of the charter must of necessity be general, and it would be ridiculous to try to force economic development through rigid and preconceived patterns. The task of the legislator is to prepare laws elastic enough to respond to unforeseen situations and events. To attempt to foresee everything, to sketch all minute details in legislation of this kind, would mean to create too rigid a framework and risk stifling all development. At the same time, if legislation is too general, then there is the danger of creating only the empty juridical shell to be filled in as the various partners desire. In our case, given the impossibility of making the treaty too detailed, the critical point of the problem lies in the question of what institution will have the power to fill the shell and thus be empowered to control and watch over the unfolding of economic factors.

This power, and let us be frank about it, is not referred to at all in the project prepared by the Brussels experts. In this project, the proposals relative to the institutions are still vague, and the executive power, as represented in it, will be very weak. The institutional framework of the common market follows closely the structural setup of the Coal and Steel Community. There will be an executive, an assembly, a court, and a council of ministers. In the Coal and Steel Community the executive, that is the High Authority, was conceived of as the most important institution, and the Council of Ministers as the co-ordinating organ having the task of harmonizing the requirements of the High Authority with the policies of the single member governments. However, in the case of the common market, the European Commission—the title itself already reflects a change in atmosphere and concepts—will have limited, consultative powers. This makes it quite obvious that the Council of Ministers will be the actual decision-making organ, and as such it will have to act unanimously, at least during the transitional period.

Thus the European Commission will have power to preside over the evolution of the common market during the transitional period, applying, whenever needed, the so-called safeguard clauses, that is, taking special measures in favor of an industry or an industrial sector when these appear to be endangered by the progressive formation of the common market. It is clear then that, apart from consultative powers on all matters on which it can request the intervention of the Council of Ministers, the only real powers of the European Commission are essentially those of preservation. In other words, whenever an industry is in danger because of the dynamism of the common market, the European Commission can intervene to save it.

Here, in my opinion, is a crucial problem worth much consideration. Under the projected treaty, the European Commission will become an organ charged mainly with the application and interpretation of the safeguard clauses, when in a healthy common market it is natural, and indeed desirable, that those industries which are uneconomic and not worth maintaining should be eliminated. The dynamism of the common market and its superiority over national markets lie principally in the elimination of less economic enterprises on one hand and the creation of conditions for the rise and expansion of healthy industries on the other. If the European Commission is meant to be able to measure up to the new economic situation and derive the best results from the enlarged market, then it is necessary to endow it with sufficient powers so that it can cope with the dangerous symptoms or crises as they emerge in one industry or a whole sector. The European Commission should have its hands free to deal with concrete problems and to try to solve them with a view to future conditions, rather than be forced to rely upon past experience and to look to the future only as a mirror reflecting the economic forms of the past.

On the basis of this same criterion, the European Commission should be allowed to act autonomously in selecting those measures which it deems best suited for the success of the common market, especially with regard to the fight against monopolies, abolition of discriminations, utilization of funds to be invested in underdeveloped areas, the reabsorption of the unemployed, etc.

The fact, however, that the project presented by the Brussels experts assigns to the European Commission only consultative functions and concentrates all the executive power in the hands of the Council of Ministers leaves no doubt that there will not be a European economic policy conceived and carried out from a common and unified point of view. On the contrary, we will have a policy which will be the sum of the economic policies of the single states, a total of all the agreements, compromises, and expressions of fine intentions, common enough results of meetings of councils of ministers, carried out in an atmosphere of diplomatic niceties and having nothing in common with a real work session as, for instance, we can observe in the High Authority.

The analysis of the Brussels experts' report led me back to the question of institutions, actually of the federal character that such institutions should have if we expect our national structures to be transformed effectively into a unified organism through the process of economic integration. I am very much in agreement with Jean Monnet when he states:

> the creation of institutions which will obey new and common rules is more important for the future of Europe than technological progress and the increase of material wealth which will be made possible by a common market. . . .

and

> while each man's experience begins anew, institutions have the advantages of benefitting from collective experience, and thus of becoming better tools, and as a result of this cumulative experience and wisdom the people who move within the confines of these institutions will see themselves gradually transformed without noticing the changes taking place in their own nature. . . . Institutions control the relationships among men; they are the real pillars of civilization.[2]

This, translated into everyday political terms, means that in order to arrest the process of European decadence, it is absolutely necessary to delegate sovereign power to a federal organization. For this reason we have fought for the success of the Schuman Plan, as we are now fighting for the common market and Euratom. Those who today raise objections to Euratom, saying that it is necessary to abandon the idea of integration by sectors, are very well aware that they are moving in the wrong direction, because, although the action committee for the United States of Europe has agreed to give priority to the fight to create a European Atomic Community, it has also bound itself solemnly to tackle as soon as possible the problem of the common market. This is not the place to make a detailed examination of the atomic energy situation. I would like to say only that atomic energy is the key to the economic future, and in this sector more than any other, we can see clearly how development on a national scale could never hope to compete with the achievements of the Americans and Russians. The nuclear sector becomes, thus, a sort of symbol. If the economy of the future will be based to a great extent on nuclear power, and if the only feasible way of developing nuclear energy in Europe is through a supranational integration, then the superiority of the supranational method will undoubtedly have repercussions in other sectors of the economy, and the atomic pool will then increase the possibility for a large common market. If we succeed in creating an atomic community with supranational attributes, then we will have reached another goal in the institutional battle.

As you have seen, I am far from being an optimist when viewing

[2] Jean Monnet, *Les Etats Unis d'Europe Ont Commencé* (Paris: Laffont, 1955), pp. 37-39.

the immediate future. The report of the Brussels Committee shows that while everybody seems to agree on the necessity of a common market, while the opinions of the experts show that they see the greater advantages of a common market over national markets, while they all praise the effective supranational experience of the Coal and Steel Community, still the executive organ which they propose to direct the creation of a common market is given none of the effective powers necessary to insure its success.

The reason for this state of affairs, however, is a political one, and I would exceed the limits of my subject if I were to attempt to analyze it.

The Case for European Integration: Political Considerations

E. N. VAN KLEFFENS / *Ambassador of the Netherlands to Portugal*

THERE ARE four introductory points I should like to make for a proper understanding of my treatment of this subject.

First, I shall not attempt a full historical description of what already has been said and done in the field of western European integration from the political angle. What I want to do is to throw such light as I can on the essential political elements of the problems of western European integration, their background, their development, and their foreseeable future. I shall have to mention from time to time several events that have taken place in my allotted field, but that will be by way of illustration, and not as my main object.

Second, by *integration* I am thinking in conformity with what I believe is by now a generally accepted meaning of the term—of the transfer to some supranational body of certain powers previously vested in individual sovereign states. By *supranational body* I mean, again in conformity with current terminology, a body having authority over the states which are answerable to it in the field over which its authority extends.

Third, although my topic is integration in the sense I have just indicated, I shall have to mention on occasion that time-honored and usual form of international co-operation which consists of states working together on a basis of simple association, each member state remaining the sole judge of the extent of his contribution, without being answerable to a superior authority. The reason is that, although some countries of western Europe are prepared to accept integration while others are not, all those countries have now and will have for quite a time to come, the same common problems, so that there is a strong bond between them, whether they are ready to accept integration or not. To consider only the countries willing to agree to integration would be, theoretically speaking, quite possible, but it would draw a picture threatening to be very one-sided, disregarding and overriding the fact that all western European countries have the same common problems to solve. That they share several of these problems with the United States and Canada would constitute an isolated examination of those western European countries which are in favor of an even more unrealistic integration.

Last, I shall have to mention repeatedly matters which superficially may seem to be not political, but economic. I shall do this unashamedly, which may seem paradoxical, since I am expected to deal with "political" considerations. But, when you look closely, you will find that these matters are either political intrinsically, or they have considerable political overtones. Take as an example the European Coal and Steel Community, Schuman's thriving brain child, which is far from being simply an economic phenomenon. As a prerequisite for Franco-German general co-operation it is a political matter of great importance. Professor Reuter of Paris said rightly at The Hague Academy of International Law in 1952, that the Coal and Steel Community is political with regard to its aim as well as to its subject matter (coal and steel) and its method. Think, also, of how marked a political character these seemingly economic arrangements have, of the convention establishing the Organization for European Economic Co-operation, which in the beginning of its preamble states:

> a strong and prosperous European economy is essential for the attainment of the purposes of the United Nations [largely political], the preservation of individual liberty and the increase of general well-being, and will contribute to the maintenance of peace.

"The real nature of the integration of Europe in the field of energy and of 'European economic integration'," said my compatriot, van der Goes van Naters, recently in a report to the Common Assembly of the European Coal and Steel Community[1] (and I am sure he was right), "is political." Many of these matters that have an economic side are also political in nature, and that is why I shall have to make frequent mention of them.

Let us look back briefly to get the proper perspective, and bring out a few salient points without which the rest might not be quite clear.

Americans nowadays are often heard to ask, not without some impatience, "why doesn't western Europe get together?" Well, certainly not for want of talking about it, for although the incentive to get together lacked strength until recently, Europeans have been talking for centuries about closing their ranks. Let me only mention, among many others, and chronologically widely apart, Dante and Pope Leo X, Erasmus and Grotius, Thomas More and William Penn (after all, of European origin), Émeric Crucé, Sully and the Abbé de Saint-Pierre, Fichte and Kant—all exhorters of theoretical or utopian proposals to keep the peace and establish some order and unity in Europe.

In the second decade of the twentieth century, group movements were initiated for European co-operation. These were, as such, something more than mere exhortations by individual authors. First in the field was that oft-derided figure who nevertheless, as Americans say, "had something," Count Coudenhove-Kalergi. We all remember the Pan-Europe movement he started in 1922, a movement of which no less a statesman than the late Aristide Briand, not a dreamer but a man of action, became President five years later. In 1924, another famous political figure, Édouard Herriot, while he was Prime Minister of France publicly advocated European union.

Then, following the nineteenth century prototypes, European customs unions were in the air.

The most statesman-like prewar approach to the integration of Europe was undertaken by Briand in 1929. His ideas were discussed by the Eleventh Assembly of the League of Nations, which decided to have their study continued by a commission. There it got bogged down—other more spectacular and pressing problems forced themselves upon the attention of the world. Instead of getting together in

---

[1] Van der Goes van Naters, "Exposé Introductif au Rapport sur l'Intégration Economique" (European Coal and Steel Community Document AC 2068), p. 1.

the interests of peace, active preparations for war were made in a number of crucial spots.

In 1939 war came, and after it a cruel aftermath which saw western Europe on the edge of an abyss. It was rescued largely because of American perspicacity and generous assistance. In the process, the old idea of European unity reasserted itself, this time with greatly increased vigor.

For the first time in history, there were very powerful reasons for western Europe to get together. Here was Toynbee's challenge in *optima forma;* a civilization and a way of life were in dire peril. Would there be a response? We now know that there *was* a response, a response which is still being worked out, and which is our current subject matter.

What was that peril? Partly, it was postwar exhaustion, a general state of anemia in western Europe. Next, there was the increasing threat of the old, but revived, Russian expansionism, allied to and galvanized by the pseudo religion of communism with its promise of all things to all men.

The alarm was first sounded in Zurich by that extraordinary, prophetic statesman, Sir Winston Churchill, who as early as 1946 advocated the creation of a United States of Europe and, as a first step, of a Council of Europe. By the following year the economic situation of western Europe had become so precarious that General Marshall, as reflected in his momentous speech of June 5 at Harvard University, felt it was urgently necessary to combine what was left of the resources of western Europe and the vast economic potential of the United States for a grandiose salvage operation. Matters then began to gather impetus. In January of the next year (1948) the late Ernest Bevin, then British Secretary of State for Foreign Affairs, suggested in the House of Commons that, if Western civilization as we know it were to survive, it would be necessary to develop what he called "some form of union in western Europe, formal or informal in character, backed by the United States and the Dominions." The idea found favor in the whole Western world, and particularly in western Europe itself—1948 saw the Brussels Treaty concluded, promoting military, economic, social, and cultural cooperation between Belgium, Britain, France, Luxembourg, and the Netherlands, which West Germany and Italy joined seven years later, an arrangement known as the Western Union. The same year saw the Convention for European Economic Co-operation and the establishment of the equally beneficial European Payments Union. A year later (1949) the Council of Europe came into being, and in 1952 the European Coal and Steel Community came into force. There followed negotiations which, as we all know, failed to be ratified, for a Western European Defense Community and a wider Western European Political Community. To end on several notes of positive achievement, I mention the European Conference of Ministers of Transport, steps to arrive at unity on matters pertaining to agriculture and food, unifying attempts among smaller groups of western European countries, Benelux, and the promising efforts and results tending toward greater unity of the northern states. And finally there was the very positive *relance européenne* of last year, which is still in full swing and being very actively pursued under Spaak's dynamic direction.

All this would not have been possible without the assistance which the United States, and also Canada, gave so generously and in so many forms to western Europe in the last decade.

Now why has all that been undertaken? Why have so many practical measures been put into effect? I think there are three main sets of reasons: a sense of the inadequacy of relatively small states in modern political and economic conditions; the shift of the world's centers of gravity as a result of the two successive world wars; and the Russian menace.

Let me begin with what I ventured to call the sense of inadequacy of relatively small states in modern political and economic conditions.

There are, in the world today, at least four giant states. Through size and sheer population numbers, China and India, with 600 and close to 400 million inhabitants respectively, are undoubtedly giants. For a variety of reasons, their influence, though great, is not the same as that of the other two, the United States of America and the Soviet Union, each of whom has not only a vast population, but a tremendous production apparatus and wide internal market. These two colossi set the pace and the tone, each in its environment and partly beyond it, in the world of today. Compared with these two, all other countries are small, even one with as extensive an area as Brazil. This smallness applies particularly to the western European states, some being smaller than others. There is a double aspect in which the existence of the two principal giants affects western European states with a certain sense of inadequacy, politically or militarily, and economically.

First, let us consider the political or military aspect. There is no western European state today which can assure its own defense. For that purpose, not one of them alone has the man power, the production resources, or the raw materials, nor are they sufficiently distant from potentially hostile centers. This inevitably results in the need to lean on others. The United States and the British dominions have become the mainstay of the western European states, individually as well as collectively, Britain itself not excluded. But the feeling the western European nations have of not being able to insure, each for itself, its own defense, has also engendered a new tendency to work together *inter se*. In view of the possibility that another major war may supervene, no western European state can afford not to co-operate closely with the other western European states.

Second, as for the economic aspect, the times in which we live call for large production centers and wide markets. Technological progress would have brought about all this even if World War I had never taken place. But that war did take place, and it resulted (my second point) in shifting the world's centers of gravity away from western Europe and toward the two principal giants. The western European nations realize that this shift of the world's centers of gravity away from western Europe, where they had been for so many centuries, has revealed a new and fundamental insufficiency in their national fabric, both in peace and, still greater, in contemplation of aggression from outside. "Our countries," said Jean Monnet on November 11, 1954, "have become too weak in terms of the present day world, of up-to-date technical development, and in relation to America and Russia as they are today, and to China and India as they will be tomorrow." As the Research Directorate of the Secretariat-General of the Council of Europe put it in a report published exactly a year ago:

> Formerly dominant in world affairs, Europe today finds herself in the position of a group of individually secondary units placed between the two world Powers: the USA and the Soviet Union. The movement for European political unification, partly inspired by this situation, has involved also a call for increased economic

integration as a corollary to, or even forerunner of, the prospective political transformation.[2]

These are words that deserve our closest attention, for no one has ever won a final victory over the needs of his time.

Third, let me consider what I have called the Russian menace. The first person to draw public attention to the need for western Europe to unite in order to meet the Russian menace was a man whom I have already mentioned as the founder of the movement for Pan-Europe. Count Coudenhove-Kalergi as long ago as 1922 wrote with considerable foresight: "History gives Europe the following alternative: either to overcome all national hostilities and consolidate in a federal union, or sooner or later to succumb to a Russian conquest."

Expansionism seems to be inherent in the collective Russian soul, which is all the more extraordinary because individually Russians tend to be docile and long-suffering. That expansionism is both physical and spiritual. From the smallest beginnings, the Russian Empire in a bare two hundred years occupied all the lands and dominated all the peoples between the Vistula and Alaska. Some urge seemed to drive the Russians on. They did not pause to develop what they occupied, going forever onward, and filling, gaslike, every space where they met no resistance. Sometimes, however, their unrelenting pressure found resistance, as their European and American record shows. Recall how Peter the Great attempted in vain to obtain a foothold on the Adriatic (think of Albania today!); how Russian armies between 1711 and 1918 were driven from Rumania a dozen times; how they were pushed back from the Rhine in 1735 and 1747, and from Berlin in 1760. Think of Czar Paul, who for a brief period was Grand Master of Malta, and of the temporary presence of their troops in westernmost Continental Europe after Napoleon's downfall. And as far as America is concerned, they are no longer in San Francisco, nor in Alaska.

To that physical Russian expansiveness is added an equally natural messianic spirit. Russia is the heir of Byzance, which had succeeded Rome—Byzance, whence came the orthodox faith of which Moscow became the guardian and keeper. Russia felt itself a new

---

[2] Research Directorate, Secretariat-General of the Council of Europe, *The Present State of Economic Integration in Western Europe* (Strasbourg: 1955).

Holy Land and a new Rome, with a new mystical message of salvation for the whole world.

This, too, is a component of Russian expansionism. The great Russian writers rejected western European concepts. The cautious approach, the sense of responsibility and of limits of western Europe, did not appeal to them.[3] From the middle of the nineteenth century there was a whole galaxy of Russian writers, whose names do not mean much, if anything, to the western Europeans of today, who thought and wrote about the destinies of Russia, which to them were —note the expansionist trend—identical with those of the world in general. Power over others was to them not so much an aim as a duty and a burden—the true messianic spirit. It was like "take up the white man's burden," only the white man carrying the load was to be a Russian, by the grace of God.

That messianic tendency is now allied to the equally ambitious, universalist spirit of Marxism, a dangerous combination if ever there was one. We all know its tenets. And as if that were not enough, there has been fused with this double-barreled expansive faith and with that urge to physical expansion I mentioned before, a fourth element, an empirical, purely technical element, a carefully thought out technique to gain and retain power, a method which shows few scruples and little respect for the traditional ethical values of the West, the end justifying the means.

That is the threat of Russia, which Occidentals here and in America all feel, without necessarily analyzing it. It is the challenge which confronts the whole Western world, both America and western Europe. The West has decided to resist this challenge. There is, in other words, a response.

To counteract our triple predicament—the emergence of giant states, the shift of the world's center of gravity, and the Russian menace—we have rejected outright two methods, abject surrender and the method followed within the Russian orbit of complete domination by the strongest member of the group. Such domination would be so completely against the Western tradition that it has been neither tried nor advocated by anyone, particularly in the

---

[3] See Hans Kohn, *The Twentieth Century* (New York: The Macmillan Co., 1949), pp. 94-95. The seventh chapter of this remarkable book contains an interesting review of this subject.

United States. And about abject surrender, General McAuliffe's "Nuts" would be the only comment needed.

No, we try to bolster our position by co-operation, and in that field we are flexible. Our strength will always be in direct proportion to the adequacy and excellence of our co-operation system. Together, the West has at its disposal incomparable resources of every kind, labor, raw materials, capital, know-how, and what we have of these four elements in western Europe alone is very considerable. To attain the best way of making use of them, we have found out that there is not just one single recipe. The Continental states of Central Europe, the Netherlands, Belgium, France, Italy, Luxembourg, and West Germany (sometimes collectively referred to as "Little Europe," as distinct from the larger group of western European countries represented in such organs as OEEC and the Council of Europe) are prepared in suitable cases to consider giving co-operation in the form of integration in the sense I have indicated above, voluntary transfer of certain sovereign rights to a supranational agency. Note the Coal and Steel Community, which, if the signs do not deceive us, will not be the last instance of western European integration, for this is only a beginning. The avowed aim of these countries is, as they declared in a resolution adopted in Messina on June 2, 1955, a wide form of integration "through developing common institutions, the progressive fusion of their national economies, the establishment of a common market, and the progressive harmonization of their social policies."

On the other hand, the northern countries and Britain have, for different reasons, shown great reserve in respect to integration, which does not mean that they will not co-operate in the time-honored, associative way, without transferring any powers to a supranational body.

Until now, the Scandinavian states seem to have had an aversion to integration. As far as Britain is concerned, that country has objections to integration which are not applicable to the other western European countries. I mention only in passing the British preference for growth as opposed to construction, for empirical solutions as contrasted to written legal texts, which come naturally to the Continental nations. The main consideration in the special case of Britain is that it is, of course, the center of the Commonwealth and Empire, and, much as we Continentals may regret it, this makes it understandably difficult for Britain to give to a supranational body certain powers which are retained by other partners of the Empire. The result would be a lopsided structure with a kind of double allegiance, a situation just as unacceptable as the dual allegiance which would result from adherence to the British Empire for Continental European states. We have to accept that stern political fact, and there seems to be justification for the hope that on her part Britain realizes that it is to her interest to enter into a close partnership with western Europe, second only to that with the nations which together with Britain form the Empire, and as close as that with the United States.

In connection with political facts, in general in the wide fields where western European co-operation is possible, doctrinaire attitudes are, I think, dangerous and can only lead to disappointment. Let us do what is attainable, but let it be commensurate with the danger we have to face.

Why are certain countries in favor of integration rather than of the old form of simple co-operation? A reply was given by them at the conference of Messina, where they declared: "Only in this manner can Europe expect to maintain its position in the world, to regain its influence, and to raise steadily the living-standard of its population."

I should like to add that an integrated area may be expected to react better in times of depression than would its individual unintegrated component parts, each of which would in such circumstances, as experience shows, at once ban imports from the others and resort to that bilateral barter which reduces the volume of trade when this is least desirable.

Beside this, integration, the supranational variety of co-operation, will in my opinion prove the best, the only really effective way to face the monolithic Russian organization. The day of the individual state, western European size, standing alone, or playing together with its equals a delicate game of adjusting balances of power, is past. Nationalism cannot satisfy needs greater than itself. To ignore it would spell certain disaster. National insufficiency in present circumstances is being realized with particular acuity in the central zone of western Europe. All this helps to explain why integration is more readily acceptable there than elsewhere.

Another very important political consideration in connection with integration is that political integration without an economic basis is inconceivable, and vice versa. The two are inseparable; just as there can be no political integration without an economic basis, so there can be no economic integration without a political framework. When the ministers for foreign affairs of the countries that are members of the European Coal and Steel Community met in Messina in June of last year, they adopted the resolution I already mentioned, in which they stated very clearly that Europe can only be united by developing common institutions, by a gradual merging of the national economies, the creation of a common market in which goods, persons, and capital circulate freely, and a gradual harmonization of social policy. Political as well as economic points are taken simultaneously. The Research Directorate of the Secretariat-General of the Council of Europe reported a year ago:

> An integrated European economy would reinforce and make more obvious the community of interest of the nations involved; its administration would require common political organs; and these, once established, would by the interpenetration of economics and politics, soon give to all Europe a single common policy in the face of the present crisis in the world.[4]

No political integration without economic integration, and vice versa. That, as a result of the laborious threshing out of all these problems which was done in the course of the last ten years, is a truth which is now more or less generally accepted. It has been acted upon in the Coal and Steel Community. It will no doubt be acted upon in other fields.

As to method, you can either integrate over a broad front, establishing an area comprising the territory of several states with one and the same social insurance system, for example, or a common single market between the partners with free circulation of persons, goods, and capital, and the necessary political organs to administer whatever there is to be administered in that unit; or you can single out one particular sector of the economic life of the nations, organizing it according to its needs. The European Coal and Steel Community is an instance of this kind of vertical or, as it is also called, functional integration. What seems worth mentioning is that to a certain extent the method to be chosen is a matter of expediency and the possibilities of the "how." I say "to a certain extent," because

[4] Research Directorate, Secretariat-General of the Council of Europe, *op. cit.*

it goes without saying that one cannot multiply ad infinitum cases of vertical integration without creating a large number of organizations presenting such complicated problems of interrelation and coordination as might well prove to be insoluble, thus robbing integration of much of its advantage, and creating new and highly undesirable problems.

The main political difficulties in the way of integration are by no means confined to the western European nations. They are inherent in the nature of things in every country everywhere. Let impatient people elsewhere, therefore, think twice before reproaching western Europe for not getting together more quickly. They themselves would be no less inclined to balk at these difficulties if *they* were asked to do a little integrating in their turn.

There are several difficulties. The Research Directorate of the Council of Europe has drawn attention to quite a few, among which are xenophobia, inertia in habits of thought, and fear of immigrant labor. For those important points I would prefer to refer you to the Directorate's remarkable report on "The Present State of Economic Integration in Western Europe" of May, 1955, for I myself should like to mention another kind of difficulty which you will not find in that report. The difficulties I have in mind are partly concerned with private persons and enterprises, and partly with individual states.

First, there are many private persons and business enterprises in each separate country whose existence is bound up with the fact that their state or government protects their livelihood or capacity to make profits, i.e., by instituting a customs tariff. When economic integration is contemplated between two or more states, import duties are sure to be raised for the people of country A, while they may well have to be lowered for country B. It is this lowering which is painful, and provokes that resistance which is capable of giving the measure, economic by nature, strong political overtones. It is, economically as well as morally speaking, impossible to disregard that kind of resistance. You cannot, as a government, tell the owner of a business, flourishing on the basis of certain protective customs duties, "well, sir, you have this flourishing business, quite legitimately founded by your grandfather and developed by your father and yourself, but it has to be sacrificed because we think it is important to establish a great international market where it is going to meet deadly competition." That clearly is impossible. If such a case arises on any significant scale, transitional measures must of course be devised to cushion the shock. We have done that when establishing Benelux, and it has also been done in favor of the less competitive mines when the European Coal and Steel Community was founded. But it is a very real difficulty.

Second, there are those difficulties which arise from the nature of the sovereign state. The sovereign state is an institution with an extraordinary degree of vitality. In spite of the fact that it consists internally of a multitude of interests in a state of unstable and ever shifting equilibrium, each sovereign state appears outwardly as a closely knit unit, with an individuality all its own, speaking to the outside world with one voice, that of the government, which interprets the needs of the internal interests as it thinks proper at the moment.

Sovereign states possess great endurance, and their undiminished existence has great emotional appeal. Since integration means a certain diminution in the exercise of sovereign rights, it provokes resistance. In the material field, each sovereign state is intent on perpetuating and advancing its own interest, having a dynamism which shows political, military, and economic forms of expression, is rather inflexible, and has difficulty in fusing with others, even if it does not actually repel them, like nuclei giving off radiation.

In the emotional sphere, the nationals of each state feel an innate allegiance toward it. Bound together, if not by kinship or language, then by customs and institutions of their own, they are conscious of the many things they appreciate or are used to in their own particular country, things they do not find the same elsewhere. Their country gives them protection, a home, friends, a chance to develop their native genius. It provides a stimulus to compete with the nationals of other states. The citizen feels that it is *his* country, the expression of his own nation's individuality, to which he is bound by hundreds of ties. We can feel ourselves good western Europeans, but if we ask ourselves which are stronger, the ties that bind us to western Europe or those that bind us to our own country, the answer in most cases would not be in doubt.

All these factors are obstacles in the way to an easy acceptance of integration, particularly because to a large extent they belong to the realm of the emotions. On the other hand, the desire to integrate is a matter of cool reason. It is this contrast, coupled with all the public and private vested interests mentioned, which makes integration so difficult and so unappealing. If integration is to succeed, it will be through persuasion, and not through an appeal to the emotions. It follows that in all our countries, governments and organs of public opinion have a very large and difficult task to perform to facilitate the acceptance of integration where it is necessary.

After all, why should we in western Europe be squeamish about transferring certain sovereign rights to a common body for the common good? Look at the extent to which in practice we have delegated authority to NATO which to all practical intents and purposes has, no matter what the lawyers may say or what NATO may be in other respects, a supranational general staff, and in so sensitive a field as national defense! We are by now quite used to that (it would have shocked our fathers). Can we not do something similar in other fields, especially within a group of nations such as those of western Europe, with a common approach to the things around us, common dangers to face, common aspirations to pursue? Let us not exaggerate, making a bogey out of national sovereignty. A lot of sovereign rights (nobody can say exactly which or how many) have to be transferred before a state ceases to be a sovereign state. The states which established the Coal and Steel Community turned over to the community important sovereign rights, but is there anyone in his right senses who would maintain that Belgium, France, West Germany, Italy, Luxembourg, and the Netherlands are no longer sovereign states? Let us look these realities in the face, and not be overly susceptible to emotional but uninformed talk about loss of national greatness.

For national greatness will remain in plenty. Nobody dreams of asking anyone to give up his national characteristics, his cultural identity and heritage, his complete autonomy, wherever this can be at all safeguarded and maintained, consistent with common safety. What we are asked to do is to take such measures as are adequate to protect us from the perils that threaten us, precisely in order that those precious and essential acquirements may be secure. What integration (where integration is necessary) aims at is not destruction, but protection, preservation, and continued development; not a drab and soulless uniformity, but security and prosperity in diversity. This, I submit, is not rhetoric, but common sense.

There are people distrustful of integration, who ask somewhat ingenuously whether nations accepting some degree of integration are perhaps weary of being sovereign states. I do not know how seriously we have to take such a question, but one sometimes has the impression that it is being asked half in jest and half in earnest. I should like to reply to that question, and my answer is an unqualified "no." No, we of western Europe are not tired and weary nations; we may go through a period of difficult adjustment, but we have the stamina and the fortitude to do it. There is a vast difference, or perhaps I should say a complete and irreconcilable opposition, between such a negative notion as being weary of something, and a positive objective such as that being pursued deliberately by those who would put integration into practice where it is an essential condition of security and survival. Does anyone think that the Russians and those who are subservient to them would be so dead set against Western integration if integration did not increase our safety and our strength? Wherever we find it necessary to integrate, we show not weariness, but vitality; not degeneracy, but robust health; not despondency, but confidence in the future, and our determination to *have* a future as free nations.

There is one special field in which the possibilities of integration would appear to be particularly promising, and that is the development of atomic energy. There no vested interests stand as yet in the way of integration. The very magnitude of the problems involved, of the resources required, and of the capital needed, all seem to point the way toward integration. Accordingly, one of the four commissions established in July, 1955, by the Committee of Government Delegates, called into being by the Messina Conference, has to deal with atomic energy (the other three committees are concerned with traditional sources of energy, the common market, and transport *cum* public works, respectively). What should be pooled in the field of atomic energy is knowledge, raw materials, and equipment. There should also be, of course, a system of supervision. There arise, in this connection, problems with a marked political character. Assuming that there will be an international European organ in charge of atomic energy (the name apparently is to be Euratom, to whom is that organ to be responsible? Responsibility there obviously must be. A solution such as has been found in the European Coal and Steel Community seems indicated, in which the executive supranational organ is responsible to a form of supranational parliament. It undoubtedly would be useful if this supranational parliament could be the same in both cases, a joint organ for the Coal and Steel Community and for Euratom; the same applies to the Coal and Steel Community's Council of Ministers and the Court of Justice.

That some western European countries are prepared to consider integration in this important field, while others are not, need not exclude fruitful co-operation between the two groups, the former to be embodied in Euratom and all countries concerned to be embodied in the organ now being studied by the OEEC. It is earnestly to be hoped that, should it prove easier to make progress with Euratom than with the establishment of a common market in western Europe, measures will be taken to make sure that a solution of this latter problem, which is at least as important and certainly of an even wider scope, does not suffer by being retarded or relegated to second place.

I shall make two more remarks, and I shall have finished.

In the first place, I should like to mention the special position of the smaller western European nations vis-à-vis integration. To the smaller nations, integration means a greater sacrifice of influence and position than to larger states. In a diplomatic congress, where what the Charter of the United Nations call "the sovereign equality" of all states makes itself felt by each delegation having a vote of equal value to that of the others, the legal and political weight of each state can make itself fully felt. But in an integrated organization this is different. Unequal representation in executive and other organs, weighted votes, and other devices may result in as many disadvantages as advantages for the smaller states. True, they will find some compensation—assuming the essential rule of "no political integration without economic integration and vice versa" is heeded—in a wider market, and this may mean a considerable increase in trade, as Benelux experience convincingly shows. But that applies likewise to their big partners, just as increased security is obtained by all. It follows that for smaller powers integration means a greater sacrifice of autonomy than for the larger ones. And yet, some of the smaller states of western Europe are more in favor of integration than some of the larger countries. I believe this is the result of the problem, and especially of the true nature of integration being better understood in some countries than in others.

Finally, let me call attention to what might be called the question of the closed or open shop. Let us assume that a number of western European states decide, for the sake of their greater security and prosperity, to proceed with political and economic integration. Does that mean that from then on they will form an exclusive society which does not admit other members? I do not think for a moment they would want to do that. In fact, I feel sure they would welcome any other like-minded free western European nations who subsequently might express the desire to join them, just as they would wish to co-operate constructively with organizations such as the OEEC.

And I believe further that they would also see the danger of a closed shop in the sense of a new high-tariff area, or an area in which imports would be based on a system of quantitative restrictions, without due regard for the need of generally increasing international trade and of observing such principles as are embodied in the General Agreement on Tariffs and Trade (GATT). Here again, things that seem to be primarily of an economic nature have strong political overtones.

An Inquiry into
Feasible Forms of European Integration

JOHN A. LOFTUS / *Professor of International Economics, Bologna Center, School of Advanced International Studies, The Johns Hopkins University*

THE PURPOSE of this article is a modest one. It is to examine the concept of European integration, to try to determine not what it should mean, but what it does mean. Once this question is posed, its answer is obvious. The concept means many things to many men.

In the first place, the expression *European integration* has no dictionary definition. It is not possible to go to a glossary and learn precisely what it means, as one might go to a glossary and learn the exact meaning of, say, *antidisestablishmentarianism*. Indeed, the term *Europe* does not express a precise geographical concept. One has only to examine the membership rosters of those various international organizations called European to recognize this. The precision of the geographic concept is somewhat, but not very much, enhanced if one refers to *Continental* Europe; but what the concept gains in precision by this qualification, it perhaps loses in fruitfulness.

In any event, whatever *Europe* may mean in different contexts and for different purposes, the term *integration* truly defies definition. It is one of those terms which spring out of nowhere into common usage. It is in this respect analogous to the term *viability*, which was almost exclusively a medical word and concept until, with the birth of the European Recovery Program, it came into use by economists and statesmen and practitioners of other arts far removed from medicine. It is similarly analogous to the more recent term *automation,* the exact physical content and economic significance of which cannot be identified.

It has been claimed that the term *economic integration* of Europe was invented within the American government and more specifically within the administrative agency for the Marshall Plan, the Economic Co-operation Administration. There may even be substance to this claim, although proof is inherently impossible. Surely, however, no one would be so brash as to claim that, to the officials of the ECA, the economic integration of Europe had a single and uniform and clear and determinate meaning. Nor could any analogous claim be made on behalf of the professional students of government or the economists. In recent years, for example, after *economic integration* had come into vogue, Professor Jan Tinbergen reissued, with only relatively minor factual variations, his excellent study on *International Economic Co-operation* under the more fashionable title *International Economic Integration.* The political integration of Europe, to the political scientists, means whatever form of intergovernmental rapprochement conforms to the predilections of the particular scholar or his conceptions of what is practically possible.

European integration seems to be more or less synonymous and interchangeable with European unification or European unity or the European movement or the European idea. It will be useful first to examine this last usage, the European idea. To the logical and pragmatic among us, this might better be called the European dream. This is not said out of disrespect or cynicism. It is not called a dream in the sense that it is divorced from reality, but in the sense that it is vague and nebulous, without form or shape, configuration or operational significance. Its content is mystical. It provides no basis for a program of action. It is rooted in a loose and dreamy sense of history, a feeling for the spiritual unity of Europe, a yearning for the return of the times and conditions under which Europe was cosmopolitan, humane, universalist, undivided, and whole, times and conditions that are supposed to have existed in the Roman Empire or the Holy Roman Empire or the Age of Enlightenment. Things that are mystical and that are not related to specific concrete action are not thereby to be scorned, but they are not the stuff out of which programs are divised and carried to execution.

Something else which more properly might be called the European idea may be discerned a step or two beyond the emotional mysticism of the European dream. It is not, strictly speaking, an idea, but a series of interrelated propositions, not necessarily forming an impeccable, logical sequence and not necessarily demonstrable. These propositions have been formulated at great length and eloquently in so many articles, speeches, pamphlets, and books that to single out one or a few would be merely invidious. Briefly, they run about as follows. Europe has served as the repository of the cultural traditions of at least Greece and Rome. Europe has made and can continue to make a uniquely important contribution to the culture of mankind. Europe represents a blend of all that has been best and most beautiful in human civilization. Specifically, Europe embodies values that are more precious than the civilizations of America and Russia. The former is too mechanized, too robot-like in its perfection of mechanical achievement, too little aware of the deep conflicts of the human spirit which are the stuff out of which a mature and civilized view of life is fashioned, and too obsessed with the attainment of material goals that are below the inherent spiritual worth of man; the latter is brutal, ruthless, prideful, and sordid.

Yet Europe is now encompassed and surrounded by these two gigantic continental powers and well-nigh suffocated by their insistent and inescapable closeness in a world that technology has shrunk. Not only is Europe crowded by these alien and uncouth giants, but it is weak; it has been ravaged by two wars and by the passions those wars have aroused. And not only is it weak, but it is fractionated, split into a multitude of geographically small states, which are rendered obsolete in relation to the technology of the present age and are divided down the very center by the Iron Curtain, which, by effectively absorbing most of eastern Europe into the Russian Empire, has left western Europe, now small and weak and absurdly atomized, as the last bastion of a great cultural tradition. The only course that is open for this beleaguered survivor and bearer of a great human tradition is to unite, to find in the whole greater strength and capacity to survive than can be presumed to reside in its constituent parts.

I pass no value judgment on these propositions, and I hope I am not suspect of having satirized them by compressing them, although in all honesty it must be confessed that they sound a little less plausible when abbreviated than when spun out with rhetoric and eloquence. My point is merely their ambiguity as a basis for any kind of action program. They do not tell us what is Europe and what is the meaning of uniting. What countries should do what in order to fulfill this mission of conserving a culture? In the technical language of contemporary discussions of European integration, do these propositions argue for federalism or for supranationality, or merely for closer co-operation, and in what respect and particulars?

It is to be noted that the propositions cited above do not contain any reference to the economic arguments for European integration. Actually those arguments are closely intermingled with the cultural considerations mentioned above and are of overriding importance. They are at least of great psychological importance, in the sense that most of the adherence that one finds to the target of European integration (whatever, in any particular context, it may be intended to mean) is based on economic considerations.

A group of students at the Bologna Center devised an interesting questionnaire on various aspects of the question of European integration. With this questionnaire they circularized all the members of the Italian Parliament. The number of responses they received, while not inconsiderable, was nevertheless small enough to justify misgivings as to whether it really is a representative sample of responsible opinion. Qualitatively, there is ground for suspicion that most of those who responded were those who are fervent advocates of European integration in some sense, so that the sample might give an exaggerated impression of the degree of support for integration. Nevertheless, the results of one group of questions are extremely interesting and are, I think, unaffected by any general sampling defects of the results of the exercise as a whole.

The recipients of the questionnaire were asked to specify, if they did favor different conceivable forms of integration, what they thought were the principal benefits to be derived therefrom. Of 227 benefit-concepts advanced by the various respondents, no fewer than

151, or 66 per cent, were clearly economic in character. It is also significant that, while many responses gave both economic and noneconomic reasons, many more gave economic reasons alone, and only two responses mentioned no economic considerations whatever. This means that among those who favor European integration in some form or other the overwhelming majority do so for economic reasons.

This is not really startling. It only confirms what can be easily inferred from the volumetric distribution of the large and steadily growing literature on the subject. What is more interesting is that most of the benefit-concepts adduced fall into the category of catchword concepts, the most popular reason by far being the concept of the common market. This deserves a moment's consideration.

The concept of the common market in literature on European integration is surrounded with not a little shoddy thinking. There is, of course, no serious doubt among economists that the size of the market has much to do with the efficient organization of production and that therefore free trade is better, at least in the efficiency sense, than nationalistically compartmentalized trade. On the other hand, the case that free trade will produce an optimum result in the welfare sense is at least controverted. A common market achieved, for example, by the customs union route can as easily be bad as good, in any sense. All depends on the character of the union area's relationship with and posture toward the world outside, that is, upon the nature of the larger economic environment into which a union fits and of which it is necessarily a part.

For example, in the concluding chapter of Edouard Bonnefous' book, *L'Europe en Face de Son Destin,* there is the statement:

> No one challenges the advantages possessed by the USSR with its area of 21,000,000 square kilometers and its population of 200,000,000 inhabitants and by the United States with its population of 150,000,000 and its area of 7,840,000 square kilometers over the states of Europe, each with its separate frontier, army, money and customs tariff.[1]

Perhaps no one challenges, but perhaps someone should, at least

---

[1] Edouard Bonnefous, *L'Europe en Face de Son Destin* (Paris: Presses Universitaires de France, 1952), pp. 231-32.

for the sake of argument and clarification. It is far from self-evident that Russia's economic strength, whatever may be the measure thereof, is entirely or primarily or indeed even significantly attributable to the size of the common market available to Russian producers or to the absence of monetary barriers to commerce arising out of the fact of a common currency. As for the United States, the physical size of the free internal market (size as measured in number of people and square kilometers) is undoubtedly a significant factor in that nation's pre-eminent and unprecedented economic power, but it is surely an oversimplification to evaluate that size as the determining factor, at the expense of considerations of economic structure and of the economic quality of the people.

Economic well-being would be indeed easier to achieve and maintain if there were a convenient and consistent correlation between the size of geographic area and numbers of population on the one hand, and on the other hand productive efficiency, distributional optimalism (a good welfare result), and capacity to develop and progress at a politically satisfactory rate. But the possibility of such a uniform correlation is negated by two factors: the existence of large countries with large populations, e.g., India and China, which are not efficient, which do not have a socially acceptable pattern of distribution of well-being, and which have yet to demonstrate their capacity to sustain the politically necessary pace of economic development; and the existence of relatively small countries like New Zealand, Sweden, and the Netherlands, which have a very creditable performance record on all three counts. Or take the extremely interesting case of Canada, a country which is geographically large and has an extremely high level of per capita income and welfare. The economic and investment relations are closer and more fruitful between the eastern provinces of Canada and the northeastern and north central states of the United States, across customs and currency barriers, than between the eastern provinces of Canada and the Canadian provinces of the Plains and the Far West.

It is evident, then, that the concept of the common market, despite its obvious merits in appropriate contexts and with appropriate qualifications and attendant circumstances, is in itself a primitive and unsophisticated notion on which to base almost the whole of the case and the effort for European integration. If we proceed now to examine the various formulations that purport to assign a more precise content to European integration, we find that they tend to sort themselves out roughly according to the following lines of distinction:

1. There is the distinction between Little Europe and Big Europe. I shall develop this distinction more fully, but for now it is enough to say that this is the distinction between the Europe of the Six (the Coal and Steel Community group) and the Europe of the more-or-less Fifteen (the Council of Europe group plus or minus one or two at the fringes pursuant to diverse individual prejudices). Just for the sake of completeness in enumeration, there might be added the notion of Pan-Europe, the idea that, despite contemporary political realities, the integration of the countries of eastern as well as western Europe might usefully be sought.

2. Then there is a set of distinctions based on the form of union visualized. It is more difficult in this case to classify clearly the various alternatives possible, but again they fall roughly into three types, each with its minutely shaded subdivision and perhaps shading one into the other. At one end of the spectrum there is federalism, which, though there are many variant specifics conceivable, involves generally the creation of some supranational entity in whose favor some or several, or many or most, of the aspects of sovereignty commonly thought to be exercised by national governments are waived. At the other end there is co-operationalism, under which is envisaged nothing more than an indefinite extension of the forms of international co-operation that have been heretofore developed among the countries of western Europe. Somewhere in between there is an amorphous something which, for lack of a better name, may be called unionism, which involves, along with maintenance of and respect for national sovereignties and national traditions, the quest for such common desiderata as a standing common military command, standing institutions for the pooling of the fruits of research, councils of prime ministers, and the extension of all possible areas of common, as distinguished from (and a little more than) co-operative, action.

3. Finally, there is the distinction between a gradualist approach and a more drastic and immediate approach, the differences between union by successive stages and approximations and union now.

Plainly, of course, these lines of distinction cut across each other. One might, for example, be a federalist or supranationalist within the geographic framework of the Europe of the Six, but advocate a gradual step-by-step approach to the ultimate goal. Or one might be a co-operationalist within the ambit of the Europe of the Fifteen, but advocate the immediate adoption of a comprehensive set of new measures of international co-operation.

It is probably not profitable for us to go at any great length into the subtleties of the distinction between the gradual approach and the do-it-at-once school. It is sometimes contended that there is a proper place for each, that there are certain things which, by their nature, can only be done gradually and by successive approximations, and there are certain other things which, if they are to be done at all, must be done immediately and by a single stroke. I am not now sure, however, that there is much substance to this.

Among examples that have been adduced of the kind of thing that must be done in a single and immediate action if it is to be done at all is the creation of a common currency. In a legal and mechanical sense, this is, of course, true. To abolish existing national currencies and replace them with a new international currency is something that you either do or you do not do—and if you do not do it all at once, you do not do it all. But if the circumstances are such that one can realistically think of doing it at all, then those circumstances are by definition circumstances of such widespread interconvertibility of currencies and such uniformity and stability of prevailing rates of exchange that the action of replacing the diverse national currencies by a single international currency has become a purely formalistic action. At that point and in those circumstances it probably does not matter much whether you do it after all, since the real, as distinguished from the nominal, goal—stability of international monetary relationships—has by definition been achieved already.

Similarly it is true in a formalistic sense that the overt and explicit waiver of any aspect of national sovereignty in favor of a supranational entity is something that has to take place by a single stroke and in a single moment of time. But if sovereignty is viewed as a political reality, rather than as a legal abstraction, it is difficult, if not impossible, to conceive of a single aspect of national sovereignty that cannot in the real world be consecutively whittled away by agreements and concessions and co-operative engagements so that it makes no practical difference whether it is formally waived or not.

In fact, to those who favor supranationality, it should be refreshing to reflect how much of the apparatus of national sovereignty already has been so whittled away—not, it is true, in favor of a single supranational entity, but by virtue of bilateral undertakings, of regional European engagements, and in favor of various global international organizations. What remains, in many spheres, is little more than the sovereign freedom of states to denounce their engagements or to find relief from them by virtue of escape clauses built into them.

In this matter of the speed at which to proceed toward integration, there would seem to be no better rule than (*a*) to be sure what it is one is trying to accomplish, (*b*) to try to proceed toward the goal immediately, but (*c*) to be prepared to accept the fact that the goal will not be reached immediately.

There is not much use, either, for us to pursue precise and subtle shades of differences between different kinds of federalism and different kinds of unionism. As a practical matter, if questions of speed and timing are ruled out, the major controversy among protagonists of European integration concerns only the choice between Little Europe and Big Europe and the choice between federalism or supranationality and co-operation without formal pooling of sovereignty. And these are, practically, not two sets of choices, but one. The real issue is between an expansion and multiplication of supranational entities within the Europe of the Six and hopefully their ultimate consolidation into a single all-embracing federal state, and an enlargement of the area of co-operation on political, economic, and military matters among the various countries now bound loosely together in the Council of Europe.

The reason why these are not two issues, but one, is that there are no prospects whatever for any formal pooling of sovereignty or the creation of any genuinely supranational entities in any wider geographic context than the Europe of the Six. This is admittedly a flat prognostication, and it emanates from one who makes no claim to be a professionally qualified political prognosticator. But one must occasionally make an assumption or two in order to carry forward a logical process, and this seems to be an assumption it is more than amply safe to make. The attitudes of the British and Scandinavian governments, and of the people of those countries, are known. Austria has not the freedom of action to cede her only recently regained sovereignty and has no desire to do so. Switzerland has not evidenced in generations any inclination to enter into more than practical and prosaic co-operation with the other countries of Europe. And any community which involved adding to the Europe of the Six the countries of southwestern and southeastern Europe would be a geographical, political, economic, and cultural monstrosity.

If it be accepted then for the sake of argument that the issue is between a more comprehensively supranational Europe of the Six and a loosely knit, but more widely co-operative, Europe of the more-or-less Fifteen, there are at least three questions to be asked and answered: (1) What is the use of a Europe of the Six? (2) What is the use of supranationality? (3) Are the two alternatives mutually incompatible?

By a Europe of the Six is meant, of course, a progressive tightening of the bonds among France, Italy, the Benelux countries, and West Germany until, hopefully, a complete federal union of these states has been achieved. A few years ago it was assumed that the line of progression would be from the Coal and Steel Community to the European Defense Community to the political community with, somewhere along the line, an economic community or at least a customs union having come spontaneously into existence. With the collapse of the European Defense Community project and the consequent stillbirth of the political community, the emphasis has shifted to a different line of progression, namely from the Coal and Steel Community to an atomic community to a set of arrangements (yet to be specified) for achieving a common market within the area and hence to further unspecified supranational ventures and ultimately to a complete federal union.

The idea of the Europe of the Six has had its roots in rather easily discernible facts of the European situation since the end of World War II, particularly after it became evident that the West must arrange for the rearmament of the German Federal Republic. But the idea also has been given a historic rationale and a cultural rationale that do not bear very close examination.

Historically it is contended that this area has in the past been a unity and therefore can easily become a unity again. Specifically it is pointed out that the area comprised within the Europe of the Six is roughly the same as the area of the empire of Charlemagne. This is an interesting historical observation, although it is not altogether accurate and its relevance to contemporary reality escapes at least this observer.

On the cultural side, Professor Northrop[2] has argued that there is to be found in this area a large and adequate measure of homogeneity in matters of religion, political alignments, and other "living-law norms." It is beyond my capacity to translate literally Professor Northrop's observations and arguments out of the esoteric language of sociological jurisprudence into ordinary English, but I think I can understand him and I think that the statistical validity of his entire case rests upon an assumption that West Germany and East Germany are not reunited. This is probably a safe enough assumption from the political viewpoint, at least for the near future, but to predicate the "living-law" viability of Little Europe upon a statistical basis that would be upset in the event of German reunification obviously postulates a schizophrenic character for German policy in adhesion to such a community, and to assume indefinite separation of East and West Germany flies in the face of the declared policy of the leaders of West Germany.

In reflecting upon the possible usefulness of a close-knit Europe of the Six, certain observations seem to be of paramount importance. In the first place, from the economists' vantage point, it is not self-evident that intimate adhesion or even complete economic union of the Six would in itself go very far toward the solution of the major intra-European economic problems, or specifically that it would result in the creation of a common market either large enough to have special significance or inherently capable of a near approach to self-sufficiency. The principal economic problems of contemporary Europe are: the relaxation or, if possible, the elimination of restrictions on trade and payments; the balancing of accounts on an intercontinental, that is to say a global, basis; a reduction of population pressure, either by migration outward or by the development of new employment possibilities; and the im-

[2] F. S. C. Northrop, *European Union and United States Foreign Policy* (New York: The Macmillan Co., 1954).

provement of industrial efficiency, by technical modernization and by the elimination of restrictionism and cartelization. None of these problems are unique to the area of the Six nor can any of them except the last be solved significantly by any conceivable action the Six might take collectively. Indeed, these problems could be and would be aggravated by any union of the Six which tended to become ingrown and autarchic. Hence, a customs union over this area, were it achievable (which scarcely seems probable), could enlarge and liberate the internal market of this area, but it would fall far short of being a panacea for the economic ills of Europe.

In the second place, the area as it is now constituted, without East Germany, could not constitute, in the present and prospective state of military technology and in the actual condition of military alignments, a viable military aggregate. No one claims that it could. Neither can it be contended that, militarily, the strength of the Six would be any greater when taken collectively than the strength of the separate parts when taken as part of a larger alliance. Even the European Defense Community project did not predicate itself on any such contention. It was nothing more nor less than a device to permit German rearmament without inviting the risks of a possible revival of nationalistic German militarism.

Finally, the economic relations and problems of Europe lie, to a very large extent, outside Europe, and they run in different directions for different European countries. This is not just a question of economics. What is true on the economic front is at least equally true on the political and strategic fronts.

All this is not to contend that a unifying trend within the Six is without meaning or value. It is just an effort to define the limits of what might reasonably be expected to be its benefits. The creation of the Coal and Steel Community has definite advantages, although, apart from the symbolic and political significance of the achievement of supranationality in some one sector, the concrete advantages of the Coal and Steel Community as such are not so great as is sometimes alleged. In any case, one must reflect on the scope of additional communities that might be brought into being pursuant to what has come to be called the sectoral approach. What is special about the coal and steel industries of Europe is their concentration mainly within the territory of the Six (although of course the community's efficacy suffers somewhat from the ambiguity of its relations with the United Kingdom, Austria and Sweden); but in how many other sectors can be found a comparable concentration within the territory of the Six? An electric power community or a transport community with similar geographic limitations would not have the same *prima facie* usefulness; a "green pool" of the Six would appear to be a small and limited thing as against a European Green Pool. And on the currently thorny and agitated question of an atomic pool, or Euratom, I can only observe that the countries of the Six, with the partial exception of France and perhaps Germany, are not the countries of Europe in which conspicuous research and development have taken place in the peaceful (and other) uses of nuclear energy, so that an atomic community of the Six, at this time, might be likened to the Coal and Steel Community made up, not of its present actual members, but of, say, Spain, Portugal, Italy, and Greece.

On the question of the uses of federation and/or supranationality, I limit myself to raising a series of questions for reflection and discussion, without attempting to suggest what the proper answers are.

1. Is federation in fact necessary for the achievement of the economic benefits associated with the notion of European integration? I note in passing that, in the United States, federation was in fact attained; that economic considerations were uppermost in the minds of most of the founding fathers; that indeed the Constitutional Convention of 1787 sprang directly out of the outcome or lack of outcome of a trade convention assembled in the fall of 1786 at Annapolis; and that on purist economic reasoning it can be established that full and effective economic union requires federation. Against all this, nevertheless, it is clear from the record that in practice a pretty good result is attainable and, within the ambit of the OEEC for example, has been attained without formal federation.

2. Even within the community of the Six, will federation in itself cure, say, France's political ills or Italy's population problem? Will it control German expansionism if that is a danger, or will it resolve forever Franco-German conflict? Note that Anglo-French conflict, which was much more long-lasting, was resolved and was

converted into an enduring and mutually beneficial alliance without federation.

3. Is nationalism necessarily bad, or if its autarchic excesses are controlled and counterbalanced by co-operative commitments, is it not in fact or in potentiality a driving force of great strength and popular appeal?

4. Given the dilution of national sovereignties by virtue of numerous co-operative engagements, is the formal pooling of sovereignty meaningful or important or necessary for the attainment of any large number of specific, identifiable, concrete results?

On the question of whether supranationality among the Six and co-operationalism among the Fifteen are necessarily incompatible, the answer is obviously in the negative. There is no reason why a federation of the Six could not function as a single nation within the councils of a larger Europe more loosely organized. Indeed, if federation of the Six were to be assuredly prevented from becoming a restrictive and self-contained autarchy, and if the benefits of its common market were not to be realized at the expense and loss of others, the federated Six would have to be aligned co-operatively within a larger Europe and a larger world.

In summary thus far, I submit that European integration has several different meanings in practice, and innumerable subshades of meaning. In a larger view, these diversities of meaning reduce themselves for the most part to a difference between a close-knit federated community (which is probably a practicable thing only within the geographical community of the Six, if indeed even there) and a loosely-organized co-operationalism within a wider Europe, or to a combination of the two. I personally favor a progressive widening of the area of co-operation and a deepening of its content, combined with whatever measure of more intimate adhesion among the Six is demonstrably useful for definite and concrete ends. I consider anything more ambitious to be neither necessary nor feasible. But my personal opinion is unimportant in comparison with the clarification of terms. Those who say they are opposed to European integration should be quite clear in mind and speech about what it is to which they are opposed (for surely no one is opposed in principle to all integrative trends and forces in Europe). Similarly all who favor and advocate European integration should be similarly clear in thought and language. And those who are skeptical about the practicability of European integration should feel under an obligation to specify what it is they question.

It is frequently said that the enthusiasm of the youth of Europe can be enlisted only in the pursuit of some goal and dream that will be larger and more creative than the petty interests of national states. This may be so. What I suggest is that it will not prove possible to arouse and sustain the enthusiasm of any of them, young or old, in pursuit of a goal that is not clear and definite—and attainable.

Finally, a very brief plea in behalf of a wider view of the problems of Europe and the world than is generally present in discussions of European integration. There is a tendency for most such discussions of European integration to assume a tone of parochialism, of (in the interesting Italian phrase) *campanilismo*. It is no derogation of the importance of European integration to point out and remember that the world is larger than Europe and larger than the area represented by Europe on the one hand and Russia and the United States on the other hand (those two alien and uncouth giants who surround and enclose Europe). What about China for example? China almost never enters into discussions of the future of Europe, but China, like Mt. Everest, is there, and China's relations with Russia, present and emerging, are of overwhelming importance for the future and the destiny of western Europe, as are, equally, China's relations with and impact upon India. And, important as is the United States, it is not the whole of the Western Hemisphere.

In the global view, the great issues are: the liberation and expansion of world trade, in which Europe has a great stake, perhaps greater than it has in the opening up of intra-European trade; the dramatic process and problem of economic development in the underdeveloped regions of the world, in which, for reasons of political stability, Europe has a vital stake; and the global strategy of the free world against Communist imperialism, in which struggle Europe has a life-or-death stake.

3

Economic Integration

Economic Integration:
Problems and Possibilities

PAUL DELOUVRIER / *Financial Director of the European Coal and Steel Community*

THE EXPERT has none of the learning which is the professor's prerogative and none of the responsibilities which are the monopoly of the ministers (a difficult term to define and a difficult role). Experts have their part to play in a discussion of European experience and prospects for the future. To the experts are referred all the impossible questions. If Europe has become the experts' Calvary, it also can be said that the experts have become Europe's Calvary. There is a good deal of conflict among experts, but the fact is that all Europeans now have the feeling that Europe must be created. The real difficulty starts when they are asked how Europe must be created.

In consequence, the question of Europe has become a quarrel about methods. Contrary to what is often thought, however (and I am expressing the view of an expert), quarrels over principles are not as serious as quarrels over methods. Quarrels over principles are basic, of course, but they are not serious, because when principles are irreducible, a compromise is reached! That is known as coalition government in certain European democracies, one of which I know very well. It is known as toleration between fellow citizens in civilian life. Nowadays between two blocs it is called coexistence. Coexistence or war, that problem is not one for the experts. Quarrels over methods, on the other hand, are very serious quarrels, and can be put on a footing with religious wars, in so far as religion is agreed to be a method to reach heaven. Religious wars are very dangerous and, where Europe is concerned, we are now engaged in a religious war over methods in order that Europe may be created. Every European people and every European politician dreams of Europe, but not of the same Europe.

The present state of affairs is the following. Since the war, Europeans have followed two main roads in endeavoring to create Europe—and I am referring only to economic Europe: first, the OEEC, or the way of association; second, the ECSC, the coal and steel pool, and to this second road Professor Ludwig Erhard has given the name of "functional way," while others call it the way of integration.

We have also witnessed another attempt. When the ad hoc assembly in Strasbourg was called together and requested to draw up a treaty for European integration, that assembly tried to define a European constitution and conferred economic powers upon the institutions which it set up. It arranged matters in a very simple manner, as jurists sometimes can when they are not economists. It was laid down that the European executive powers set up by this treaty would have at their disposal the economic powers of all the states after a transition period of five years, and the whole problem of economic integration was resolved in one single article. I cannot criticize this path, which logically I believe to be the best—logically, because the logicians tell us that in the end economic Europe can be created in its entirety only if a political Europe exists beforehand, that is to say, European political institutions. There I believe that the logicians are right, but this whole affair of Europe from A to Z was born completely illogically, and it is a consolation, not perhaps for the professors, but for the ministers and certainly for the experts, that European construction should be illogical.

After the rejection of the EDC, the triumphal way leading to a political Europe had to be abandoned for the route leading to an economic Europe. There was thus a return to strictly economic considerations and there was again revealed, in its simplicity and its clarity, the conflict between the associationists on the OEEC path, and the integrators or functionalists on the path of the coal and steel pool. And today, looking at the assemblage of the existing European economic institutions, the picture is as follows. First comes the ECSC, the coal and steel pool, with six members. Next there is the Western European Union, whose statute confers upon it certain economic attributes, and which has seven members, including the United Kingdom. Then there is the Council of Europe, which also touches upon economic matters, and which has a membership of fifteen states. There are the Conference of European Ministers of Transport, with a membership of sixteen; the OEEC, numbering seventeen; and the Ministerial Agriculture Committee, which operates within the framework of the OEEC and has eighteen members. There are still other smaller groups. There is Benelux, in which only three states participate. There are experiments in joint marketing made by from three to five of the northern states. And, last, the European countries come together in two other groupings: NATO, which, especially at the beginning, carried on certain economic and financial activities from the armaments angle; and the European Economic Commission in Geneva, where the Europeans meet the Asiatic countries.

This listing, except for the last two categories (NATO and the Geneva Commission), suggests to me, speaking as an expert, a very small idea, a very small reform, which nevertheless has a revolutionary aspect. These various European organizations should be asked to have their headquarters in the same city, for Europeans and the European official services are reaching the point where they know nothing of one another because they are scattered to the four corners of Europe. Let us leave ministers free to move about, but the experts should be grouped in one place.

Here now are some reflections about the two ways selected for European economic integration, the association way and the functional way or the way of integration through the ECSC. I should like to venture some conclusions which are not entirely orthodox. First, both the ways chosen for the attempt to construct Europe are quite irrational. One is as completely illogical as the other. The coal and steel pool is illogical and there would be no point in a lengthy explanation to that effect; the isolating of these two activities from the rest of the national activities to put them both into a joint market is an idea which could never cross the mind of an expert. It is completely irrational. But the OEEC, too, is just as irrational as the ECSC, and that also can be seen clearly. The OEEC was in fact set up so that, through mutual association, the different countries in Europe might try to revive their commerce. It is not the OEEC's duty to eliminate all the obstacles to trade. The OEEC deals chiefly with the fixing of quotas, quantitative restrictions, but in actual fact it has no real competence concerning customs tariffs. This did not matter very much as long as quantitative restrictions were at a very high level, but nowadays, when it is the percentage of liberalization which is high, the fact that the OEEC has nothing to do with customs tariffs paralyzes its action to a considerable extent. To have entrusted to this organization only a very small part of the obstacles to trading is truly irrational. It is therefore comforting to know that both these present organizations are irrational. The European slogan of a joint market of 160,000,000 consumers is perhaps irrational, but I believe, effective.

The second conclusion, which is not entirely orthodox either, is that, in practice, far from being mutually exclusive, far from interfering with one another, these two types of European organizations have ended up by being of mutual assistance. The OEEC has helped the ECSC. If the system of the European Payments Union, which was built up through the efforts of the OEEC, had not existed, I do not know how the ECSC could have worked properly. On the other hand, the OEEC, in developing the liberalization of trade, in having the quota system abandoned, made it possible for the ECSC to work, and prevented its irrational nature—in having cut off coal and steel from everything else—from giving rise to difficulties of too serious a nature. But this aspect is not always clearly perceived. The existence of the coal and steel pool has greatly helped the OEEC. All those who do not like the six-country integration transfer their efforts to the OEEC, so that, whenever the six-country integration makes any progress, the OEEC can immediately be seen bestirring itself to make fresh progress too. There is a spirit of emulation and rivalry and, let us face it, the United Kingdom is only attached to the OEEC because she detests the six-country organizations. And when the six-member organizations seem a little out of luck, because the atmosphere has cooled off, the United Kingdom moves away from the OEEC. As soon as there is talk of a European renewal, however, the OEEC gets back to work and the United Kingdom cleaves to the Continent once more.

Take, for example, the last European renewal exercises. As soon as the six countries of the ECSC discussed doing something about atomic power and the classic sources of power, the OEEC discovered that, a year earlier, it had appointed a commission to deal with power and the atom and that this committee's report had not yet been seen. The rapporteurs were summoned immediately. They had forgotten that they had to make a report, but within three months a report was drawn up, and the race between Brussels and the OEEC led to our having the joy of receiving two very good reports upon the atom. I consider, therefore, that that was very important in the past, and as I have been an expert in the two institutions, you may believe me when I say that the two institutions have helped each other more than they realize.

The third conclusion is that both institutions are going through a crisis in relation to the functional way, the way of integration. Nothing would be gained by giving a lengthy description of this crisis, brought about by the rejection of the EDC. People are still talking about European renewal. Many people are anxious to know whether this European renewal within the six-country framework will finally be handled by the parliament. Regarding the organization of the OEEC, there, too, is a crisis, inasmuch as this association allotted to itself as its principal task the suppression of quotas in Europe and the establishment of a multilateral payments system. It has fufilled the main part of its task and I may say today that it is getting to the hard part, to some extraordinarily difficult things. The ultimate goal, regarding freedom to place orders, is convertibility.

So far it has not been possible to do anything about this, and the freedom limit for commodities is set at 100 per cent liberalization of trading. This goal has almost been achieved, and once you have reached 100 per cent liberalization of trading, you must go on to exercises on customs tariffs, or exercises on joint markets, that is to say, study the artificial aids to exportation, the procedures whereby countries compete abnormally, and all these are exercises calling for much longer and more careful study, and much more difficult adjustments. When I add that, beyond the European problems, the question of convertibility and the question of customs tariffs arise in a world-wide setting, and point out that the same experts who officiate at the OEEC also meet one another at GATT in Geneva and at the meetings of the International Monetary Fund in Washington, you will realize that, over and above the European quarrels, there is also the quarrel between the regionalists and the universalists.

There are those who say to themselves that there is no point in getting excited over putting an end to the little European quarrels if they can be submerged in a universal settling of these matters. And, strangely enough, people who handle monetary matters have an organic reaction which is universalist rather than regionalist. Governors of central banks have a planetary outlook.

Thus, we have drawn three conclusions. Both institutions, both ways of creating Europe, are equally irrational. They are not as much in opposition as people like to say; today they are undergoing a crisis.

Let us look, therefore, at some future prospects. My personal conviction is that as long as the politicians have decided for the time being not to create political Europe, the two ways of creating economic Europe will coexist for a long time. The way of association, the OEEC way, is irreplaceable as long as the United Kingdom declines to associate herself with the efforts of the six countries to set up a joint market. I do not know how long it will take the British to notice that the Commonwealth is no longer anything more than an old boys' association which meets every year in a different town. Everybody asks what everyone else has been doing for the last twelve months; everybody says, "What are you going to do tomorrow, old chap?"; then each one goes home and does what he likes. This is not my summing up of the meetings of Commonwealth prime ministers; it was a British minister who said it to me, but I prefer not to give his name.

There will come a day when the British will notice that the Commonwealth is an old boys' association. On that day, I believe, they will attach themselves to Europe, to the Europe of the six countries, in some manner in accordance with whatever form has been adapted by the Europe of the six in its evolution. But, for the time being, it is essential to keep up an organization in which the United Kingdom and the countries which usually follow the United Kingdom will encounter the men of the Europe of the six. If six of the sixteen countries wish to progress more rapidly than the rest within the union, there will be nothing to stop them. Already, among the six themselves, there are three, united under the name Benelux, who have made greater progress than the others toward joint marketing.

But if the OEEC is to subsist, if it is essential that it should subsist, it also must reform itself and must renew its manner of envisaging its task. Its chief tasks set after the war have been practically completed. Today we are engaged upon exercises of a different kind. The European countries must, within the framework of the OEEC itself, make an attempt to define an economic policy which, if not joint, will at least be coherent. The next test for the OEEC will certainly be—supposing that it occurs—the arrival of a depression, even a slight one. Then we shall see whether the mechanics of co-operation, which were efficacious thanks above all to United States aid during the postwar period, when there were inflation crises to be gotten through, can stand up to a depression crisis. Moreover, I believe—and I am not saying this from the critic's point of view—that if we had a minor crisis, the mechanism of the OEEC would facilitate the adoption of energetic measures to cope with this economic situation without relapsing into the exaggerated protectionism and Malthusianism which we experienced between the two wars. But to this end, at ministerial level, the OEEC Council would need to meet more frequently (we have observed the constraining virtue of a council of ministers—when someone is not playing the game, they are embarrassed). It is the experts' hope (since I have decided to reveal the thoughts of the experts) that ministers will meet more often than at present, in order that the ministers, too, may feel embarrassed.

As to the second, functional integration way, the ECSC way, there too I believe that it is indispensable to make progress. Progress is already being made in many ways at present. Just now the ministers meeting in Venice have received a report from the Brussels experts on Spaak's authority. The experts have answered the three basic questions which had to be answered before further steps could be taken along the path of integration. The first question was: "Should integration be continued by sectors, or should economies be integrated globally?" To this question, ever since the Rome Conference in 1953, the experts had been replying that integration by sectors, through the admission of successive sectors, would certainly be an impossible method, and that it would be preferable to take the method of global, but gradual, integration—that is to say, to arrive at a customs union and a joint market by a progressive suppression of all the obstacles and through adjustments of legislation, rather than by the addition of fractions of economy. The only fraction of economy which the experts set aside for special treatment was the question of atomic energy.

I believe that they were right, because the problems raised by the atom are new problems. There is as yet only a very small atomic industrial structure in the six countries concerned, and, contrary to a certain tendency leading a number of people to think that the joint market is more important than Euratom, I am not certain on that score. Intellectually it is clear that the joint market is more satisfying to the mind, for one can envisage all barriers falling at the same time for the whole collection of economies. If those who believe in the atomic era are right, however, if through industrial use of the atom we are on the eve of a second industrial revolution which will change not only the forms of power, but all industrial processes, then I am prepared to state that Euratom is something which is of capital importance, although the progressive lowering of customs tariffs is certainly very important also.

We have seen joint markets in operation and in consequence we are all aware of the fact that they have customs tariffs, though lower ones. The French Union, for example, is the joint market composed of France and her overseas territories, and yet there are customs duties there, too. For a long time our country had tolls, and nowadays, when people hear "joint market," they imagine that frontiers are about to disappear as the tolls did. Alas! even when one crosses the frontier between Luxembourg and Belgium frequently, one is nevertheless held up at the frontier, where the word *customs* is no longer written on the office and worn on the cap of the agent inside, but instead there is the word *taxes*. Ah, well, from that angle, the frontiers of Europe will remain for a long time tax frontiers. Consequently, I fear that public opinion will be somewhat disappointed by the outward signs of the joint market, so that, although I professed my inability to choose regarding the importance between the joint market and Euratom, I am prepared to say that Euratom, in my opinion, should be pushed forward as energetically as the joint market, even if it appears that its fruits would be less satisfactory. There, then, was the first question which the experts answered.

The second question was: "Is it necessary to continue along the way of the delegation of powers, the supranational way, or can we content ourselves with organizing a joint market in partnership, by means of decisions reached unanimously, as in the case of the OEEC?" Here the ministers, very courageously, had said, when referring the question to the experts: "We have no bias in this matter. Get together, study thoroughly all the mechanism necessary to set up the joint market, and from the objective study of these mechanisms you will be in a position to deduce what is required by way of an institution." Well, in three months in Brussels last year, we experts did indeed endeavor to find out objectively what were the minimum institutional needs to make a joint market work. And in the end, if you read the Brussels report, you will see that we have only arrived at a malleable situation in this respect which satisfies no one.

I am convinced that the European Commission study was carried out as objectively as possible and that all the experts present in Brussels knew beforehand, from all their meetings in the past, that in order to constitute a real joint market a supragovernmental authority would be necessary. We are no longer living in the nineteenth century, in the era of liberalism, when the state had no great functions. At that period, free trade on convertibility of currency could have created a world-wide joint market. Today, faced by the collective conscience of every nation, the state assumes major economic responsibilities, for, if there is a crisis, who is responsible? The government. If there is inflation? The government. In our own times, what public opinion would really consider an unwarrantable situation would be when, in organizing a joint market, no real authority was set up.

To tell the truth, in the Brussels report the powers given to the European Commission have been camouflaged, minimized in words. In actual fact, if the report led to a treaty and if that treaty were ratified, I can assure you that the European Commission provided for in the Brussels report would have some extremely interesting attributes and extraordinarily wide powers.

There is a third problem which the people in Brussels have solved already. Does the general joint market call only for the suppression of customs barriers? Does it call for something more? Does it call for the harmonization of working conditions, a harmonization of labor regulations, transport laws, credits, and so forth? That is the most critical point, the point at which, in the brain of the expert, his professor aspect is useful to his minister aspect— and, if he is a hybrid being, he has these two sides to his brain. Well, certainly, it will be much easier to set up a joint market if a certain number of harmonizations have been effected previously. I recall in this connection, the avatars of the Franco-Italian Customs Union, for I was an expert in that union too. When we met in 1947 to set up the customs union, we considered the following questions. Will it be necessary for salary conditions, credits, and monetary conditions to be unified? Well, I believe that was theoretically right, but the Franco-Italian Customs Union never saw the light of day.

So in Brussels, in the reply we gave, we endeavored, profiting from the lessons of the ECSC, to show that it was possible to set up a joint market without any prior uniformization or equalization of conditions. From the point of view of theory, the work done in Brussels could be called into question, or even severely criticized, because the monetary aspect is practically inexistent therein. This was not because the experts present in Brussels were unaware of the basic importance of monetary problems for a joint market or an economic union, but because here their ministerial, political side came uppermost. Experts fear the governors of central banks. As I told you, governors of central banks are for the most part universalists and seek convertibility, rather than European unification, which would perhaps end up in a public central bank. Furthermore, the idea of a common currency is closely allied to considerations of population. On this last point I will say nothing. The experts said to themselves: "Don't let us talk about monetary matters in this framework; if the successive stages for suppressing customs duties which have been provided for in order to build up a common policy are really respected, a certain degree of monetary unification is bound to come about." It was perhaps an act of faith, but it was the only practical way, at that stage in the work, of dealing with the matter.

Experts have no thoughts and must nevertheless have ideas; they are asked to keep their sentiments to themselves—but believe me, sentiments and high thinking are what the world is led by all the same. Experts are called upon to instill something rational into the irrational, but they know that the illogical, the irrational, is in the end the most important. And then, they are themselves in search of men who will give Europe a soul—and ministers who will give it a reason for existence. When these men have done their work, born of the basic preparatory preliminaries, they will always find experts to harness the forces they will thus have unleashed.

European Integration:
Commercial and Financial Postulates

MICHAEL A. HEILPERIN / *Professor of International Economics, Graduate Institute of International Studies, Geneva*

GEOGRAPHICALLY, the term *Europe* applies to the Asian peninsula which extends from the Atlantic Ocean to the Ural Mountains, but it is quite obvious that this is not the area with which we are principally concerned here. Allowing for the political realities of our times, the integration of Europe can only include that part of its full geographic area which is not imprisoned behind the Iron Curtain and which is tantamount to the membership of the OEEC. It is to this group of countries that the term *economic integration* was first applied, in the fall of 1949, by Paul G. Hoffman, then Marshall Plan administrator. In more recent years, the scope of the Europe-to-be-integrated has been narrowed down further to the six countries which organized the Coal and Steel Community in 1951. It is these countries which are discussing in precise detail the ways and means of establishing an integrated economic union. Spokesmen for some of these countries, however, especially J. W. Beyen, Foreign Minister of the Netherlands, have made it clear that they would view with favor a future expansion of the integrated group to other countries of like mind.

In what follows I shall be concerned, therefore, mainly with the six members of the Coal and Steel Community, but whenever necessary I shall extend the scope of my argument to the OEEC group as a whole and even to a group wider than that, including North America and other overseas regions of the free world. For, as will be shown below, conditions of successful integration in western Europe involve policies the scope of which extends far beyond the seas.

So much about the term *European* in the phrase *European integration*. The second term of this phrase calls for a more lengthy elaboration, which will take us directly into the real subject matter of this chapter.

The term *economic integration,* whatever might have been its earlier history, only recently became a slogan for action, or what the French call more respectfully *une idée force*. In October, 1949, when, as already mentioned, Paul Hoffman used it with great emphasis in an important speech delivered before the OEEC Council in Paris, that organization was suffering from early growing pains and was losing sight, or so it seemed, of its great potentialities and wider goals. Paul Hoffman came to remind the OEEC Council that, in addition to the task of balancing Europe's dollar accounts, it had a second, and very important task. He told his audience:

> The second [task]—and to say this is why I am here—is to move ahead on a far-reaching program to build in Western Europe a more dynamic, expanding economy which will promise steady improvement in the conditions of life for all its people. This, I believe, means nothing less than *an integration of the Western European economy*. . . . [The emphasis is mine.]
>
> The substance of such integration would be the formation of a single large market within which quantitative restrictions on the movements of goods, monetary barriers to the flow of payments and, eventually, all tariffs are permanently swept away.

This appeal had far-reaching repercussions. In the first place, the OEEC developed from then on into an agency for the progressive elimination of intra-European import restrictions, other than tariffs, and for the restoration of multilateral payments among its members. The Liberalization Code and its progressive enforcement, and the European Payments Union with its remarkable achievements over the past six years, are the products of this evolution.

The other momentous development which grew out of Paul Hoffman's "Integration Speech" was the formulation of the Schuman Plan. The spiritual father of the latter, Jean Monnet, was—and most likely continues to be—far more interested in a political federation of France, Germany, Italy, and the Benelux countries than in the economic integration of Europe as such.[1] His steadiness of purpose, a particularly favorable constellation in western Europe at the time the project was launched, and the backing which the government and the public opinion of the United States are always prepared to give to federal projects in which America's own sovereignty is not involved, jointly brought about the miracle of the Coal and Steel Community. For, indeed, nothing was less likely, a priori, than the ratification by the parliaments concerned of legislation placing the coal and steel industries of the respective countries under a supranational High Authority. The unlikely, almost impossible, having come to pass, much thought and effort were henceforth directed to the conceiving of other such supranational bodies which might integrate, one by one, important branches of industry of the countries concerned. This sector-by-sector approach to economic integration was, until recently, the most important alternative to the so-called common-market approach.

For the past six years there has been a good deal of controversy, on both sides of the Atlantic, concerning the relative merits of the two approaches. In the realm of practical achievement, however, the Coal and Steel Community has remained to date the only experiment in sector-by-sector integration. The project of a "green pool" for agriculture, once sponsored by Pflimlin, of France, never had any chance, considering the strength of agricultural protectionism in Europe, and has faded out of the picture, as have other such projects. Monnet and other leading protagonists of European federation addressed themselves, in the climate generated by the Korean War, to promoting political federation and especially the European Defense Community, which, strongly backed by the United States, suffered eventual shipwreck in the French Parliament. Having recovered from that blow, the statesmen of Little Europe took in hand once again the economic approach to integration. The foreign ministers of the six countries are now in session at Venice to discuss and, it is hoped, to approve a detailed blueprint for the establishment of a common market which has been elaborated during a year of well-nigh con-

---

[1] Nor was he the only one to see in the coal and steel pool an instrument of political action. The last time I saw Count Sforza, in the Italian Embassy in Paris, on April 15, 1951, just after he, as Italy's Foreign Minister, had signed the Schuman Plan treaty, I asked him what results he expected from it. "It will breathe new life into the Council of Europe," was his unhesitating reply.

tinuous discussion by a group of experts appointed in June, 1955, by the Messina Conference of the six and headed by Belgian Foreign Minister Paul-Henri Spaak.[2]

It may be well at this point to turn our minds back to the end of 1952. It was the time when the debate over the European Defense Community was in full swing, when the Coal and Steel Community was getting under way, and when a fresh breeze of economic liberalism stole over western Europe, bringing in its wake a generalized "rediscovery" of monetary policy as an instrument of checking national inflations, balancing international payments, and paving the way for convertibility and freer trade. It looked as if the time were ripe for a major attack against economic nationalism and for swift moves in the direction of reviving the multilateral pattern of international trade and payments.

This was when I first developed a favorable attitude toward the economic unification of the six countries of the Coal and Steel Community. I confess to a considerable amount of skepticism concerning the Schuman Plan and outright opposition to the idea of proliferating other sectional arrangements on the same model. For a liberal, there was much danger in such an approach, for its eventual outcome could hardly fail to be either chaos or superstate planning on an unprecedented scale, a boon to economic planners and state Socialists of the countries concerned, but a danger to the liberal pattern of international economic relations.

It occurred to me that if the six countries were to talk about unification at all, they should bring into the picture, as soon as possible, the idea of establishing complete free trade among them. My notebooks show the record of a visit I paid to Robert Schuman, at the Quai d'Orsay, on December 10, 1952. On that occasion I suggested to the distinguished French statesman the launching of what I called the Second Schuman Plan, involving nothing less than the establishment of free trade among the six countries. Schuman appeared to be interested and not unfriendly to the idea, which was quite evidently, however, one that had not retained much of his attention previously. I was hoping to take up the idea again on another occasion, but be-

---

[2] Since these pages were written, the Venice Conference has adopted the "Spaak Report" as a basis for the negotiation of two treaties, one dealing with the establishment of a common market among the six countries, and the other with an atomic agency of the six to be called Euratom.

fore the month was over there was a government crisis in France and Robert Schuman ceased to be Foreign Minister.

This episode merely serves to place me within the framework of my subject. I thought of a common market[3] at a time when I hadn't realized that it already was being given very serious consideration among cabinet members and experts of one, at least, of the six countries. I confess, however, that I first favored the idea merely as a defensive measure against the growth of sectional agencies of the coal and steel pool type. It wasn't until later that I found a *positive* reason for upholding this approach. The reason was my gradually acquired conviction that only inside a wide competitive free-trading market in the heart of western Europe could European capitalism be rejuvenated and reformed. Now this I consider today, and have considered for a number of years, to be an essential desideratum not only for western Europe, but for the entire Atlantic world. Only if European capitalism can become socially acceptable, i.e., be regarded by the man in the street as the economic system which serves European masses best, will communism really be defeated in those western European countries where, as in Italy and France, it continues to keep large sectors of the population spellbound.

In the United States, capitalism has undergone in the past thirty or forty years an evolution which has not yet been paralleled in western Europe, except in a few particular instances. American capitalism is built today on the idea of growing mass consumption of mass-produced goods, with a corresponding rise in living standards for all, and with an increasing spread of property ownership even among the low income groups of the population—ownership not only of durable consumer goods such as automobiles, but of houses, of individual life insurance, and even, the latest step along the road to the wide spreading of property ownership, of industrial stocks and shares. This is America's answer to nationalization, to public ownership, to socialism, and it is an answer which has proved to have great appeal to the "little man" who has benefited so much by the evolution of the recent decades. This, too, I believe, should be the road for European capitalism to take. A common market without internal tariffs, quotas, or other restrictions and without cartels and other business arrangements restricting competition is the framework within which European capitalism can become an economic

[3] Albeit under the name of "European Free Trade."

system for the millions. As an American, as a liberal, and as a friend of Europe, I therefore favor everything that will establish free trade among the largest possible number of countries of western Europe.

In December, 1952, and again in February, 1953, the government of the Netherlands seized its five partners in the Coal and Steel Community with a bold proposal for the establishment of free trade among them, a gradual process to be supervised by a supranational body combining them all, an arrangement to be open to the participation of other similarly inclined countries. The author of that project was J. W. Beyen, Foreign Minister of the Netherlands since September, 1952. A banker by profession, one-time head of the Bank for International Settlements in Basle, Dutch delegate to the Bretton Woods Conference of 1944, and, after the war, an executive director of the International Monetary Fund and of the International Bank for Reconstruction and Development, Beyen was well-nigh predestined to bring this economic and free-trade approach to European integration into the very active debate over the political integration of the six countries.

In April, 1956, Beyen delivered a major address at the Istituto per gli Studi di Politica Internazionale, in Milan, on "Progress Towards a New Europe as Viewed by a Dutchman." In that speech he recalled the origins of what later came to be known as the Beyen Plan.[4] Expounding the opinion of the Netherlands government, Beyen said:

> in order to make the Political Community of the Six truly viable, it was necessary to entrust it, from its very inception, with the task of the economic integration of Europe and this, *of course,* not by sectors of production but—what might be called "horizontal integration"—through the establishment of a general common market.

I myself have italicized the words *"of course"* in the above quotation, for they are of capital importance. Beyen has long been a believer in a common market, i.e., in the establishment of free trade among the six members of the Coal and Steel Community. He never opposed, as far as I know, the sector-by-sector approach as such, but has never regarded it as a suitable means of achieving an integrated

---
[4] See my article entitled "Beyen Plan for European Free Trade," *New York Herald Tribune,* April 11, 1953.

European economy. The "of course" of the above quotation is a fighting phrase and, as far as I can see, the battle has been won by the adherents of the common market. Or, a little less optimistically, one might say that it has been lost by the adherents of the sector-by-sector approach. For the recommendations of the "Spaak Report" include side by side a program for action in the field of atomic energy, the Euratom, and a program for the establishment, over a period of twelve years, of free trade among the six countries. The triumph of the common-market approach will not, of course, be final until these recommendations have been adopted by the respective governments, ratified by parliaments, and carried through in practice. This means that the road ahead is arduous and full of pitfalls.

In stating above that the sector-by-sector approach to economic integration has failed—a statement which may strike some as rash— I was thinking less of the fact that the common market has been endorsed by the Spaak Committee and may become, by tomorrow, a program of action encompassed in a treaty signed by the respective governments, than of the fact that, after roughly four years of operation of the Coal and Steel Authority, nothing has happened in the six countries to further the growth of liberal trade policies, except the continuous pressure from the OEEC concerning the application of its Liberalization Code. Free trade in coal and steel does not appear to have influenced by contagion other sectors of economic life. Should Euratom become a reality tomorrow or the day after, it will be marginal to the national economies of the countries concerned. It is quite clear that the road to economic integration is that which involves the suppression of obstacles to trade and payments.

Whether this means that economic integration must necessarily be equated with free trade is another matter. The economy of the Western world had enjoyed a very high degree of integration during the several decades preceding the outbreak of World War I. Even though most countries practiced tariff protection, who can deny that there was in existence a close-knit world economy characterized by intimate organic relationships between the price systems and the market mechanisms of the various countries? The world economy of those days enjoyed a common measure of values, even though there was no common international currency. This was due to the general acceptance of the gold standard and to the way in which all the important trading nations conformed to common standards of monetary policy. Tariffs existed, but the most-favored-nation clause eliminated most discriminatory practices. There were no import quotas, no exchange control, and population movements were either free or only moderately restricted. Capital movements followed the line of economic advantage, and currency convertibility, based on a common standard of values, created an atmosphere of confidence favorable to foreign investment. The basis of the system was currency convertibility and the absence of quantitative restrictions, as well as the general acceptance of the price mechanism as a guide to economic decisions. These are, in the light of past experience, the basic prerequisites of economic integration. It is idle to speculate how the system might have evolved had it not been destroyed by World War I. It was never reconstructed after 1914, not even during the short period which separates the end of post-World War I inflations from the outbreak of the Great Depression.

Seen in a broader perspective, what we need today is economic integration over as wide an area as possible of the non-Soviet world. This we can have almost for the asking, given strong United States leadership. Great progress has been made in the direction of convertibility since 1952. The OEEC has gone almost as far as it could in the direction of eliminating quantitative restrictions within Europe, while the greatly improved dollar position of most countries has made it possible substantially to liberalize dollar trade as well. The final hurdles to be taken are difficult, but by no means insuperable, especially if both sides of the Atlantic continue to experience the present high level of economic activity.

Should a less formal kind of economic integration come into being, under the impulsion of effective United States policies of foreign trade liberalization and underpinning convertibility, it will be much easier to establish a common market among the six countries of Little Europe. In a general climate of freer trade and under the umbrella of convertibility, it will be much easier to achieve free trade among the small number of neighboring countries which are involved in the program outlined by the "Spaak Report." Having greater opportunities to trade outside of the group, individual members of it may be less reluctant than they are now to abandon their intragroup protectionism.

Although, for the reasons briefly set out above, I have arrived at a favorable opinion concerning the integration of the economies of the six members of the Coal and Steel Community, I find that it is the broader if somewhat vaguer kind of integration outlined above which constitutes the principal task for, and challenge to, the statescraft of the Western world. But since we can have no assurance that this great task will actually be performed, there is every reason for as large a number of European countries as can agree to do so to combine into a free-trading area. Here again, the larger the group the more beneficial will prove its economic integration into a common market. There is nothing magic about the figure six. The integration of the six will only make full sense if it is carried through in a way that allows for expanding the group to other countries of like mind.[5]

Let me turn next to the word *postulate,* which appears in the title of this paper. A postulate, according to the *Shorter Oxford Dictionary,* is "a prerequisite of some actual or supposed occurrence or state of things," and according to Webster it is "a condition; an essential prerequisite." With these definitions for a guide, and equaling *integration,* now, with *common market,* it would seem clear that the small group of countries envisaging integration could only benefit from a complete customs union, and this on two conditions: (1) that membership be open to other countries as well; and (2) that it should practice as a group a liberal trade policy toward the outside world. There is no advantage whatever for France, Germany, Italy, and the Benelux to organize into a free-trading area surrounded by prohibitive trade barriers against the rest of the world. Each member of this group derives far more wealth from its trade

---

[5] Since this was written, the Venice Conference, referred to above, has been fully successful and it was followed by a treaty-drafting conference which met in Brussels at the end of June for the purpose of drafting the common-market and Euratom treaties. The first phase of this conference was preliminary; the second opened in September. The immediate effect of its having been convened on the basis of the "Spaak Report" has been very considerable. In particular, the United Kingdom, at an OEEC meeting held in Paris in July, strongly supported the idea of a study of the possibility of establishing a wider free-trade area comprising a number of other countries besides the six. By the beginning of 1957 there is every reason to believe that the United Kingdom and the Scandinavian countries, and probably the other members of the OEEC will decide to establish a free-trade area. This would mean that trade would be free among all of the countries concerned, but only the six members of the common market would have a common outside tariff.

with the outside world than from its trade with the other members of the group.

In order to become a free-trading area in the first place, the six integrating countries must move as fast as possible toward their chosen goal, i.e., eliminate with the utmost speed the economic barriers which divide them. A gradualistic program of progressive reduction and elimination of trade barriers may easily bog down somewhere along the way and result in nothing more liberal than another preferential tariff system. Now the benefits which members of such a system obtain are at best doubtful, whereas there is no doubt whatever as to the unfavorable effects upon their trade due to the animosity preferential tariffs create among countries which do not belong to the system.

Of this, the authors of the "Spaak Report" appear to be fully aware and the program that they have outlined, although its realization extends over a period of twelve to fifteen years, is a blueprint for a customs union with complete free trade within its borders.

It is difficult to say at this time what the chances are of the "Spaak Report" becoming a reality. There are elements of opposition in most of the countries involved, but, broadly speaking, five of the six are more than likely to go along with translating the blueprint into reality. The sixth country is France, where the difficulties are greatest because of the country's ancient, entrenched, and embattled protectionism.

Experience as well as logic tend to show that there can be no integration, economic and otherwise, without paying the price. In political terms, the price is the surrender of some parts of national sovereignty; in economic terms, the price is the surrender of economic nationalism. Integration without tears is a mirage of wishful thinking. It does not follow that the tears must be bitter and the transitional hardships unendurable. If the commercial postulate for integration is free trade (at least when we speak of a small group of countries), then machinery for facilitating the transition toward a free-trade system is the financial postulate. This involves some kind of a reconversion fund, out of which workers affected by the changeover could be given free training and, if need be, transportation to a new place of work. Such a fund would also compensate losses of those businesses which cannot make the adjustment, however hard they might try, and which must be liquidated. It would finally assist financially the reconversion of yet other businesses which can be adapted to the free-trade conditions with the help of new investments. If the fund is large and its organization very efficient, the transition period from the present state of affairs to the free-trade situation can be made reasonably short. The "Spaak Report" provides for a Readaptation Fund, which is to assist the transfer of labor to new jobs and alleviate such transitional unemployment as might occasionally develop, and an Investment Fund, which is to assist, through investment loans, the readaptation of business to the new conditions resulting from a common market. The experience of Benelux shows that, in the manufacturing sector at least, disturbances are much smaller than they are usually alleged to be and that, in an expanding economy, the freeing of trade involves no major cases of hardship.

The Benelux experience is very instructive in more ways than one. It shows that even under the best of conditions the process must take time and that the twelve to fifteen years allowed in the "Spaak Report" are not an unreasonably long period. It also shows that it can be accomplished without any supranational authority to administer it. It demonstrates conclusively that there is no need for prior harmonization of social policies of the members of the customs union (thus disproving a very recent and insistent French claim made in connection with the common market). Finally, the experience of the Benelux also shows that the success of the customs union depends upon each of its members putting its monetary house in order and maintaining realistic exchange rates with its partners and with the outside world. This point, to which insufficient attention is paid in the "Spaak Report," would call for greater elaboration than it is possible to give within the limited space of this chapter. Let me therefore merely intimate that five of the six countries envisaging a common market at the present time have roughly correct exchange parities, while the sixth, France, clings desperately to an over-valued currency. This will have to change if France is to be a helpful partner in the development of free trade in western Europe.

To conclude, there is every reason for the architects of the common market to persevere in their effort to integrate as much as possible of western Europe by means of free trade. The area, it must be hoped, will be gradually widened to include the United Kingdom, the Scandinavian countries, Switzerland and Austria. And, if the United States should embark upon a policy of effective trade liberalization, there need be no fear that these European developments should result in a new preferential system. After all, most of Europe's prosperity resulting from foreign trade is due to the scope of overseas commerce and not merely to intra-European transactions. There is thus, in the end, no conflict, but indeed great organic cohesion between the development of free trade within Europe and the building of a liberal and inclusive North Atlantic Community.

The Coal and Steel Community as a Case Study in Integration

GIUSEPPE PELLA / *President of the Common Assembly of the European Coal and Steel Community*

THE EUROPEAN COAL AND STEEL COMMUNITY occupies a key position in the development of an economically integrated Europe. This process of integration, which started with the end of World War II and has expressed itself in many differing proposals and forms, found its first realization in the Organization for European Economic Cooperation. Here we have an example of how political movements have been able to frame international institutions in the effort to create an economically unified Europe or, if some among you find the use of the term *unification* too strong, of how they have succeeded at least in eliminating some of the divisions and particularisms which have characterized European politics and economies during the late war and in the period immediately following it.

In my opinion it would be an error to look at this process only from the point of view of what has been achieved following agreements made by several European nations, because that would give the impression that European integration is not a natural outcome of forces brought together by the innate exigencies of the European economy, but is the artificial result of a definite political line followed by the individual governments.

I would like to clarify this concept further, because there is no sector of human activity which is more susceptible to interference from outside than that of economics. And when we speak of European integration it must be clearly understood that we are not speaking of a preconceived plan to bring about such economic development in one way or another, but simply the desire to create the indispensable requisites for the free expansion of an integrated European economy.

It is a very well-known fact that a well-balanced economic and financial development of European countries, especially with regard to their relations with other areas, cannot be carried out unless there is a development of the European economy within the larger frame of the world economic expansion. Any other attempt to resolve the existing disequilibria would imply a return to restrictive principles and would force the use of methods which, by limiting free international commerce, would lead inevitably toward autarchic systems.

On the other hand, the technological progress and the development of two great economic powers, one to the east and the other to the west, while raising the Continent of Europe to a position of particular historical importance midway between these two systems, also have rendered it indispensable that Europe reach an economic capacity which will enable it to preserve its political independence. Only through such preservation can we hope to save Western Christian civilization and be able to develop that progressive social action characteristic of the new times, which has appeared in various forms in all European countries.

The common market, which represents the immediate goal of European integration, must not be considered as a measure for controlled or, worse yet, planned economies, but must be understood as an effort to eliminate those factors which restrain the development of a free market. Thus, the goal of economic integration is not the channeling of economic forces toward a given direction, but on the contrary the removal of the barriers that hold back the natural growth of these forces.

The peculiar position—I would almost be tempted to say the preeminent position—which the Coal and Steel Community occupies in this process derives essentially from the fact that the community itself has a supranational character and it forms, even though in the restricted field of its competence, a common market. This supranational character and this common market are not found in any of the other institutions, even though the efforts in international cooperation, as for example in the OEEC, lead necessarily toward the same goal, though no explicit declaration in this sense has been made.

On the basis of the fifty-year treaty which set up the Coal and Steel Community, the member countries renounce a part of their sovereignty in favor of an organization in which the executive power is vested in the High Authority, the control power in the Common Assembly, and controversies are resolved before a special Court of Justice. A Council of Ministers of the six countries involved represents the link between the supranational and national powers.

There is much to be said about this fundamental characteristic of the Coal and Steel Community, especially if we should want to examine the really novel political elements which it brings to play in the field of European relations. But we must restrict ourselves to economic matters, and here the essential problem can be resolved only by pooling together some specific activities and by assigning the exercise of these functions to special institutions which, though created by single states, are completely autonomous. Only then can we really speak of integration. If the provisions and regulations which direct these specific activities remain in the sphere of competence of the individual countries, then regardless of how much we may try to co-ordinate our efforts and in spite of the fact that some agreements can be reached, we will always have separate economies, at best running parallel and converging toward the same goal. Only through the institution of an organism which operates on a level higher than that of individual governments, and in favor of which the governments renounce their competence in the particular field derived by their sovereign rights, can one hope to have a unified economic policy and the assurance that in the shaping of this policy the structural differences of the various components of the integrated community never will be lost sight of.

This brief résumé of the peculiar character of the European Coal and Steel Community, which is usually referred to as a supranational organism,[1] explains how within the ECSC it is possible to plan and

[1] I would like to point out that I use the term *supranational* as it is commonly accepted in the language of the supporters of European integration, without wanting to get involved in a discussion of its legal and political attributes, which, apart from complicating the discussion, would also make it academic.

actually to put in operation a common market, a market that is without quantitative restrictions, without duties, without tariffs and discriminatory practices, without a double standard of prices favoring the internal market at the expense of the exporters, a common market in which there can be free circulation of investments and of manpower, a large unified zone in which goods, the manpower needed to produce them, and the necessary capital can circulate freely.

This indeed is the final goal of the economic integration of Europe. As for the legal structure which the integration eventually will take, it must not be set up rigidly from aprioristic conclusions, but it should develop naturally in such a manner as to render possible the efficient functioning of the common market on the largest possible scale. These are the principles which have inspired countries to enter the Coal and Steel Community and consequently have brought about the first experiment of a common market achieved through a supranational organization.

It would be presumptuous to give a positive judgment on the achievements of the Coal and Steel Community after only three years of its existence. The charter provides for a transitional period of five years and so we are still in the organizational stage showing the repercussions which economic fluctuations have had on the coal and steel industries. But if it is too early, perhaps, to draw a balance sheet for these first three years, it is possible to follow the main activities of this period and at least draw some conclusions which may tell us whether or how far the Coal and Steel Community will succeed.

In this brief summary I am not including a discussion of the concrete results gained by the Coal and Steel Community in such fields as investments, international transport, where an agreement on the standardization of fares has been reached, and labor, where much has been done to solve the problem of re-employment, to insure a free circulation of the labor force, and to provide the workers with adequate housing facilities.

A most instructive estimate of the probable success or failure of a general common market can be had by studying the reaction of the Coal and Steel Community to two opposite phases of the business cycle.

The year 1953 and the beginning of 1954 were characterized by a regression and stagnation of all economic activities both in the countries of the community and in other Western countries. The coal and steel industries, because of their importance in economic life, and because they are particularly sensitive to variations in the economic cycle, could not escape the effects of this situation. As a result, the volume of orders in the steel industries dropped heavily from an over-all tonnage of over 12 million to less than 6 million tons between the end of September, 1952, and the end of December, 1953. Steel production had declined from 3.6 million tons per month during the last semester of 1952 to 3.3 million tons as the monthly average for 1953.

In the coal industry, due to the lack of elasticity which characterizes it, production remained stationary. Stocks registered large increases, however, regardless of the fact that the work day had been reduced in many of the coal areas of the community.

It was during the period of low economic activity, however, that the first effects of the common market, which had become operative on February 10 for coal and on May 1, 1953 for steel, were felt. Steel producers were forced to intensify their sales in those areas of the community where demand had been relatively high, as in Germany, the Low Countries, and Italy, without becoming involved with traditionally protectionist markets. So it was possible to avoid heavy curtailing of production in order to keep the regression within safe bounds.

The coal market also responded favorably to the situation, with an increased exchange within the community. This traffic, made possible by the abolition of restrictions, the circulation of the products and in some cases facilitated by the equalizing mechanisms recently set up, certainly contributed to prevent the accumulation of large coal stocks in those areas where the demand had always been weakest. Within the community the economic situation showed an improvement, especially in the building and automobile industries, beginning with the second quarter of 1954.

A tangible sign of such improvement was the increase of orders registered by the steel market. This increase first took place in Germany and Italy, due both to greater internal demand and to orders received from other countries, while a similar expansion was occurring also in France, the Saar, Belgium, and the Low Countries as requests from other areas of the community mounted. Thus the over-all demands placed on the steel industry rose from 7 million tons in the March–April period to over 10.8 million tons at the end of 1954. There was also an increase in the production of steel over a period of time, which by the end of the year had reached 4 million tons monthly and an annual average of 48 million tons, an all time high. Steel production for 1954 was 43.8 million tons, which was 7.6 per cent higher than the annual averages for 1952 and 1953. Prices did not rise appreciably, as is the case with a steel market in the process of expansion, due mainly to the livelier competition as evidenced by the developments in the exchange, the application of regulations publicizing price lists, and the toning down of discriminatory practices, thus relieving the consumers from the burden of higher prices.

This expansion of the steel market did not stop in 1955, as production rose to 52.6 million tons, and it can be safely estimated now that to satisfy all the needs of the market there should be an annual production of about 50 million tons. In this situation characterized by a very lively demand, prices of steel products have increased only slightly and have never reached the high levels of the period following the outbreak of the Korean War. This is due mainly to the regulations implicit in the operation of a common market. Another positive result which can be studied in this connection is that while the common market was a stabilizing factor in this sector of industry, it also contributed to the maintenance of reasonable export prices. The United Nations Economic Commission for Europe has underlined this fact, pointing out that in 1955, in spite of the high cycle, the difference between export prices and internal prices of the community was relatively small.

This, however, was not true during the last months of 1955 and the beginning of 1956, when there was a tendency for export prices to rise. The High Authority has immediately taken cognizance of the phenomenon, and it has intervened directly with the steel producers, and by its action has achieved stability in export prices.

The coal market registered a rise in demands in October, 1954, determined by the expansion in the steel industry, with benefit to the whole common-market community. German stocks were rapidly absorbed. The same happened later in Belgium, and in some instances there was even an incipient shortage of some types of coal. Coal from the Lorraine and Saar areas moved particularly in the direction of southern Germany, while that mined in Belgium was more easily absorbed, due to reciprocity arrangements, by the Low Countries. At this same time coal exports have been greater than at any time since the end of the war, with Great Britain purchasing coal from Belgium, Germany, France, and the Saar and the Scandinavian countries getting coke from Germany.

But it is interesting to note that in spite of this heavier demand on the coal market, prices, with the exception of the Dutch mines, have not tended to rise. In 1955 and throughout the first months of 1956 coal production rose, even hitting a record in some sectors such as those producing coke. But this increase must be read in terms of larger power consumption, which in 1955 was 6.5 per cent over 1954, while for the same period coal production increased only by 2 per cent. The problem here lies in the fact that coal production within the community is not sufficient to supply the needed power potentials, and this deficit has to be made up by importing from other countries, as was the case last January when 2,655,000 tons had to be imported. With reference to this problem, the European Coal and Steel Community has channeled its efforts to assure these needed imports and at the same time to maintain a reasonable level of prices through a rational transportation policy and a well-planned system of distribution.

But even during such a period of great demand, coal prices for members of the community have remained almost unchanged due to the system of price ceilings which the High Authority enforced up to April, 1956. This price-fixing policy would at first seem like a direct intervention in the play of a free market, but it was resorted to because of the existence in Germany of a particular sales system which tended to limit competition. This intervention has now become no longer necessary, due to the reorganization of sales in the Ruhr brought about by the community and to the return to normal conditions of competition.

As expected, this decision has created a rise in the price of coal, justified by greater production costs, and especially by salary increases. This fact has brought to light the fundamental problem of the coexistence between an integrated sector and the rest of the economy still under the jurisdiction of the individual countries. Some countries, in fact, faced with this rise of coal prices, have made proposals for the adoption of measures which could keep coal prices at as low a level as possible, measures which at present are being studied by competent members of the High Authority and especially by a mixed commission whose task is to work out agreements with interested governments and to come up with solutions which, though retaining the indispensable features of a free market, will guarantee as much as possible the maintenance of stable prices in the present high economic cycle.

Another aspect of the operation of a common market which must be considered is the unprecedented expansion of trade which, between 1953 and 1954, had taken place at a rate three times faster than the increase of production. This development, which is typical of a unified market and of the vigor with which the greater possibilities for trade exchange are exploited, has also, without doubt, exercised a moderating influence on the level of prices during a period of economic expansion. Was this intensification of commercial activities due to other factors, such as the high business cycle and the climate of liberalization being brought about by the activities of the OEEC, or must we look for its first cause in the opening of a unified market? The answer may be found in the following data.

From 1953 to 1955, exchange of products within the sector of the community member countries increased by 93 per cent, while the exchange increase of other products has been only by 59 per cent. If we go one step further and limit our attention to comparing the exchange of the community's products and other goods, such as non-ferrous materials, cement, lime, building materials, machines, and vehicles, we can see that the movement of steel, scrap iron, and iron ores among the member countries had increased by 153 per cent between 1952 and 1955, while for the same period the movement of the other goods mentioned above registered an increase of about 59 per cent. These are encouraging figures for those who are convinced of the value of large and free markets as factors for economic progress.

This brief examination of the statistical data relative to the three years of operation of the common market demonstrates how the system of the European Coal and Steel Community has proved that it is possible in a period of stagnation or recession to cushion the negative and dangerous effects, and to stimulate instead an acceleration in industrial production with evident advantages to the consumers and the producers as well. These considerations could also be applied if we examine one particular steel industry, such as that of Italy, in a state of inferiority with respect to that of other members of the community due to the lack of raw materials, to the structural difficulties which scatter steel production, the overabundance of manpower, and the scarcity of individual orders.

In spite of this, and contrary to some pessimistic forecasts which had been voiced here and there when discussions began on the Schuman Plan, the Italian steel industry reached in 1955 a record production of 5,393,000 tons of steel, that is, twice as much as in 1938; and for the period from 1952 to 1955 per capita consumption of power and steel in Italy approached the average of the whole community. Without doubt many factors have contributed to these results, such as the expanding economy and, above all, the investments which have been made. It can be maintained, however, that a common market of raw materials has been a determining factor in this particular situation, and on the basis of the experience of the last three years it can be said that the institution of a common market, well regulated and disciplined, brings economic advantages which not only affect the over-all average well-being, but also benefit the single areas which make up the common market. Of course, it is always necessary to keep in mind the characteristics peculiar to each area.

It can be said without hesitation that the operation of the Coal and Steel Community has provided a positive experience. In saying this we must always remember the particular character of the Coal and Steel Community, and above all of the orbit in which it moves. The Coal and Steel Community is, in effect, an example of integration by sector, an achievement of what is usually referred to as *vertical integration.* I do not wish to be drawn here into a long discussion of the advantages and disadvantages of vertical integration versus horizontal integration, but two points should be made.

One point is that the term *common market,* as generally used in speaking of the coal and steel market within the area of the community, is not completely suitable, because when it is applied to only two economic sectors, it suffers, as it were, from a disability from birth, since a common market should involve all economic factors. In fact, while the abolition of quotas, customs duties, and other barriers to trade make possible a free movement of goods, all the regulations which are intended to discipline the market of the community and to bring about a regime of free competition cannot by themselves lay the basis for effective competition among the various industries of the community. Thus we have an imperfect common market, since, while some general principles are stated, the individual entrepreneurs are still subject to economic, fiscal, credit, social, insurance, and other such policies which differ from country to country. It is evident that an economic sector as basic as that of steel and coal cannot be totally separated from the rest of the economy.

The second point is that if we apply to other sectors of economic life the same approach which has been used in the case of the coal and steel sector, we will risk having one day a European economy subdivided into many sectors, and thus, rather than integrating, we would be dividing Europe into a number of tight economic compartments. From the political point of view we would have, in addition to the states which I shall call political, numerous states which I would define as economic, increasing thus the division rather than bringing us closer to the realization of a unified Europe.

For these reasons I believe that the system of sectoral integration can be applied only in a few instances such as that of transport, industrial power, and nuclear energy, sectors which nowadays are fashionably referred to as infrastructures, that is, as representing the bed rock of the entire economic life and necessary to all industrial production. It seems feasible that the integration of the infrastructures could bring about a complete integration of the Continent, obviating the creation of the above-mentioned tight compartments.

The positive lesson which can be learned from the operation of the Coal and Steel Community lies essentially in the fact that, although the market is an imperfect one, it has given the expected results, and I would say that it has given more than had been expected, not only in the field of production, but also in the social field, inasmuch as the functioning of the Coal and Steel Community shows how a market economy based upon free competition can lend itself to the fulfillment of social goals as well. This is an extremely important point, because it shows that social justice can be achieved within liberty, in democracy, in a market economy, within competition, and that it does not require as an indispensable premise an unchecked statism, which leads to the extermination of liberty in the political field and a stifling of private initiative in the economic field.

From a strictly economic point of view I believe that it is possible to state that the common market of steel and coal has reached, or is on the road to reaching, the objectives which are of particular interest in order to judge whether this is the right road to bring back European economy, not to the position of pre-eminence which it has had in world history, but at least to that level which is indispensable in order to provide assurance to the people of the old Continent. These four objectives can be summed up as follows:

1. To adapt the size of the market to the capacities of modern production, and to stimulate modernization of plants and industrial equipment.

2. To set up a regime of competition within the common market, and thus ensure Europe's competitive position in the world market.

3. To abandon the a posteriori, anti-cyclical policies which up to now have been used to correct economic phenomena, in favor of a policy preventive in character and directed toward envisaging continuous economic expansion.

4. To dedicate to the solution of social problems a good part of the resources which will be derived from the prevention of economic crises and from improved production.

In making these remarks, one cannot forget that, if on one hand the common market of the Coal and Steel Community includes two basic products, on the other its development is tied strictly to the demand for by-products of coal and steel, which are still outside the aegis of the common market. We are thus in a situation in which the increased demand for by-products of steel and coal, regardless of how the steel and coal market is regulated, cannot help being affected by the disequilibria which occur in the general market. Moreover, since the more complex manufactured goods are those which are affected advantageously by a more modern system of production and by specialization, this would lead to the conclusion that greater benefits for all could be gained if the common market were expanded to semifinished products as well.

In the end, always in the light of what can be learned from the experience of the Coal and Steel Community and applied to bringing about a European economic integration, one must recognize the soundness and the efficacy of the juridical system, considered, naturally, as a means and not as an end, upon which the community itself is based. It is undeniable that the common market of coal and steel would not have reached the point which it has reached today if it did not have at the base a supranational organization, and I am using this term here with the reservation which I mentioned earlier. Above all, the way this organization has functioned, its ability to discern the disequilibria existing from area to area, and remedy them, and the possibility that the setting up of a common market could mean that the strong would get stronger and the weak weaker, constitute in my opinion a clear confirmation that in order to reach the stage of a supranational authority we must work by trial and error if necessary, without being tied down by preconceived terminologies or political factors. This is not said here to mean that a stop should be placed on the process of European economic integration; but one should not confuse the final goal with the point of departure or with the transitional phases during which it is not so important which road or method is followed, as long as the road and the method allow a forward stride and, above all, help to create those premises and those ties whose growth, day by day, will bring about the union of the economies of the European countries.

In conclusion, I believe that it can be said that the experience of the Coal and Steel Community shows how a pool can become a vital construction, especially when it deals with sectors the integration of which will have no disturbing influences on the economic situation. And now, for the reasons already mentioned, I am referring specifically to power, and in particular to atomic power. Since this is an absolutely new economic activity, there do not exist those positions and those vested interests which, besides representing great difficulties, carry all sorts of inconveniences in the passage from a national to a common market.

The experience of the Coal and Steel Community has shown that the road to a common market is the right one to follow. The common market, which we believe should be as large and as free as possible, presupposes gradualness, to permit the necessary readjustment for passage from the regime of the single market to that of the unified market, thus eliminating possibilities of violent crises.

I will not discuss further the constitution of this common market, its organization, or the systems best adapted for its functioning. The essential point is not the scholarly and lofty discussion of system. It is the departure from the study phase, with caution and courage, for a phase of realization in which, perhaps, an empirical approach is more appropriate than the insistence upon fixed plans which can present all manner of difficulties and inconveniences. But even following this pragmatic approach, which is without doubt the preferable one from the tactical point of view, we should always keep our eye on the unique example of the common market, partial and imperfect though it is, but which today is in existence. One cannot fail to realize the undeniable success of this first experiment.

European Integration
and the World Economy

GIOVANNI DEMARIA / *Visiting Professor of Economics, Bologna Center, School of Advanced International Studies, The Johns Hopkins University*

LET US SUPPOSE that integrated Europe were to be a political and economic reality tomorrow. The destiny implied in this hypothesis is one which presently-divided Europe, no longer possessing centers of political gravity, no longer cherishing great hopes, and with national economies of uncertain future, may well be about to face. Let us further suppose that there were to be a European legislature, a supreme court, a European currency, an inter-European commerce commission similar to the Interstate Commerce Commission in the United States, and, finally, decentralization and spatial centralizations of various economic activities which would no longer be dependent upon political fantasy or the particularistic and chauvinistic interests of individual states, but upon rational economic factors. The Europe thus hypothecated would still be a Europe with an extremely varied economy embracing a broad range of differences and local colorations. In particular, my hypothesis implies that the European economy would be based essentially upon a multiplicity of competing enterprises, whether public or private.

Very probably these enterprises would have broader dimensions than at present, for the advantages of a large market and the economies which large size often assures would be decisive in this regard. There would be much more powerful machines and equipment, larger and better power plants, and a Europe-wide rather than state-wide system of transportation. The number of small enterprises would probably be numerically reduced, not only because some would be eliminated as those of great dimensions emerged, but also because local monopolistic situations which previously protected them would disappear.

Labor organizations would differ no less profoundly from those of the present. European unions would probably assert themselves in various industries. In others there would be regional unions, federated on a national or semi-European scale with exclusive collective bargaining contracts.

It is not possible to set forth in purely quantitative terms either the economic consequences of an integration of Europe or the political and economic problems which would arise simultaneously with the international situation emerging from so radical a transformation of European economic activity. Yet one general conclusion seems indisputable. The European economy would be very complex and efficient and would require a type of general European-oriented economic policy, the major aspects of which may be glimpsed in the outline of probable relationships between united Europe and the economic world at large.

Above all, it should be observed that in estimating the effectiveness of a complex economy emerging from the economic union of Europe, one must neither disregard the various governmental policies designed to limit competition which are currently operative in individual European states nor compare these with the foreign economic policy most likely to be adopted by the united Europe of tomorrow. It may be said that as a result of European economic union the anticompetitive positions today manifest in every individual European state would be considerably attenuated and that it would be relatively easy to introduce an antitrust law on a Europe-wide basis. One may also be reasonably safe in asserting that both the law and the courts would be much more decisively opposed to monopolistic practices in the various sectors of economic life. Were it not so, it would be difficult, even impossible, to conceive of enduring European unity.

For the same reasons I also maintain that *dirigiste* economic policies within Europe would be well-nigh impossible. If they were attempted on a wide scale, the very future of a united Europe would be cast into doubt. In this connection, it is enough to remember the psychological and political resistance of various European nations to the German attempt in World War II to impose the Berlin Indemnity Bank, the authentic organ of a European economic plan even though camouflaged as an arrangement merely for the clearing of inter-European payments. And this was the case even though Germany at that time was at the summit of its military power!

Little by little the idea will take hold that there is a European interest in having a variety of competing markets operating within an area as broad as Europe itself. Jurisprudence will establish European rules of conduct; European courts, in their turn, will interpret these in a European sense and apply them to specific cases. And yet European political leaders will frequently find it possible to move toward this goal only under the pressure of circumstances or because of emergency conditions.

But what shall we say about the economic policy of a united Europe vis-à-vis the rest of the world?

At this point my hypothesis no longer serves to guide the reasoning which follows. In the final analysis, the answer to my question is more the product of intuition and sensitivity, comparable to what may be called an historical experience, than it is a rigorously reasoned reply.

First, in regard to importations, I say that there is a strong probability, rather than just the possibility, that a united Europe would require high tariff barriers against importations in order to protect its own industries, agriculture, and labor. General European legislation of this type would seem likely as would also legislation discriminating against industrial products coming from outside Europe. The same may be said about protectionist measures in favor of labor, naval, automotive, and air transport. Other restrictive practices would relate to extra-European banking and insurance companies.

Naturally, some of these protective tariffs would be imposed initially to insure certain fiscal returns, but, little by little, others, mainly protective of European production and trade, would be imposed, not in logical consequence, but as a political consequence of these originally introduced.

Against what kinds of extra-European activities would such protective or restrictive measures be principally directed? Many responses to this query might be made, of which some would appear to be reasonably good guesses. It is probable that the European worker would want protection against non-European labor, especially colored labor, and, in any case, against labor with living standards inferior to his own. It is my view that the history of North America would be repeated in nearly every detail by a united Europe.

It is also likely that the numerous pleaders of the cause of infant industries (and of short-term protective measures which now encounter so many obstacles within the restricted confines of individual states) would find more favorable opportunities once there were established a single European market much larger than any local market. There would very probably be created, therefore, a substantial number of infant industries enjoying protection against the competition of extra-European industrial products. This would appear to be borne out by earlier experience, when we remember what happened following the creation of the German Empire, the British Commonwealth, and the French Union, all of which felt obliged to resort to extensive protectionism in order to encourage or sustain new industries.

In my judgment, the steel and textile industries would take precedence among the major industries to be protected, more so than others, unless an effort were made to protect certain large sections of Europe which, in the absence of well-equipped industries, could endanger European unity because of psychological restiveness reinforced by poverty.

Nevertheless, for a long time to come, considerable industrial importations from the North American continent would be required, at least until European industrial know-how had reached the level of that obtaining in the most progressive extra-European countries. At the present time the disparity between the two continents is very great, and decades, at least, will be required to overcome it, given the fact that in the industrial field the construction of the necessary foundations requires much time and that there is no possibility of reproducing in a simple way the most advanced North American industrial methods. Patents cannot be acquired and utilized freely. The technical preparation of others cannot necessarily be copied. All the infrastructures can be created but very slowly. Russia, for example, in spite of its attempt to imitate the

North American pattern through a rigorous economic policy and professional training, has required decades to bring itself near to the halfway point.

Another reason which leads me to believe that the distance to be covered in industrial development would not soon be spanned is the social security policy of all the European states, a policy which, being more extensive than that in North America, would necessarily impose greater burdens upon European industries and therefore weaken their competitive position in world trade.

We may turn now specifically to European agricultural production, protected and unprotected.

With the best intentions in the world, European agriculturalists could not avoid asking for extensive help in order to plan for the production of certain agricultural commodities in substitution of those thus far imported. Imagine what could be obtained from the Sahara brought to life with the fissionable energy of Euratom. Perhaps, similarly, radical changes could be achieved in the manner of storing cotton, wool, grain, sugar, and meat.

In general, extra-European agricultural products would encounter more serious obstacles in united Europe than in the past or today in disunited Europe, the individual states of which may easily come to terms with nations and markets abroad. Similarly, and in addition to these changes, it is conceivable that the present international conventions relating to grain, sugar, and other agricultural products, as well as conventions which fix maximum and minimum prices and which establish export and import quotas for participating countries, will be abandoned sooner or later.

And what would happen to the exports of united Europe? It seems almost inevitable, especially as far as exports to non-European countries are concerned, that internal prices in Europe (which could only reflect those of a detached competitive area), substantially cheaper European labor costs, and the progressive improvement of techniques of production would give many European industries such improved possibilities for expansion and export as to oblige the most progressive non-European countries to restrict excess to their own markets and also to resist penetration into other, less developed, non-European markets. Should all these conditions and possibilities be realized, then nothing seems more certain than that we would witness in the industrial field all over the world the formation of large self-sufficient industrial areas, self-sufficient in considerable measure, if not in entirety. In particular, the expansion of industrialization in Europe could make this an independent geo-economic-political area.

Naturally these events would impose upon each of the areas in question not only problems connected with conserving its own natural and industrial resources, but also those of military protection, since industrial overproduction in the type of industrial economy I have predicted for a united Europe must be sold to non-European areas, which for many reasons will not be able to organize themselves on a self-sufficient basis, especially with regard to production of industrial goods. In making this assertion, I start from the assumption that this is the time, not for romantic dreams, but for the examination of concrete industrial problems regardless of whether they assume a favorable aspect or not. There is no reason to resort to idealistic symbols or to introduce, at least for the present, algebraic or arithmetical formulations.

It would be helpful, indeed, if one were able to define qualitatively the broad lines in which industrial traffic between Europe and the areas outside Europe will develop. But here again the matter is too speculative and open to criticism. One thing is sure, however. Given the hypothesis of a greatly increased European industrial complex, there would follow a great movement of industrial goods within the European market, while at the same time there would be a strengthening of commercial relations between Europe and non-European areas. I will try to sketch an imaginary model to show this reorientation of industrial traffic for the future.

It seems to me that with regard to industrial exports from Europe to non-European areas the most important would be exports of industrial plants, machinery, rolling stock, chemical and electrical materials, radios, clothing, printing presses, and cosmetic articles, all directed toward Latin America, Africa, and Asia. Regarding agricultural exports it would be such primary materials and by-products as tobacco, alcohol, beverages, and processed leather which would set the pace.

With reference to European importations of industrial and agricultural products from non-European areas, it would be impossible to go back to the traditional structure existing before World War II. Except for spices and delicacies and for some nonferrous metals (coal, tungsten, nickel, cobalt, zinc, copper, molybdenum), a substantial reduction of imports is to be expected, at least in the long run.

As I mentioned previously, in a united Europe it would be possible to resolve the problem of shortages of basic raw materials essential to industrial transformation. Synthetic rubber, coal, wool, and perhaps even cotton can be produced largely within Europe or in adjacent areas, or perhaps can be substituted for completely by the revolutionary development of synthetic products. Consequently, except for some metals and some nonmetallic minerals, European economic development would be conditioned, so far as imports are concerned, essentially by stocks of oil, spices, and forest products, and at the beginning by imports of natural fibers, fats, and animal products.

The maintenance of a high level of European trade with non-European areas would therefore depend, above all, on the possibility of the economic development of non-European areas, of the great continents from which Europe would draw in exchange on a temporary or permanent basis such things as the minerals already mentioned, fats, fruit, tropical products, seeds, meats, etc.

As a result of the redistribution of European and extra-European economic functions carried out along the above lines, there would be a strengthening of some currents of world traffic which today are overburdened or underdeveloped. Likewise there should be a notable increase in commercial relations with Central and South America and with Africa and Asia. European commerce with Asia would certainly increase rapidly.

The present five-year plans for India and China are oriented toward the creation of the greatest possible industrial power, which will require heavy imports of capital goods for many years to come. A united Europe could enter this trade without having to impose upon itself a planned economy along the same lines. The requirements of this trade could easily be met by the large enterprises which would develop in united Europe. It must be remembered that countries with planned economies prefer to deal with great private enterprises to fill their orders rather than with other planned economies, especially in the cases involving long-term industrial orders. This consideration I think is of decisive importance.

With regard to the North American continent, however, the

situation would be much as I have already suggested. European importations of industrial goods from this area would be inevitable for all of the period required to close the gap between European and North American industrial development and to build up the accumulations of capital which cannot be financed completely from European savings. Europe also would have to import financial capital for investments.

Substantially, at the beginning—a rather long period historically speaking—there would be a kind of industrial integration between the two continents, but the rhythm of this integration would diminish as obsolete European industrial equipment was replaced with modern equipment of North American type.

Whether all of this is realized or not will depend to a great extent on the attitudes, policies, and reactions of the non-European areas toward Europe. In the study of these latter problems, it is usually forgotten that commercial relations between united Europe and non-European areas would be determined by the bargaining position of the contracting parties. United Europe's bargaining position would depend a great deal upon its military position, but also upon the military and bargaining abilities of other blocs. Finally, the flow of world trade would depend upon the spirit of international co-operation which up to now has been fostered in European, Arabian, South Asiatic, and the Central and South American countries, principally by the United States.

The economic development of a united Europe could be great enough in the long run to require no further outside help for the development of its industries and agriculture and for the self-correction of its inferior social status resulting from lack of education, disease, malnutrition, and the poverty of some of its classes and regions. Collaboration with the great North American continent would then take above all, perhaps exclusively, the form of scientific and technical assistance.

The economic development of a united Europe could indeed be such as to assure from the outset its participation in international economic co-operation on an active rather than a passive basis. Europe could thus envisage as one of her future goals the civilization of these continents which she entered as a colonial power and from which quite justly she has been forced recently to withdraw in face of the inevitable pressures of popular patriotism. In fact, a united Europe would be far more acceptable to colonial and semi-colonial countries than the present states of disunited Europe are or could be.[1]

I began by hypothecating the existence of a united Europe and then drew from this some conclusions. But all of my constructions, including the initial hypothesis, are of the future and not of the present. It is easy to accuse me of having presented a fantastic and imaginary development of events. But looking at the dynamism of the last twenty-five years, starting from the time of the Great Depression when so many radical and unexpected changes took place, one can scarcely avoid the conclusion that further changes, no less radical and unexpected, can very well take place within the next twenty-five years. Were this to be the case, the present phase of our history would be the prelude to that of a united Europe tomorrow.

[1] My perspective is purposely projected into a long, though not necessarily very long, period of time and is developed within the limits of an hypothecated "diffused spirit of international cooperation." If we abandon this hypothesis, quite different consequences could be envisioned, the most important of which, as I see it, being the economic reorganization of the world on racial bases. But here we are sliding into a frightening nightmare, with an industrial integration of all the white areas, including the Soviet Union, on one side, and one of the colored areas on the other.

4

Political Aspects of the Question of European Integration

The Dynamics of European Integration

HENRI BRUGMANS / *Rector, College of Europe, Bruges*

WHEN DISCUSSING European integration, the average European stresses perhaps too often the gloomy prospects of non-unification. His arguments, of course, are justified. Our countries cannot be successful if they deal separately, for example, with the problems of atomic energy or defense. And one can easily assume that Africa will be lost to us, if we continue to reject any form of "Eurafrican," plurinational, and multiracial co-operation.

I do not see why people seem to prefer to put the European case in a rather negative form. Why not put the main emphasis on what European integration would *permit,* rather than on what it can help to avoid? True, we do not want to overplay our hand and compete with the totalitarian states in promising a kind of earthly paradise, once Europe is united. In this respect, lack of modesty is lack of realism, and in the past most prophets who seemed to have the keys of human happiness when they were in opposition, created ruin and misery once they had seized power. Our younger generation is therefore extremely cautious when confronted with political messianism, and rightly so. Nevertheless, why should we abstain from what Lenin called "scientific dreaming," from long-term policy and creative imagination? For once, let us think about the new dynamic forces which would—or rather *will*—be freed after and by the unification of our Continent.

We start from the assumption that such forces are potentially present, but that they are unable to become active under the present circumstances. This assumption may be called an optimistic hypothesis for which there is no evidence. But without such an assumption, not only is our debate useless, but so is our staying in a Europe which would be decadent beyond help. Moreover, time and again, a student of European affairs is struck by the considerable amount of powerful will (and not only so-called "good will") still to be found in the hearts and minds of our ordinary people. The raw material is still there, but initiative is nearly always discouraged by the present state of affairs.

That is even true for nations which are comparatively sound and active. Even in Benelux and Scandinavia there is a widespread, although latent, feeling of malaise and stagnation in spite of wonderful technical achievements like the drying up of the Zuider Zee and the remarkable systems of social security. I sometimes ask myself if people would not prefer a bit less security and a bit more adventure. Our European ship lies on a sand bank. Parts of it are beautifully kept and well in order, and we are told that there are supplies for an indefinite period. We hold elections and are constitutionally "free," but nevertheless, we envy our grandfathers who fought their political campaigns with such excitement. Unfortunately, we are more and more skeptical about internal politics, as we realize that the basic problems of today are no longer put in national terms—at least, not in Europe. Surely, from time to time, there is a sudden outburst of traditional political passion, when, for example, the Belgian left is mobilized against King Leopold or the Belgian right against anti-clerical legislation, or when workers in Holland or Denmark go on strike in a period of boom, refusing the proposals of the employers, the arbitration of the state, and the leadership of their trade unions. But all this remains on the fringe of historic events.

In short, Europe is living in a state of psychological frustration, of uneasiness and latent revolt, not because its population is miserable or exploited or oppressed, but because there is no inspiration, no perspective, no movement which stirs up the vital forces which, however, do exist.

Unfortunately, we have to face the fact that the federalist movement in Europe has not succeeded in crystallizing the secret energies of our peoples. In many countries the movement exists as an effective pressure group and is to be given credit for having organized numerous local branches where "the grammer of a new European political language" is taught. But the movement is limited nearly everywhere to a civic élite (including left-wing and trade union leaders), without a larger rank and file. In short, I do not believe that this situation is going to be reversed. The dynamics of integration, as far as I can see, will not become revolutionary before integration itself is achieved. Federation is a solution, not a myth.

Disappointing as this is, I do not think that we hereby have pronounced the verdict of federalism. From the historic point of view, nobody can expect a revolution to appeal before it is made. Even in 1789, there was not the slightest prefiguration of a republican undercurrent in France. And still, four years later, the King was beheaded and a new republican calendar started: *"L'An de la République."* No theory and not even a progressive program had been put into practice. Events had taken place, and life had been more eloquent than any orator, more persuasive than any barrister, more illuminating than any educator, more convincing than any pamphleteer. Two generations later, Cavour pointed to a comparable state of affairs when he said, with an apparent paradox, that "Italy was 'made' . . . now we had to 'make' good Italians."

There is, perhaps, one more reason why federalism in Europe has remained until now remarkably modest and "governmental," in spite of its far-reaching aims and the militant spirit of its supporters. I refer to the general situation today, when no responsible democrat would willingly take the risk of preaching the gospel of systematic opposition.

During the nineteenth century, the Protestant right-wing anti-revolutionaries in my country always stressed the importance of continuity and the danger of undermining public order by too radical reforms. Maybe, they said, these reforms will have good results, but nobody knows before they have been tried. And above all, in going too far too fast, you weaken the authority of the state as such and create a moment of transition and uncertainty when the old is dead and the new not yet entirely strong, so that the demons of anarchy may get their chance. Therefore let us replace carefully one stone with another, instead of blowing up the whole house in the hope that we can later build a better one.

The argument of the anti-revolutionaries might be a pretty strong one at a time like ours, when not only the demons of anarchy are wide awake, but even more the totalitarian brain trusts. True, we might well bring home to public opinion the fact that an unintegrated national army in Europe is ineffective as such. But can we go beyond that statement and call the recruits to conscientious objection for Europe's sake? I am afraid the result would be more defeatist than federalist. Or can we ask people to refuse national taxation with the unanswerable argument that the national state can no longer fulfill its task? I am afraid that Poujade would, for the first time, agree with us.

In conclusion, the federalist movement in Europe finds itself in the deplorable situation of a doctor who would have liked to operate upon his patient, but knows that such an operation would probably mean death. It has to be extremely careful in putting forward its full doctrine. It proclaims the historic end of the national era in human evolution, but it knows that the Bastille of the nation-state is not only a prison, but also a democratic bulwark which should not be destroyed by violence. The Jacobins could trample the flag of Louis XVI. The European federalist cannot do the same thing with his national flag, which is not only the label of outdated political machinery, but also the symbol of a beloved fatherland and of a precious democratic tradition. We have to protect what we attack, at the same time. For all these reasons, federalism has not yet developed its real force of renovation and has sometimes come to be interpreted as a force of social conservatism instead of the opposite.

But the dynamic potential of federalism exists. And, what seems even more important, there is no alternative. Whatever the mistakes and misdeeds of the federalist organization, it is the only democratic political force, which, as such, embodies a relevant and clear idea. True, one can belong to a traditional party with full loyalty and conviction. Nevertheless, it remains probable that neither liberalism nor Christian democracy nor democratic socialism, those three main currents of political life in Europe, are still able to generate lasting enthusiasm. Their ideologies appear much less clear than before World War I. Most of their respective programs have been fulfilled. And, even more important perhaps, the solidarity of all democrats against totalitarianism is so vital that there is in fact much more which unites Socialists and Conservatives than there still remains to divide them. A bit more planned economy or a bit less, but when the struggle for world freedom is at stake, the debate becomes more a matter of technique than of principle. Therefore, it should be possible to find a very large common ground between a left wing which would not be doctrinaire or utopian, and a right wing which would look beyond vested interest and prejudice.

Such a constructive compromise, somewhere in the center, has not been reached everywhere. In Germany, for instance, government and opposition quarrel systematically on every issue, even when one cannot see where the alternative solution would be. But public opinion is not fooled. It feels vaguely but strongly that the debate is artificially dramatized. People shrug their shoulders and pass by. Unfortunately, their diminishing interest in national politics means that they lose faith in democracy.

While Europe today desperately lacks political dynamism, it is futile to expect it from national party systems. Whether the traditional parties continue to fight each other as Saint Georges fighting dragons, or try to find a permanent basis of reasonable co-operation, the result may be more or less satisfying, but it will never give much inspiring hope. Only new facts can create a new impetus, and those facts can no longer come from within the national states, nor from the parties which run them. They can only come from a world situation on which no Continental power of Europe can any longer have an influence, as long as it acts separately. In other words, we cannot hope to play our political part, as long as we remain disunited. Or, putting the same idea positively, only European unity will again confront us with the real political issues of the twentieth-century world. Here alone lies the road to dynamic action. Those who refuse it accept stagnation, apathy, disintegration.

European federation, however, is not an aim in itself, like the salvation of our souls. It is a means to an end. How can it better the situation? What are the problems which can be solved more efficiently, once Europe is united?

First is the need for central Western headquarters to co-ordinate and direct operations in the political war. Whether we like it or not, communism has declared war on the West, not as a geographic entity, but as a civilization. It wants to destroy the ground we stand on and continues to say so, just as frankly as Hitler used to announce his plans in *Mein Kampf*. Even today, in the period of de-Stalinization, Khrushchev does not hide the final aim of Communist strategy, and a return to Lenin is certainly not an abandonment of world revolution. On the contrary, at an earlier stage, many students of the Soviet Union announced that the realistic Great Russian Stalin was much less dangerous for us than the global revolutionist Lenin. On the other hand, it may very well be that in Russia itself the revolution is now behind us and that the profiteers have taken over. Let us not forget, however, that the French Revolution really started to become a menace to its neighbors when "Thermidor" had taken place. It is a normal phenomenon in history that a revolution, when it has completed its progressive task, turns toward the outer world and wants to revolutionize it. Communism may well be dead in Russia. Ideologically, it may have exhausted its vital force. But this does not mean necessarily that we can live in peace as far as the USSR is concerned. Bonaparte was only too glad to take over the centralized Jacobin state and its formidable police machinery. He gave it a new institutional form, a new ritual, and a well-disciplined striking military force, all because internal economic difficulties made "glory" a necessary opium.

I do not believe for a moment that we will see Bulganin or another marshal riding up the Champs Élysées or Piccadilly, at the head of triumphant Russian infantry. I mentioned political warfare. In our time, the old guard of those post-revolutionary conquerors is comprised of the members of the different politburos in all non-Communist countries of the world. Political warfare is also partisan warfare behind the lines. We have to meet that challenge and must do what we can to resist the attack while attacking ourselves with any method short of military conflict. But I repeat, we need global political strategy, if we do not want to continue the present state of affairs, which is the sour product of Western amateurishness and planless political improvisation.

Perhaps I am wrong and underestimate the forces of internal disintegration within the Red Empire. Even so, we cannot remain passive, hope for the best, and speculate according to our optimistic or pessimistic temperaments. We have to discuss the problem openly "on the highest level" and then act together accordingly.[1] Is it an

---

[1] Upon a question put by John Loftus, the author came back to this point, making his views more precise. Being asked if he felt himself in agreement with a certain declaration made by Foster Dulles at an earlier stage, concerning a policy of "roll back," he replied as follows: (1) Although responsible American statesmen never played with the idea of military "liberation" of the

established fact that we can accelerate the coming defeat of communism, as Burnham called it, just by being nice toward the ruling class in the USSR? Many people seem to take that as an article of faith, as an undebatable axiom. As soon as we notice the first signs of relaxation, they say, we have to respond positively and open negotiations. In other words, we have to see how far we can go to meet their desires. Still, we have to prepare a list of possible concessions.

It might be that, on the contrary, a policy of definite firmness is, in those circumstances, more necessary than ever. I personally believe it, but I do not want to pose it as dogma. I do feel, however, that we need an exchange of views in this field, a full-dress debate between Europe and America, on the basis of serious reports, searching for scientific evidence. What we need is a common ground of undisputable "sovietology." What we need next is a series of common political decisions in order to push back the Iron Curtain and change the present precarious status quo to our advantage. And

---

eastern countries, this has not been brought home strongly enough to public opinion in western Europe. In fact, a good many Europeans think that the issue is between preventive war and status quo. It does not occur to them that the Communists, from their side, reject alike and with equal conviction both hot war and non-intervention. It is not sufficiently realized in the West that the ideological conflict can only be prevented from becoming an armed clash if we are prepared to take the necessary steps for winning the political contest.
(2) The Iron Curtain as it exists today does not correspond to any historic, geographic, or cultural reality. It was just the demarcation line which the Red Army reached, but was not able to cross, between 1945 and 1948. Therefore, this artificial frontier between our two worlds will not remain. In some way or another it will move, either westward or eastward. But how can we expect the Iron Curtain to be moved eastward if we abstain from any active policy in respect to the enslaved countries? Inevitably, the victory will remain with those who constantly look beyond the barrier and want to expand their regime. It is, therefore, our duty and our interest to study the evolution in the Communist Empire carefully and to prepare for the day when freedom will return to Leipzig and Prague, Koenigsberg and Warsaw, Budapest and Belgrade, Bucharest and Tirana. Unfortunately, the verbal declarations about "roll back" were not followed by the outlining of a concrete policy, and it is to be feared that a new June 17 would find the West just as unprepared as was the case in 1953. Von der Gablenz was right when he wrote recently that "the inhabitants of the Soviet zone look to us for hope and inspiration, but we look Westward and are not seriously concerned with the fate of those who expect our leadership."

what we need above all is that those decisions should be loyally carried out everywhere as a result of agreement between equal partners. There will be in those decisions a normal proportion of human error, but I do not see why this proportion should be larger, if we decide on a larger world-wide scale. At any event, we will no doubt make new mistakes, but it will amount to immense progress if we can avoid the old ones.

A final example on this point is colonialism. It is certainly true that American public opinion has a tendency to judge anti-colonialist movements too sympathetically, because they are reminded of their own emancipation from the English crown. That is a rather biased, oversimplified, and unrealistic approach. Those who are on the spot know that the nationalist leaders of new, ex-colonial countries are far from being just progressive liberals, good tolerant democrats *in statu nascendi,* and pioneers of modern parliamentarism. They know about fanaticism, cruelty, race hatred, and the blind will of destruction. On the other hand, the Americans, less directly concerned as they are, perhaps understand better that if a human community has come to a certain stage of self-affirmation, it is useless to ask whether it is "ripe." It will simply fight against those it sees as foreign oppressors and refuse any solution short of national freedom. Is the truth in this drama with the old experienced colonizers or with the champions of emancipation? One thing is certain—the Western world has to find an answer in common and, after having agreed upon a common line, follow it together. If only 50 per cent is true of what is told about the political and economic activity pursued by allied citizens on their own behalf, for reasons of private business and benefits, that means that our own people give direct help to the enemy. It is better to make mistakes together than score isolated points for one country or one firm.

What I try to express here is in itself nothing very revolutionary. At the latest meeting of the NATO Council, Dulles warned the allies that military defense was not enough and that we are faced, all of us, with a world-wide problem which we will solve only by a common political effort. That seems a platitude rather than a revelation of deep wisdom. In theory, nobody would refuse to pay lip service to the idea. But in practice mankind always tries to forget those elementary truths which are annoying and simple, and which the French call *vérités de La Palice.* The real stumbling block in this case is not a lack of logical understanding, but the principle of absolute national sovereignty. That, too, seems to be obvious, but if the West has been retiring for so many years already, it is mainly because it sacrificed common strategy to sectional interest and traditional prejudice.

We, the West in general and Europe in particular, are faced with catastrophe in North Africa, but we can only watch, hope, and pray, because we cannot interfere in France's home affairs, and to help her would mean to interfere in her future plans. We had to follow passively the evolution in Cyprus, knowing that we were all directly concerned. The Balkans alliance was broken up; the traditional friendship between Britain and Greece collapsed; the anti-Communist Greek government saw its very narrow parliamentary majority even menaced by a patriotic storm at home, but according to standards completely antiquated, this was just an internal conflict within the British Empire. At most, the Council of Europe could put the question on its agenda and have it debated in the abstract.

Absolute national sovereignty is the enemy of the Western cause. Sometimes, one would wish that the United States were less respectful of national independence, especially because it is blamed for being imperialistic in any event. In fact, however, such a solution is impractical, because public opinion would not understand and there would be mobilized against America the whole force of Communist-led, nationalist envy, hatred, and sentimentalism. "In the house of the hanged, don't talk about the cord." For the same reason, do not talk about American hegemony in Europe. Everybody knows that it exists, but people feel humiliated and irritable about it. Their inferiority complex, which can be explained only too easily, revolts against reality, without trying to change it. A void, purely formalistic but psychologically strong attachment to the sovereign nation-state, that is, to the past, paralyzes our strength and helps the enemy.

If, on the contrary, the United States would find in our part of the world not a group of quarreling, powerless satellites, but a federation speaking with one voice, the whole picture would change. Even then, I do not promise an automatic solution of all our problems, but it seems obvious that a new start would be made. We would not see foreign ministers of comparatively great Continental states speculate on disarmament and coexistence. We would be freed from that kind of morbid anti-Americanism which is one of the consequences, as well as one of the causes, of our decay. In short, European federation would bring about the shock we need, it would make possible a lucid, common policy between equal partners, replacing the merely technical alliance we have today in our popular, unself-conscious, hesitating NATO. It would make possible a political headquarters of the West.

Doubtless, such a headquarters would be unthinkable without democratic control. But in history, the executive branch always comes before its democratic opposite number, the parliament. Is it not likely, therefore, that there is so little interest in Atlantic democracy just because of this? People see that SHAPE gives a very good performance, but does not receive enough political guidance. In comparison with SHAPE, NATO looks rather weak and, as long as it remains comparatively powerless, it would be unwise to put it under direct parliamentarian, supranational control.

That is why the proposal of Senator Kefauver and his friends, asking for a kind of consultative assembly of the free West, has been so coolly received. We know such a consultative assembly without a government to give advice to, to criticize, and, as the case may be, to overthrow. We know Strasbourg and have learned the lesson of the Council of Europe.

Therefore, let us first create an effective executive power and then a parliament of the free. But how can we conceive any kind of Atlantic government, any kind of political headquarters in the struggle for freedom, without bringing out the overwhelming superiority of the United States? Obviously, the supporters of national sovereignty in Europe want to avoid such an "hour of truth," as the Spaniards call it in their *corridas*. They go on paying lip service to Atlantic solidarity, occasionally even using it as an alternative to European federation, but finally leaving things as they are, i.e., letting them deteriorate.

European integration would create in our Continent a new, formidable world power, "a new giant," as *The Observer* called it some years ago, when it was reasonable to suppose that the Continentals would be reasonable and unite. Such a world power could never be neutral between the blocs, as neutralism is today a kind of escapism, a political form of resignation and hopelessness. Our "new giant," however, could not dream of remaining out of trouble in world affairs, and, psychologically, the new feeling of strength would overcome the present feeling of distress, so widespread in Europe disunited.

European integration would at last make the road free for Atlantic solidarity, with all its institutional consequences. The condition, however, remains that we be prepared to give up the lamentable privilege of fighting, one after another, our own "sovereign" rear-guard actions and being "sovereignly" defeated. We have to learn that it is better to win together than to lose separately. How can we clear up our relations with the USA as long as we are quarreling between ourselves over the canalization of the Moselle and over the Saar?

A political Atlantic headquarters, however, even controlled by a democratic assembly, is not enough. Political machinery is never enough. It has to be inspired by a common loyalty, generously given by the citizens. Mentality and morals are more important, especially in an ideological conflict, than material and machinery. We must not only build up our military, economic, and political strength. We have to do more than just understand the driving forces of Soviet policy. We have to realize that the victor in this political world war will be the one who has the deepest belief in the valor of his cause.

We may, of course, doubt the loyalty which the present Soviet government can mobilize. We can try to persuade ourselves that, after all, things are not as bad as that because Russia was, in 1941, the only occupied country where a real mass movement emerged, spontaneously, in favor of collaboration with the German *Wehrmacht*. True, that movement lost its impetus rapidly when the population realized that the Nazis were "just another type of Bolshevik" and not even Russian. Even so, nearly a million Soviet citizens did wear the German uniform, as soldiers, or as *Hilfswillinge* ('helpers'). The national minorities particularly often rose in arms against Moscow, and in the Ukraine the German troops were, in many cases, welcomed as long-awaited friends who were expected to disband the *kolkhoses*. Here, in fact, was a card which Hitler refused to play or which he played when it was too late. Would there be a possibility for us to do better? In principle, yes. The Nazi army could hardly act as liberators, but when we proclaim that the cause of freedom is our cause, we need not necessarily come in conflict with our factual behavior. We must in any case take this possibility seriously and not forget that we are attacked by a regime, not by a nation. The "revolutionary defeatism" which has been a regular weapon in the Communist arsenal since Lenin can also be used in our camp.

Nevertheless, it would be irresponsible if we relied upon the weakness of the enemy alone. It would be far too easy to create a special service for psychological warfare and take it for granted that it is just as important to weaken the enemy as it is to strengthen our own force. *We* have to overcome communism, the Russians cannot do it for us. True, they know better what it means and the most modest Soviet subject is a better "sovietologue" than many of our best advisers on Russian affairs. Nevertheless, the élan also has to come from ourselves.

In this connection I think we meet European problems again. For the very considerable difference between Europe and America in the field of civic consciousness—a difference very much to the Europeans' disadvantage—can only be explained by a psychological factor which derives from the decline of patriotism. Whether he realizes it or not, whether or not he thinks of himself as a good citizen of his national state, each European today is a less dedicated patriot than his father and grandfathers were. Let me explain what I mean with an example.

When Belgium was attacked in 1914, there was a strong Socialist movement in the country, which was more or less revolutionary and antimilitaristic. Moreover, the Flemish question was becoming a burning one. The Nationalist Party in Flanders, which became active after the war, called itself the Front Party, because it was thought that the anti-Belgian spirit had started on the Yser front. This was understandable, because there was too often a mental gap between the officers (the majority of whom spoke French) and the rank and file (who were mostly Flemish). Finally, unpopular as the German invaders undoubtedly were, they could hardly have been looked upon as banner-bearers of a despicable regime.

How different the situation was in May, 1940. Considerable steps had been taken toward the solution of the Flemish question and, consequently, the movement of the Nationalists had lost ground. The Workers' Party had ceased to be a revolutionary or even a systematic opposition movement. Moreover, it had relentlessly denounced Hitler as a devil. In these conditions we would expect that the morale of the Belgian troops would have been much higher in World War II than in World War I. And yet, the opposite was true. The political problems were less complicated, but there was less genuine enthusiasm in 1940 than there had been in 1914. If there were to be war now (which I doubt), the morale would certainly be still lower. This is, indeed, a crucial point for our argument, as the conflict between communism and ourselves is a conflict of morale. Is it too much to ask that NATO and SHAPE should face these facts and see what can be done? They are looking around for cultural activities, in order to make the Atlantic Alliance look less brutal. I, for my part, would be content if they could look on the question in a soldier-like way, that is to say, without forgetting that a soldier is not a robot to be armed, clad, supplied, and entertained, but also a human being of the twentieth century, who has a right to know why he has been mobilized and for what cause he is expected to fight.

I am told that in fact nobody is asking such complicated questions. That is a bad sign, like a patient who is no longer hungry. I met some German SS soldiers during the war and can assert that they knew for what they were expected to die, if that had to be. Until the end, the Allies met German troops with a very high morale nearly everywhere. In order to obtain similar results today, the East German Soviet army, or *Kasernierte Volkspolizei* as they call it, devotes 50 per cent of its training time to what is called "ideological education." On our side, however, nothing serious is undertaken in this field, and the letters which I receive from my former students who do their military service are totally uninspiring as far as their reports about their experience as "citizens in uniform" are concerned. In one country, there is a little bit more *bonhomie* and in another somewhat more *laisser-aller,* but the general picture is rather disturbing, so much the more as my young friends are not, of course, neutralists or nihilists.

There are exceptions. In Britain (doubtless the European country where traditional civics are still comparatively unquestioned) the problem seems to be less acute and a systematic effort in this field is made.

At the other extreme there is Germany. This country has to prove that it can rearm and make a really effective contribution to Western strength, without indulging once more in what is vulgarly called militarism. Here is a definite challenge, especially as the younger generation is overwhelmingly cured from any kind of false hero-worship. Germany, which has not been called to arms until recently, faces a challenge. The government and general staff have to convince the population that rearmament is necessary and that it will serve the cause of freedom in a new, democratic style. A strong, positive reluctance has to be overcome.

Elsewhere, however, the trouble is that military service as such is not questioned by anybody. Apparently, routine seems to be enough. But this is the great illusion for which we shall have to pay heavily unless we change our minds, face the facts, and act accordingly.

Something must be basically wrong, when a younger generation mentally refuses military service, not for reasons of principle, but because they think it is a bore. And that is precisely how people feel about military service and national defense! I would say that people unconsciously no longer believe in the national community for which they are supposed to take up arms. The moral authority of the government is not great enough to persuade them that its cause is worth fighting for. Moreover, the government does not take the trouble to put its cause before the people. It acts as if things were still self-evident.

I think something quite different seems evident, namely, that the national states which distribute the uniforms are no longer the real masters of the situation. They only act as if they were. Everybody knows that if there were to be an attack from the east (whether we consider that as unlikely or not), there would be no French army to defend France nor an Italian army to defend the peninsula, nor Dutch, Belgian, and Luxembourg armies to defend Benelux. This conception is obsolete. The existence of a common command in peacetime (a revolutionary reform which Clemenceau brought about only in 1917, when the enemy was *ante portas*) is sufficient evidence that national defense is over. Everybody knows that today Germans and Frenchmen, with or without a European Defense Community, are allies in fact, and that America is the leader of a world-wide group of nations which considers itself in danger—and rightly so. But the ritual has outlived the faith. The fiction is stronger than reality. In such conditions, can we be surprised if our young people have the feeling that they are fooled, if they feel uninspired, and if their officers do not know what to tell them? Is it surprising that there is latent moral disintegration?

The dynamics of European integration would not, to be sure, bring us the fulfillment of a beautiful age-old dream. It would do infinitely better. It would at last bring us in harmony with the facts. As an example, during the first years of the struggle between revolutionary France and non-revolutionary Europe, external discipline was at its highest in the ranks of the old hireling armies. But the French had something better—they belonged to a community of which they were proud. This decisive advantage was lost, however, when the idea of a national people's army, of "the people in arms," was taken up by those who fought the French troops in Germany and Spain. At that moment, Germany and Spain recovered their grip on the real data of the century, and they won. We need only look at Goya's works from that period and listen to the songs of the national guerilla.

This is only a comparison. I realize that Europe is, for the moment, still uninspiring to the masses. I have given some of the reasons. But if it is possible at all that we in Europe recover civic feeling, that can be done only for and through Europe united. In spite of the fact that we are deeply rooted in the part of our Continent which we call our fatherland, this fatherland no longer suffices as a political and civic unit. It is becoming in fact what the Canton of Geneva is for the modern Genevois, a "little fatherland within a larger one."

This means a mental revolution and each revolution in history means that a community has to pass through a dangerous period of uncertainty and transition. But is there any alternative? National patriotism, respectable as it is and of lasting value, can no longer save itself alone. It has to be saved by integration into Europe and the militant Atlantic world. The only community of which the modern European can possibly think as great, powerful, and inspiring is the plurinational body politic of the free. Moreover, for the Europeans only one kind of Atlantic Community would be psychologically acceptable—the one in which they would act as Europeans —strongly and without the inferiority complex of "poor relatives," a complex which has remained, curiously enough, in spite of our rapid economic recovery.

European integration is not the solution of our problems, but the prerequisite to their solution. Dynamic impetus can only start from there.

Germany and Europe

ALFRED GROSSER / *Lecturer, Institut d'Études Politiques, Paris*

DISILLUSIONED SERENITY prevails today in all discussion of German and European matters. In order to retrace this development and also to study the degree of consonance between this disillusionment and reality, we must cast our thoughts back over the evolution of European problems since 1947; we must then examine the internal situation in Europe, particularly regarding Franco-German relations and finally Germany's role in the East-West struggle.

Germany in Europe

The failure of the Moscow Conference in April, 1947, ushered in a new period in the history of the postwar world. It marked the real beginning of the Cold War and the dividing of the world in two. Its repercussions were felt particularly keenly in France and Germany. In France, it led to the instant departure of the Communists from the government and an ever-widening rift between Communists and non-Communists. In Germany, it hastened the geographical separation of the country which was both cause and effect of the world separation.

In conjunction with, and owing in part to, this world division, the European idea gained ground. General Marshall's offer had been the beginning of its career. In all its applications, it was to bear the twofold stamp of constructive internationalism and fear-inspired anticommunism, these two feelings varying in form and proportion with the men of the moment and according to the trend of world events. Instruction JCS 1779 given to the American Commander-in-Chief was as strict regarding denazification and demilitarization as was Instruction JCS 1067, which it superseded on June 11, 1947. The preamble ran thus, however: "A well ordered, prosperous Europe calls for an economic contribution from a productive and stable Germany." On July 12, delegates from sixteen countries accepted the American view and stated in Paris that "the German economy should be integrated into the European economy so as to contribute to a general improvement in the standard of living."

This went without saying. Why, then, had the failure of the Moscow Conference been essential to its discovery? During the following year, West Germany was to be among the countries benefiting from the law of April 3, 1948, governing European aid, and was to become a member of the Organization for European Economic Co-operation, established on April 16. True, it was only represented by the commanders-in-chief. Four years later, however, a German was to be elected chairman of the OEEC. In May, 1948, at The Hague, the European movement called for the establishment of a federal Europe. The notion of abandoning sovereignty appeared in the constitutions of certain European countries, especially in the 1946 French Constitution. It was possible to foresee the integration of a Germany not as yet sovereign into a Europe which would have inherited from each of the other nations that part of sovereignty which Germany lacked. This was not to be, and West Germany became a state destined to adopt as egocentric a policy as the rest.

It might be said that Chancellor Adenauer's policy since 1949 has been more European and less self-centered than the foreign policies of the other western European states. His efforts were of a very special nature and, as far as we are aware, unprecedented in history; his foreign policy consisted in obtaining the right for the Federal Republic to have its own foreign policy, the aim of which was the abolition of independent foreign policies in Europe. With the ratification of the Paris Agreements, he obtained satisfaction on the first count, but an integration of European policies is no longer contemplated. It is obvious that the Chancellor's Europeanism was not, and still is not, shared by all German governing circles. For some of them, the conception of a united Europe was the crucial factor in gaining sovereignty and equality of rights, which, once attained, would make integration lose all its appeal. It is nonetheless obvious, however, that for a wide section of German opinion, especially among the young people, August 30 is the date which, rightly or wrongly, marked the end of an integrated Europe. To our way of thinking, the basic cause of this failure lay in the very idea of rearming Germany. We shall try to prove this, taking France as our example.

SCHUMAN PLAN, GERMAN REARMAMENT, AND EDC IN FRANCE

The debate on ratification which took place in the Assemblée Nationale in December, 1951, is summed up in an extract from Pierre Schneiter's speech: "The majority of the French people were favourably impressed by the initiative taken by Monsieur Robert Schuman in May 1950." Indeed, none of those opposed to ratification attacked the general principles of the plan. They criticized its methods, not the constructive policy toward Germany which it advocated. The virulent anti-German speech made by General Aumeran led Robert Schuman to remark, without raising a single protest:

> With all due respect to General Aumeran for whom I have the highest personal regard, I would like to say how glad I am for my country that he is the only one, or almost the only one, in this assembly to advocate towards Germany and Europe the policy he has just defined before the House.

It thus appeared to be generally recognized that the coal and steel pool was, in essence, a step toward an economically coherent Europe and that the treaty justified hopes of social justice and the abolition of nationalism. It is of particular interest, in order to grasp the full difference between the ECSC and the EDC to read once again the speeches delivered in favor of the first by two men who were among the bitterest opponents of the second. André Denis, who was to be expelled from the MRP for his opposition to German rearmament, was a warm advocate of the ECSC. Marcel-Edmond Naegelen, who was to be Socialist candidate for the presidency of the Republic in January, 1954, before being expelled from the SFIO for having voted against both the EDC and the Paris Agreements, stated in this connection on December 11, 1951, in the name of the Socialist parliamentary group:

Ladies and Gentlemen, during the vote which will be taken in a few moments, the Socialist group will be giving its support, not to a Government whose policy it does not always fully approve, but to a great European policy to which France is committed, for which she may take the credit and for whose honour she is responsible.... It has been argued—this constituted the whole tenor of Monsieur Pierre André's speech in calling for an adjournment —that this great plan entails certain risks. We know that this is so. We know that nothing great or new is ever done in the world unless some risks are taken.

A large majority of the Assemblée, whatever their fears as to German "development," finally supported the rapporteur, Alfred Coste-Floret, who asserted that:

Germany is in full development, indeed this development has never ceased, and it is just at the time when we might start becoming anxious as to its outcome that the Schuman Plan has made a timely appearance in order to maintain stability and to deprive the German national State, and moreover the French national State, of the right to dispose of its heavy industry for military purposes.

It is true that Schuman had declared that the ECSC had no connection with the plan for a European army and, in reply to Loustaunau-Lacau, rapporteur for the National Defense Commission, who was advocating the contrary, Prime Minister René Pleven had stated: "We might be listening to a Communist."

It is not for us to go into a detailed account of the EDC at this juncture. Let us merely note the existence at the outset of the intention to render the unpopular idea of German rearmament acceptable to French public opinion by merging it into the popular conception of a united Europe as expressed in the Schuman Plan. Next came the agenda adopted on October 26, 1950, which only referred to the question of rearmament in a negative manner, when expressing "the determination not to allow the rebirth of a German army and general staff."

It is true that EDC supporters could put forward very similar arguments to those which had been valid for the ECSC. In his speech of August 29, 1954, Coste-Floret said:

We are well aware that present-day Germany's two sources of

power, as recent history will show, are, on the one hand, the Ruhr arsenal—we have founded the European Coal and Steel Community in order to neutralize this—and, on the other, the German national army, which we would likewise seek to neutralize by incorporating its soldiers within the framework of a non-national army. The development of Germany cannot be ignored; the point is to direct it into the right channels.

In the course of the debate held in September, 1953, Legaret had voiced similar views:

> The European idea, one aspect of which is apparent in the Defense Community, would seem, to our mind, to offer Germany for the first time a new faith, and one which is capable of firing her imagination and of stirring her young people to enthusiasm, as it might our own. For the first time since the French Revolution, a great idea is offered to mankind, an idea to which hate and war are foreign. We who conceived it must find a way to foster it in Germany, or else we shall have lost our chance of guiding German will instead of submitting to it, as has been our fate on three occasions.

Meanwhile the opponents invoked four different types of argument:

1. The "traditional" German menace. Throughout the country, this emotional approach constituted the essence of all Communist propaganda directed against the EDC. Without stating the fact clearly, it was assumed that France would have to bear the brunt of what was considered to be congenital German aggressiveness. Pierre Lebon, a Gaulliste, stated on August 28, 1954: "Germany invaded us in 1792, in 1814, in 1815, in 1870, in 1914 and in 1940. I have only gone back as far as 1792, but the problem is a very much older one than that."

2. The new German threat. Once rearmed, West Germany was capable of dragging the whole of the Western world into a war with the East in order to obtain its reunification and to reconquer the territories situated beyond the Oder-Neisse line.

3. Even if the Indo-China war were to come to an end, France's military commitments outside of Europe would result in the Federal Republic's military supremacy on the Continent.

4. The rearming of Germany was against the interests of German democracy.

It would seem essential to distinguish between the fourth and the first arguments, even if certain politicians (like Herriot, for instance) only used the arguments of type four somewhat belatedly and in order to cloak the extent to which their thinking was really governed by a basic anti-Germanism. In his report in 1954, Jules Moch, aware that in Germany French opposition to the EDC was represented as being prompted solely by such considerations, said:

> First of all Germany. Might she feel injured and driven to fresh ventures, if we refuse to let her have her divisions? Doubtless so, if our opposition appears to be the will of the conqueror intent on trampling the conquered under foot, and if we revive certain aspects of the policy followed between the two wars. If, however, we explain frankly to our neighbours that our aim is still disarmament, that we do not wish to depart from it in order to rearm them while present negotiations are still in progress, but that our object is to return, with all other nations, to a controlled, low level of armaments sufficient to preserve internal order in each country and to fulfill their international commitments; if, at the same time, we give Germany back her sovereignty in other spheres and offer to settle the question of our occupation forces and of her reunification—as I took the liberty of suggesting to the Prime Minister during a conversation—and along lines which I will not explain here so as not to add to a subject which is already too extensive, for what possible reason could the majority of Germans refuse to support this policy of reason and peace? It is perhaps not that of the present Bonn Government; their home policy, however, is none of our business. And I presume that we are not being asked to ratify the Paris Treaty in order to back one German political group against another.

At the time of the debate on the ratification of the Paris Agreements, in 1954, Daladier stated:

> Even to-day, six million German workers in their non-Communist Trade-Union group, with a Social-Democrat as chairman and a Christian Democrat as vice-chairman, are making a stand against this rearmament. What should be Republican France's reply to these German workers, these true democrats of Federal Germany? Their antagonism links up with that of the majority of German youth. Of recent times, we have heard protests from very many of the parents of these young people invoking Article 6 of the German Constitution which recognizes the conscientious

objector. This shows to what extent Germany had become pacifist after her disaster. It is obvious that, if the Agreements are ratified, the clause relating to the conscientious objector will not long remain in the German Constitution. We have heard of a Franco-German understanding—I prefer this word to that of reconciliation, for we have in no way offended Germany, it is quite the reverse. We have heard of an honest understanding. I myself am as much in favour of this as anyone here. I appreciate the immense value of an honest understanding with Germany. Would it not be better, however, to reach this understanding with the young people, the trade unions, the German Socialist Party and the forces of democracy, rather than with the Ruhr magnates or the political leaders, certain of whom figured on the American list of war criminals? This is the question I would put to you.

Herriot was to take up this theme the following day, December 23:

> Side-by-side or opposite, there is another Germany endeavouring to break free, release herself and set out, in her turn, upon the road to liberty. There are the young people, the trade-unionists and the socialists. There are also, and I say this in no spirit of controversy but because it is a historical factor in the constitution of Germany, the Protestant churches and their following who are diametrically opposed to the other view.

But by this time, the situation had changed in Germany, where the failure of the EDC had effected a separation between the idea of rearmament and that of a united Europe. Another change was thus brought about; anti-EDC arguments were taken up by certain EDC supporters as soon as the EDC had been rejected. On August 28, 1954, Max Lejeune, Socialist Chairman of the National Defense Commission, had declared:

> The German soldier, who has always regarded himself as the keeper of the German people's conscience, will instantly take up within the nation those traditional propensities we have learned to associate with him, especially since the higher grades of the German army, whether integrated or not, come, ten years after the war, straight out of Hitler's Wehrmacht.

On August 31, Paul Reynaud bewailed the rejection of the EDC in almost the same terms:

Yes, ladies and gentlemen, the Wehrmacht who marched down the Champs Elysées and through every town in France, the Wehrmacht to whom the German democrats refer when they have been telling us for years in the Strasbourg Assembly: do not allow the German General Headquarters to re-form itself and take over the Government of Germany, for we know too well the old, bloodstained story of such pressure from the German General Headquarters! You are well aware that they possess the dynamism of the German people in the highest degree. As a nation, they are not static, always on the move, restless. It is the men of the "young and merry war," the soldiers, the former Nazis who will resume control of an independent Wehrmacht.

It is not our task here to go into the merits or demerits of the case for German rearmament. Moreover, it is our belief that, even without it, the reconstruction of Europe would have been threatened by the twofold centrifugal attraction exercised upon France by the North African problem and upon the Federal Republic by the question of reunification. But we are forced to admit that the rearmament problem acted as political dynamite, the very role attributed to it in an American work published in 1950 with a preface by General Eisenhower.[1]

Happily, however, the structural aspect of integration is not everything. There is a real integration of the Federal Republic which is especially apparent, despite difficulties which must be spoken of in the framework of Franco-German relations. It is generally admitted that such relations constitute the only possible cornerstone of any European edifice. We therefore wish to draw up a somewhat brief table of the difficulties with which they are faced and of the progress they have made to date.

FRANCO-GERMAN RELATIONS

A. The Importance of History

Many people on both sides still approach the question of relations with the other country from a conception of its history, which is as

[1] Howard S. Ellis and Research Staff of the Council on Foreign Relations, *The Economics of Freedom. The Progress and Future of Aid to Europe* (New York: Harper & Brothers, 1950), p. 231.

positive as it is inaccurate. Despite the very similar conclusions eventually arrived at by French and German historians as to periods and events which had previously been highly controversial, public opinion continues to hold as established fact the absolute rightness of one country's past and the utter blackness of the other's. This leads to emotional attitudes which constitute a political factor both because they affect the electoral body and because they are adopted by a far from negligible number of parliamentarians or journalists who can imperturbably put forward, as historical evidence, assertions for which no historian would assume responsibility. (Two examples: German aggressiveness is supposedly demonstrated by the invasions of 1813 and 1814; Clemenceau's policy is alleged to have aimed at the extermination of twenty million Germans.)

For the most recent past, namely, the period which began after the close of World War I, some special observations are called for:

(*a*) *The Weimar period and the rise of Hitlerism.* Much remains to be done on both sides before we can arrive at a serene and considered appreciation of what constituted French policy between 1919 and 1932. As for the internal evolution of Germany, one is very glad to note that, after several years of uneasiness and silence, German research has been resumed with remarkable earnestness and objectivity. One need only take as an example the monumental work on the decay of the Weimar Republic published under the auspices of the Berlin Institute of Political Studies.[2] For the 1919-1945 period generally, the Munich Institute of Contemporary History and the *Vierteljahrshefte für Zeitgeschichte* are accomplishing a task which should be better known abroad—and in Germany (where nevertheless considerable publicity is afforded them, thanks to the supplements to the weekly *Das Parlament*).

(*b*) *The Hitler period.* An eminent German politician said a short time ago that the Germans only had the right to ask the French to forget the past if they did not forget it themselves. The formula is excellent. But it could also be said that in any case the past should not be forgotten, but should be known and lived down. On the German side, the tendency to silence as to the extent of the horrors of the regime leads to misunderstandings and injustices in

---

[2] Karl Dietrich Bracher, *Die Auflösung der Weimarer Republik,* Schriften des Instituts für politische Wissenschaft Berlin No. 4 (Stuttgart und Düsseldorf: Ring-Verlag, 1955).

assessing the psychological and political realities of the period following World War II. On the French side there is still too much ignorance of what national socialism meant for many Germans, and in this connection one can but regret the almost complete absence from French book shops of works devoted to the German opposition to Hitler. A translation of Inge Scholl's little book was published recently, and Gerhard Ritter's thick volume on Geerdeler is scheduled to appear next year, but the successive and increasingly detailed general studies by Peschel, Rothfels, and Weisenborn remain unknown to the French public except for references in reviews or in more general works.

B. Political Difficulties

In the realm of political difficulties, the essential debate today obviously concerns the Saar and the Moselle canal scheme. No useful purpose would be served by going into detail here concerning those questions which have been examined so often. Let us simply note that the Saar question became inseparable from the reparations problem after the great speech delivered in Stuttgart on September 6, 1946, by United States Secretary of State James Byrnes; that, as of 1950, the idea of equilibrium within the ECSC made its appearance; and that, in French public opinion, the canalization of the Moselle has become a test of German good will—Germany, it holds, having so far made no sacrifice for the European cause. But the return of the Saar to Germany after the referendum upset the French very little, despite Schneider's excesses. In fact, the Saar question is much more a barometer than an essential phenomenon in Franco-German relations.

C. Deeply-Rooted Differences

The deeply-rooted differences are numerous and probably have better grounds than most political disputes. We shall mention only the principal ones.

(*a*) *Two anti-communisms?* In Germany, the Communists are today considered as the "collaborators" of a detested occupying power who, through a puppet government, is oppressing eighteen million Germans. In France, if the situation is no longer exactly like that of 1944 (the Communists had been comrades in the Resistance and claimed to practice friendship with a country of which France was the ally), the problem of communism nonetheless continues to exist for a very large part of the population in economic and social terms and not in connection with East-West relations.

(*b*) *Two trade unionisms?* The aims and methods of trade unionism are fairly different in the two countries, largely because there still exist differences of social atmosphere, especially inside industry. Something in the nature of a comparative dictionary should be drawn up containing such words as *class struggle, productivity, paternalism, co-direction,* etc.

(*c*) *Two Catholicisms?* It seems to us that it should be stated that a section of French Catholics has gradually become hostile to the Europe of the Six Countries for fear of seeing the innovative aspect of Catholic life in France suffocated by the dual pressure of Italian Catholicism and of a German Catholicism in which the conservative tendency would prevail over the socializing and "anticlerical" tendency which had dominated the Bochum *Katholikentag* in 1949. Whether it be in regard to East-West contacts, social intercourse, relations between the hierarchy and laymen, between church and state, or contacts between Catholics and non-Catholics, one is obliged to note differences between French Catholicism and German Catholicism, even though within each of them diverging tendencies exist.

(*d*) *Two conceptions of citizenship?* A point which has been so much talked about that to mention it is enough is that of two conceptions of citizenship—on one side, sense of duty to the state, but too much submission to the *Obrigkeit,* and on the other, defense of the rights of the individual, but anarchism. It remains to be seen how much reality there is in this opposition, and how much is a mere cliché.

D. The Links Which Do Exist

But these difficulties must not hide a reality which is much more encouraging—the extraordinary multiplicity of the regular contacts which exist between similar circles in the two countries. Here are some examples:

Confessional groups: On the Catholic side, especially through such organizations as *Pax Christi,* contacts are frequent and very wide-spread. On the Protestant side, there exists a Franco-German Fraternal Council (*Bruderrat, Conseil Fraternel*) which is unique of its kind.

Trade unions: Study tours and discussions between militants and leaders are developing rapidly.

Political parties: Through direct contacts, through the international unions, through the European assemblies, it has been possible to diminish ignorance and tension considerably. Naturally, there still remain differences and difficulties which there seems no point in examining here.

Youth: The *Bundesjugendring* and the French Council of Youth movements have set up a joint permanent office, although neither of them has established a link of this nature with representatives of the young people of any other country.

Municipalities: Two associations of mayors have to their credit numerous *jumelages* and exchanges.

Cultural fields: Universities, schools, cinema clubs, young people's musical societies—the list of fields of activity in which cordial and regular Franco-German contacts are in existence could be continued.

Economic sphere: Let it suffice to recall that the two countries are each other's best supplier and best customer.

Much could be said as to the techniques of the contacts and of the exchanges leading to a concrete knowledge of the neighbor's achievements and preoccupations. Let us simply say that official departments and private bodies, which, in the course of the last ten years, have applied these techniques, are able to draw up a balance sheet which is much more favorable than would be supposed from a perusal of the press, which reacts almost exclusively to the political news of the day.

We believe that this observation might be made with regard to the Federal Republic's relations with any other European country. The Germany of Bonn is more closely linked to the Western countries than any Germany has ever been, but at the same time she is being increasingly tempted by the idea of reunification, which draws her toward the east. It is this paradox, this dual nature of the Federal Republic, at one and the same time a "normalized" Western state and an incomplete country, which makes the German question so difficult of analysis.

The Division of Germany, the Division of the World and Europe

Since the end of the war, the division of Germany has been both the cause and the effect of the division of the world. Every disagreement between the victors emphasized the splitting up of the vanquished nation and every emphasizing of the split aggravated the over-all disagreement. The divergencies between the allies in Germany sufficed in themselves to bring about the geographical division of that country, but the process of schism was hastened by the fact that, almost everywhere in the world, there was dissension between the allies themselves. From 1946 onward two camps had been formed, each of which was seeking to use "his" Germany in the struggle against the other camp. The more the tension mounted, the more was Germany divided. The more Germany was divided and incorporated by hostile parties into the two blocs, the more the tension mounted. It would be easy to describe in detail the functioning of this mechanism.

Since last year there has been a separation—and a very distinct separation—between the two elements. The division of Germany is regarded as an accomplished fact, and concurrently the tension has reached its lowest point since 1945, the symbol of the lull being the first Geneva Conference of 1955, which in fact consecrated the splitting in two of Germany. To our way of thinking, this forms one of the most remarkable aspects of the present international situation. It is not easy to interpret it and to attribute to it a positive or negative value. The following might make some contribution.

1. There would probably have been no relaxation of the tension without the ratification of the Paris Agreements. In any case, there would not have been a Four Power Conference. The United States would not have agreed to negotiate with the East as long as the Western camp was not organized, and the USSR presumably would have continued to content themselves with propaganda slogans instead of making definite gestures such as signing the Austrian treaty. Before ratification by the French Parliament, it was questionable whether the Paris Agreements would not increase the tension considerably, would not provoke too lively a reaction from the Soviets, would not set in motion an unprecedented armaments race. Soviet diplomacy had done everything possible to make it appear that such a development would be inevitable. A section of

French public opinion was opposed to the Paris Agreements because they believed in the Russian affirmations, in the concrete effects of a denunciation of the Franco-Soviet Treaty. Mendès-France, on the other hand, was convinced that this was only a way of exerting pressure, and that, on the contrary, ratification would lead to the Four Power Conference, which was desired by the quasi unanimity of the parliament.

2. But no sooner had the Four Power Conference been secured than it became practically pointless so far as the unification of Germany, which had been regarded for years, however, as its essential aim, was concerned. For a variety of reasons, the USSR cannot accept a united Germany within the framework of NATO and the WEU, and the Western powers continue to think that negotiations with the East are impossible until union has been achieved. It is true that reunification continues to be talked about. There is at least one American note or speech on the subject every second week, and at the end of the Soviet leaders' visit to London the Foreign Office issued a special communiqué stating their firm desire to obtain German unity. These declarations of intent are issued, however, in the majority of cases at the request of the German government and, to put it bluntly, mainly in order to please the latter—a state of affairs which is especially distressing for the Germans. It does not bear out what Chancellor Adenauer had promised. To his way of thinking, the union of the Western powers, confirmed by the ratification of the Paris Agreements, should have induced the USSR not only to negotiate, but actually to agree to reunification on Western terms. This line of thought, pronounced misleading on many occasions by the German opposition, is no longer tenable today. But, for all that, the Social Democrats cannot boast of victory. The rejection of the Paris Agreements would not have led to reunification and would have prevented contacts such as those of Geneva and London—the reply to which might well be that Germany has drawn little benefit from such contacts.

Thus we arrive at the confirmation of what has been regarded as unmentionable since 1949—the diplomatic importance accorded to the Federal Republic has always been less a question of its internal authority than of the degree of tension between East and West. The stronger the tension, the greater the heed paid to the voice of Germany in the concert of Western nations. The Federal Republic did not become an increasingly valued partner as it gained increasing juridical sovereignty. Rather its sovereignty increased with its increasing value. Moreover, if it were held in higher esteem, it is because of its vital role in the struggle for supremacy between the two blocs, a struggle in which Europe was the center of gravity and which was fought out mainly in the armaments race.

Today the two camps are far from being reconciled, but favorable conditions do exist and must be taken into consideration. First, the Western powers have at length realized that the building up of the classic military forces in Europe is not the way to meet the economic and psychological challenge which is awaiting them almost everywhere in the world. Second, a kind of political truce has been concluded on the European Cold War front simply because the line of partition seems to be permanently fixed and because there is hardly any no man's land left to dispute, while in Africa and Asia the situation is, in the language of the military communiqués, much more fluid. Third, although conscious of their opposing interests, the two blocs have increased their diplomatic exchanges, partly, perhaps, because both have serious internal troubles, de-Stalinization in one case and serious dissension between allies in the other. The growing emphasis on the economic aspects of East-West rivalry, the shifting of the center of gravity, the numerous contacts are all factors which tend to play down the role of the Federal Republic. Gone is the time when Chancellor Adenauer was the most respected of Dulles' advisers in regard to the planning of Western diplomatic strategy. Not that the personal ties between the two men are any the less close; the Adenauerian view of East-West relations is just not adapted to the world situation of today.

German diplomacy is at present at a deadlock because it lacks both immediate ends and the means thereto. It is driven to manifest itself in actions dictated rather by ill-humor than by a well thought-out policy. "Ah! you have talks with Moscow without us. Your first concern is no longer with reunification! All right, we are going to negotiate with Moscow all by ourselves!" Immediately some sections of the French and British press are ready to raise the ghost of Rapallo and of the German-Soviet Pact of 1939. Thereupon Bonn goes into reverse, not, however, without somewhat bitterly observing that France and Great Britain do not hesitate to confer with the East, without giving much consideration to the interests of their

German ally. Here we touch upon the greatest weakness of the Western camp in Europe, the lack of real and lasting trust between partners who in theory are bound by countless treaties and agreements. This lack of trust leads each country to reproach the other in contradictory terms. The French are not conferring with Moscow? Then they are not making any endeavor to bring about reunification. They are conferring with Moscow? Then it is in order to secure benefits at the cost of keeping Germany divided. The Germans are speeding up rearmament? Just like those Germans to make trouble when everything was quiet! They are not speeding it up? There you are, as usual, the Germans do not keep their promises! German diplomacy refuses to negotiate with the East? How they love the Cold War! They are talking of negotiating? Then they mean treachery. We are exaggerating only slightly and wish that public opinion in other countries would acquire the habit of studying dispassionately the problems connected with the Federal Republic's relations with the East.

In theory, these relations are restricted by the paragraph in the Paris Agreements which says:

> The Three Powers retain the rights and the responsibilities heretofore exercised or held by them, relating to Berlin and to Germany as a whole, including the reunification of Germany and a peace settlement.

Since then, however, there has been a resumption of diplomatic relations between Bonn and Moscow. If the Federal Republic were able and wanted to, the other Western nations would certainly not be capable of preventing her from bringing about the "fundamental change" referred to in article 10 of the Paris Agreements.[3] It so

---

[3] "The Signatory States will review the terms of the present Convention and the related Conventions
(a) upon request of any one of them, in the event of the reunification of Germany, or an international understanding being reached with the participation or consent of the States parties to this Convention on steps towards bringing about the reunification of Germany, or the creation of a European Federation; or
(b) in any situation which all of the Signatory States recognize has resulted from a change of a fundamental character in the conditions prevailing at the time of the entry into force of the present Convention.
In either case they will, by mutual agreement, modify the present Convention

happens, however, that the only conceivable "fundamental change" would mean a transformation of the relations or rather lack of relations between Bonn and Pankow, a transformation which German diplomacy spurns with horror. Indeed, while the USSR has recognized the Federal Government, the Western powers—and at the request of Bonn, moreover—still abide by the joint statement issued in London on October 3, 1954, by the United States, British, and French governments.

> They [these governments] consider the Government of the Federal Republic as the only German Government freely and legitimately constituted and therefore entitled to speak for Germany as the representative of the German people in international affairs.

In Germany, this text is interpreted as meaning "legitimately *because* freely constituted," forgetting that Bonn has an ambassador in Madrid. Although, after all, Great Britain and France have no fundamental dislike of de facto contacts with Pankow, contacts which would not involve a de jure recognition, from the German side there is a call to bear in mind the 1936 precedent, when German anti-Hitler elements were deeply discouraged by the spectacular way in which the Western democracies appeared to approve of the regime, especially on the occasion of the Olympic Games. This comparison, this reminder, holds equally good for the Three Powers and for the Federal Republic itself. The population of the German Democratic Republic would certainly not understand how the freely-chosen rulers of West Germany could co-operate with the heads of the totalitarian regime, whose speedy end they hope for.

What would happen, nevertheless, if reunification seemed so impossible in these circumstances and at the same time so desirable that the West Germans began to follow or urge other rulers to deal with Pankow, even at the cost of political concessions today considered unacceptable? This is the question the international press is beginning to ask itself when thinking of Adenauer's successor. When in London, did not Bulganin hint that the USSR had plenty of time and was awaiting the coming to power in Bonn of rulers

---

and the related Conventions to the extent made necessary or advisable by the fundamental change in the situation."

whose attitude would be less rigid? It is obviously impossible to foretell exactly what will be the trend of German politics in a few years' time or even after the 1957 elections. It is, however, possible to hazard two observations.

1. The Chancellor has been playing a very dangerous game in helping to foster the legend of his own indispensability. He is largely to blame if foreign countries, and in particular the United States, underestimate the soundness of German democracy and the firmness with which it handles foreign policy. He has thus injured not only his old Socialist enemies and his new liberal opponents, but also his own party, who are now concerned about the mortgage which their leader is putting on their future. The diplomacy of Bonn is too well established to disappear with one man. Doubtless it will experience greater political activity, less straightforward, less stable, and more dangerous than that of today. But activity, complexity, and risks are no more symptoms of totalitarianism than order and stability are symptoms of democracy.

2. When certain Socialists, on the one hand, and the demagogic Schneider on the other, are getting ready for discussions with the Eastern bloc, they have great difficulty in determining their substance. This is because the intensity of German anti-communism has no equal save in the United States. Public opinion in both France and Britain is far more inclined to a reconciliation with the USSR even at the cost of a slackening of Western ties, than is German opinion. That opinion would have to undergo a vital change before the threat of German-Soviet reconciliation could be exploited successfully. The Federal Republic is much too scared of Moscow to desire a tête-à-tête sincerely.

In point of fact, it is much more a difference in key than a real political split, since no one has proposed any concrete method of extricating German problems from the present deadlock. The Chancellor still holds that talks with the USSR are out of the question and that the army of 500,000 men must be raised speedily, if Germany is to become an influential ally of the Western powers; Schneider appears to believe that it is advisable to frighten these same Western powers, to stir up public opinion against them, and also to bring pressure to bear on the USSR; finally, the Socialists, and in particular their greatest expert on foreign policy, Fritz Erler, would like German diplomacy to resemble that of Pineau, in other words to be more realistic, more "open," than that of the Chancellor.

It is true that questions of key are important in diplomacy, but they are not enough to hide the lack of any real content. Whether it is considered a matter for regret or not, the Federal Republic's foreign policy is today at a standstill, sterile. What was hoped for from the West—sovereignty and equality—has been obtained. As far as the East is concerned, what is being claimed seems to be beyond reach. Moreover, neither one side nor the other looks upon her as a first-rate power.

This exasperating situation is at the bottom not unlike the French situation. France is certainly represented at the majority of discussions of world affairs, but her diplomacy is so handicapped by the Algerian question that it is reduced, like that of Germany, to giving itself merely the impression of activity. We cannot here go into this aspect of the tragic situation in Algeria. Let us simply note that its effect is to rule out any international action on the part of France just as much as Germany is ruled out in the international sphere by the question of the impossible yet indispensable reunification. Europe's present sickness derives not from one or the other difficulty encountered by Euratom or in the Saar-Moselle dispute, but in this kind of paralysis which is creeping upon the two greatest Continental states.

Neutralism

ALDO GAROSCI / *Commentator for RAI;*
Libero Docente, University of Rome

THERE MAY BE a certain logic in the fact that an Italian was chosen to speak here on the subject of neutralism. The word *neutralism,* at least in its common usage, seems to me to have had its origin in my country at the time of World War I. At that time Italy, alone among the great European powers, had remained neutral, while the other powers had been dragged, almost immediately, into the conflict. For Italy, participation in the conflict was not the type of decision which was the natural outcome of planned foreign policy, as when a nation prepares for war, strengthens its defenses, or purposely nurtures antagonisms, but it was mainly a political decision, based on whether or not it would be advantageous to go to war. In modern states, however, such a decision cannot be taken by a prince who weighs the political consequences, nor can it be taken only by cabinet officials, but such a decision must be made by the parliament, which implies a struggle for public support and public realization of the dire consequences which might endanger the life of the state itself. It means an arousing of passions. This is what happened in Italy with interventionist groups clamoring for entry into the war, and their opponents, the neutralists, fighting them back, all in a climate charged with emotion.

A variety of emotions had to be appealed to in order to effect intervention. Democratic zeal, which favored solidarity with the Latin Sister, the French Republic, was let loose against the Central European autocracies (ignoring, of course, the autocratic regime in Russia, with which Italy would also have to be allied). The pro-

French tradition of the Risorgimento was recalled, when French aid had been instrumental in the achievement of national unity. (Later, of course, it had to be admitted with some bitterness that it was only through the destruction of imperial France that Italy's unity was completed and the young kingdom attained the capacity to act as an equal among other nations. This situation, as Chabod points out in his study on Italian foreign policy,[1] left a seed of remorse and sorrow in the conscience of the Italian King and also mixed feelings among liberal leaders of the party of the right then in power, who were regretful that Italy owed its final unity and political freedom of movement to such political upheaval.) Recalled also was the Irredentist movement, together with the revolutionary ferment of the action groups, which were still vexed at having been restrained by the King's policy, and which conceived the war as an action conducted by volunteers.

Last, there was called into play the concept of a "necessary test," the necessity for the nation to prove its worth, and it was this newest means of motivation for bringing together and cementing disparate elements, which even opposing groups could not withstand. The logic underlying this concept was that Italy had been created by diplomacy and had grown up following a policy of "clean hands," and now she must prove to herself and to the world that she had a right to exist as a state, by paying her tribute in blood, by going to battle like a state, and by gaining the crown of victory. The old idea of Italy's mission in the world was charged with overtones of mysticism and necessity for action, so that the intellectuals forgot their ideals and their studies and the democrats who had chafed under Giolitti's parliamentary regime dreamed of taking their revenge. In other words, this was interventionism.

Only through an understanding of this tangle of passions can the situation be seen in its true aspects and can it be perceived how those who opposed intervention on political and humanitarian grounds, and called themselves neutralists, came to be labeled traitors, philo-Germans. There was even talk of lynching and summary execution. Giolitti had expressed this neutralist position by stating that much could be gained by Italy without entering the

---

[1] Federico Chabod, *Storia della Politica Estera Italiana dal 1870 al 1896*, Vol. I: *Le Premesse* (Bari: G. Laterza, 1951).

conflict and that it was ridiculous to become involved in a bloody war without the slightest necessity. This was also the thesis of the Socialists, who claimed that Italy could stand out as an example of how one European country could rise above the play of passions and interests and how, in a conflict which would leave all participants bleeding and would arrest the pacific evolution of peoples, Italy could stand apart and act as a great "Red Cross" organization.

Since that time, in Italy, neutralism has lost most of its political meaning and has acquired emotional content. And it was this emotional element which exploded with particular vehemence in the aftermath of the war, stirring mass resentment following the disillusion which accompanied what was called by Italians the "mutilated victory."

It is well known, in fact, that during the period of disillusionment which in the immediate postwar period replaced the euphoria of peace and, for the Western nations, of victory, those civilizing forces which the war effort had rudely repressed or forced to conform, reasserted themselves and, in a certain sense, sought a revenge. The struggle between interventionists and neutralists in Italy did not come to an end in 1914, but was renewed from 1919 to 1922. Neutralism now became the rallying point of all those who had lost faith in the ruling class and in the practical and ideological ability of the state and the motherland. As such, the forces of neutralism became the object of repression and proselytism on the part of its adversaries, the posthumous interventionists who had evolved into Fascists and who eventually triumphed with the March on Rome. Mussolini's boast that he could launch the Italian people into a war "in any direction and against any enemy" was interventionism at the pure stage of the negation of ancient idealistic bonds, the rejection of the subtle web of traditions, all of which are important factors in determining the necessity of a war. War becomes a tool of the state, which uses it ruthlessly, regardless of necessity or justification, and forces a whole population to identify their ideals with its action.

But Mussolini's violent language betrayed a consciousness of despotism and an awareness that the country, subdued and stunned —and even seduced by the dreams of glory, as during the Ethiopian war—was not entirely convinced. Italy had never recovered that self-assurance that makes issues of foreign policy immediately clear and evident to all levels of the population. Actually, neutralism, crystallized as the opposition to the arbitrary power of the state and to war as a proof of such power, as well as to risk, still remained, though repressed, the dominating psychological trait of the Italian population. Neutralism was the real winning force. Thus it happened that postwar neutralism metamorphosed itself into an attitude of lack of confidence in the Fascist state, found new sympathizers among some of the former interventionists, those Western democrats who had seen in intervention a way of supporting the democratic states, and eventually developed into one of those factors which prepared the road for the collapse of fascism and forsook the German alliance in 1943.

I have retraced here the history of the old Italian neutralism, so different from the present one, but still related to it, in an attempt to show how certain resentments can be transformed into corrosive forces, and sometimes into tools for action. Furthermore, the history of the early Italian neutralism seems to me to be, in some ways, unique; by neutralism is not meant merely preference for a neutral policy, but an inference that wars and alliances are to be considered arbitrary acts of the state and as such an abuse of power toward a peaceful population and the normal course of events.

Neutralism of this type was not evident in other European countries at the beginning of the war in 1914. Analogous phenomena did occur, however, during the war. For France it is enough to recall Caillaux and his attempts at a negotiated peace. Caillaux came to be considered a traitor and was tried before the high court. Interventionism here was called *jusqu'auboutisme,* and the reaction to it came with the victory of the *cartel des gauches* and of pacifism in 1924. It is enough to recall American isolationism, which in part was a return to the traditional policy, but was also a reaction to Wilson's policy and played no small part in assuring a succession of Republican presidents in the postwar period. It is enough to remember German pacifist literature (from Tucholski to von Gerlach, Ossietzky, Remarque, Brecht), as well as the British reaction against those ideologies which were believed to have brought about the war, culminating in the mission of the Labourite Lansbury to Rome to talk peace with Mussolini.

Here we have a profound reaction against the past, and to some extent against the very policies of European governments, which were attacked, rejected, defined as fallacious and attributed either to dangerous miscalculations or to the degeneracy of some individuals. The reaction first originated with leftist elements whose attempt to create the Internationale had been frustrated by the war, but it eventually pervaded all sectors of public opinion. The fruits of it were to be seen when, faced with the Nazi menace, there was so much talk of peace and neutrality on the part of statesmen in search of a compromise with the German dictatorship. This reaction was composed of the following elements:

1. War had come to be recognized as useless to achieve those ends which it claimed to achieve. War brought neither national prosperity nor security, nor did it guarantee domination on the world stage.

2. War was no longer attributed to the wickedness of the enemy, but to some evil factors existing within the frontiers of every country (here can be seen the success of the *Schuldfrage* polemics); they are the *marchands de canons* of all countries who instigate war to increase their profits, the Kaiser, the unscrupulous politicians like Poincaré, who plotted with Isvolski to render the Franco-Russian alliance automatic.[2] They are the military itself, striving for glory and for control of the nation.[3]

3. Also considered responsible for war were ideologies, those ideals invoked during war which animate armed forces and statesmen. The first such ideal to come under attack was, of course, that of the fatherland (the fatherland is a bourgeois concept, etc.). But, curiously enough, the fatherland was not the foremost scapegoat, for neutralism, even when it was directed against the very policies of the state, and therefore against the fatherland, preferred to insist upon other elements. The one most open to criticism was the democratic or humanitarian justification of World War I—*la guerre du droit et la civilization,* the war to end all wars, *l'ultima guerra,* the war to make the world safe for democracy. It was this automatic reaction that tended to minimize the danger of Ger-

[2] The seed of this theory on the origins of the war was already implicit in Wilson's condemnation of secret diplomacy—as if there could be a kind of diplomacy secret and public at the same time, and as if "alliances" were not normal instruments of state policy, and not simply a shameful ruse for bringing about wars.

[3] The fallacy of this generalization was fully proven during World War II, when nearly everywhere the generals were the first to organize capitulations and were opposed to intervention—in other words, they were neutralists.

many's renewed power and aggressiveness in 1934 and of the spreading of fascism in Europe. The idea of anti-Fascist war became a taboo, even among those people in the various countries who professed to be opposed to fascism, since it took the aspect of a preventive war. With this approach to the problem, which in itself had the seeds of the new neutralism which was to grow in the postwar period, it was not possible to arouse a strong popular reaction to aggression until the crucial moment when one's frontiers were violated. We find a vivid confession of this shortcoming in Leon Blum's book, *A l'Échelle Humaine.* Blum recognizes his mistake, but asks himself whether it would have been possible for anyone at that time to avoid an emotion which appeared so elementary.

The result was that with the outbreak of the war in 1939, Daladier, after the proclamation of a *repli impérial,* found no better ideological justification for the war than to declare that *"la France se bat pour la France,"* thus leaving himself open to the attacks by those who had refused *"mourir pour Danzig."* After all, a country which claims to fight only for itself (as Salandra also had done in 1914, speaking of "sacred egoism") cannot hope to gain the good will and support, in countries not yet involved in the war with the enemy, which could be aroused by the vision of a new, peaceful, and ordered arrangement of the world following victory. In other words, if France is fighting only to safeguard its interests, the rest of the world will at best shrug its shoulders. In vain Jean Giraudoux, the able writer in charge of propaganda, tried variations on this theme, trying to sell the idea that France is *l'ordre,* harmony, the garden spot of Europe beloved by all, but he was able to awaken only a weak and mixed reaction in spite of the fact that there was some truth in his slogans. Even inside France the assertion that France was fighting for France did not stir great enthusiasm for the war, until the invasion. In this attitude there is an evident distinction between defending the government's policy, in which doing one's duty is sufficient, and defending one's country, when sacrifices and heroism are in order.

The extreme to which this refutation of ideologies (which in fact was a refutation of ideals) was carried can best be seen in the different attitudes of Roosevelt and Wilson.[4] When it became a

---

[4] The comparison of propaganda material for the period that preceded the two world wars would make an interesting study. It would show the changing

question of giving an official title to the war—a strange custom, implying that each war has its particular motives and goals—President Roosevelt, after considering many suggestions, chose that of "The War for Survival." This was, more than any other, an idealistic way. It was not simply the danger of German domination on the Continent, which the United States did not like, but might have tolerated, that led them to intervention. It was rather the particular form of domination, with its aggressive character which was inseparable, in many respects, from the Nazi regime. President Roosevelt was well aware of this, and his policy toward Germany and Japan constantly risked an attack. And yet, when the war began, he chose to classify it in terms of *Realpolitik,* in terms of sacred egoism and strict necessity, in terms that could apply to any war, rather than clothing it in idealistic terms. This illustrates the degree to which Roosevelt was forced to make concessions to public opinion, against his own convictions, which were indeed more idealistic than he wished to show, believing that his people never would have fought another war except for reasons of state!

But we have anticipated the course of events, for it was during the interwar period that the working of the neutralist sentiment, and its relation to political problems, could be clearly seen. Here we have just touched on some of its causes and its development and on some of the basic problems. The fact remains that the aspirations of European states appeared to fall far short, when compared with actual possible achievements, of the enormous sacrifices required.

France had had her revenge on Germany, had reacquired the "lost" departments of Alsace-Lorraine, and had improved and consolidated her position as a colonial power, which put her, for a certain time, in a dominant position vis-à-vis the Arab world. But she had not been able to restore the position as a great power which she had enjoyed before Bismarck's unification of Germany. To do this, it would have been necessary not only to destroy German unity, but also to bring about a drastic resettlement of populations and industries, which France, due to the heavy wartime loss of men and capital, could not hope to do. The best policy for her to follow under the circumstances was one of security and the status quo, as she did

---

role of ideals in analogous situations on the part of men such as Wilson and Roosevelt in substantially similar positions and predicaments.

through the creation of the Little Entente. It was the disillusionment of not having been able to achieve her aims, and the certainty of not being able to achieve them, even through a more complete and brilliant victory, that weighed heavily upon French public opinion, paralyzing it in the face of Hitler.

In addition, a great deal of the moral leadership which France had exercised before 1914, such as that internal upheaval caused by the Dreyfus Affair, and which stood out as a model to other Europeans, had been weakened considerably by the breakdown of the moral unity of Europe; hence the mockery for the war for law and civilization. At the time of the Popular Front, France seemed, for a moment, about to recapture this leadership, but she let the opportunity escape through her passive policy toward the Fascist aggression in Spain. In reality, by this time this had ceased to be purely a French situation, and France was acting, so to speak, as the interpreter for the new political position of Russia with regard to the West. It is important to understand the moral collapse produced in France by the German-Soviet Pact and the inability of France to reassert its moral leadership by espousing the cause of anti-fascism.

An understanding of the vicissitudes of the interwar period is essential in order to understand present-day French neutralism, as well as that of the other European countries. In Germany, neutralism did not take root. Having been defeated and having lost both the hope for world hegemony and its key position on the Continent, there could not be such radical rejection of war. The Germans believed that a less foolish and more energetic policy than that followed by William II and his cabinet could obtain results and regain some of the ground lost with World War I. Domination of Europe seemed to have been missed, not because of lack of potentials, but because of remediable errors, or even because of betrayal. In fact, the Reich had reached or forged for itself a position somewhere between that of a world power, a goal that could be achieved, and that of a medium-sized state satisfied with its position and hence conservative. From this originated the varied reactions which were to explode in a second attempt at world conquest. The neutralist alternative never existed, it was only a choice of internal politics.

We have already spoken about Italy. Paradoxically enough, Italy had fulfilled, through the war, her primary objectives. Not only had she acquired the Irredentist provinces, but she also had gained an important position in the Adriatic. There were no great powers pressing at her own borders, save France, again too involved in Central Europe to be a cause for worry; she had no obligations and her hands were free. Moreover, she had proved her ability to participate in a coalition war, and she was not to be overlooked as an element in the European military equilibrium. But due to her well-known lack of raw materials, to the precarious state of her industries, to the wartime loss of wealth and markets, and above all to the internal turmoils that plagued her—consequences of the efforts necessary not only to wage and win the war, but also to bring about her intervention in it—Italy was paying a great deal more than other nations for the dire consequences that unbound nationalism had spread in Europe. The Fascists cleverly exploited this sense of frustration of the Italian people by insisting that the war was not really won because the victory was not properly utilized, thus creating the myth of the mutilated victory. Italy, they began to say, could become a great power, even an empire, but it was necessary to keep alive an aggressive spirit of intervention, suppressing once and for all neutralists and pacifists. In doing this Fascism exploited an uneasiness that was real, the sum and substance of which was that Italy had become a European power in her own right at a time when the other great powers were on the road to decline; and now it became necessary to risk national existence once more in order to reach—artificial and indeed unobtainable aim—the status of a super-power.

In reality, as with everything that is untimely, it was one thing for the dictator and his propaganda organs to pay lip service to these assertions and another to expect the nation to make them its own. Thus in 1940, when the decision had to be made as to whether or not to enter the war, neutralist points of view were quite strong, even among Fascist leaders. The deadlock was broken only by the spreading of the fiction that Italy would not be involved seriously in the war, but was preparing only to sit at the peace table, and finally by the personal decision of the dictator. But there was none of the emotion and enthusiasm that accompanied intervention in World War I.

In Great Britain neutralism seemed to characterize a situation in which the country appeared to have lost sight of her European role; however, except among some extreme Labourites, it never took the form of an unconditional renunciation of participation in foreign affairs. For some time, the disillusionment of World War I led the British ruling class, and public opinion as well, to seek a haven in the League of Nations. Actually, the collapse of the British willingness to maintain an international political position and to bear all the risks entailed in it occurred, for a brief, but decisive moment, at Munich. However, because of the difference between the crisis of the British state, which was the crisis of a great empire, still remaining a world power and first-rank member of international society, and those crises taking place in other European countries, British neutralism was tempered and never absolute. On one side Britain, through Henderson and Lansbury, paid lip service to pacifism, while on the other, with the Ottawa policy, she seemed to embody the will for imperial self-sufficiency. This never for an instant, however, implied a complete lack of faith in its own body politics, or even indicated a tendency to abrogate its own political responsibilities.

If we now pass from the study of neutralism in World War I to that in World War II, it is easy to discern in this the result of that state of mind which had characterized France and Italy after World War I. It should be remembered, however, that both Italians and Frenchmen fought, though in different ways and by different means, but always with great enthusiasm, to end World War II and to destroy naziism and indigenous fascism. No doubt they were also animated by the desire, in so doing, to save their own existence as nations. In a certain sense, the Italian fatherland had never been so popular as during World War II, when the partisan war had the active co-operation of the peasants. But if the people rebelled, in self-defense, against the Nazi occupation, which stood as an obstacle to a return to peace and liberty—a miracle which had seemed a reality on July 25, 1943—it never occurred to them that they were fighting to restore the Italian state as a power or as an international political entity. The Resistance, an act of faith in the worth of one's country—later equated with a political idea—was also a loud assertion of the insufficiency of the old political order. These people who had greeted the end of the war with tumultuous joy, even though defeated, took up arms again for liberty outside the bounds of the state.

The states which were reborn through the Resistance found themselves as much in a state of contradiction and weakness as had their predecessors; just because the Italian or French flag was flying again atop the public buildings did not mean that confidence was restored in the state as the safeguard of national interests at home and abroad. Following World War I it was said that the aims of the war effort had not been achieved; the same could not be said after World War II, when at least the invaders had been forced to flee, and freedom had been restored. But in reality the political situation had become worse even than the precarious state of affairs which had preceded the war. France had lost her role as a colonial power, a loss more apparent than real at the time, but one which caused her to wage another war, thus intensifying the disillusionment in the ability of the state to fulfill its mission. France did have "status" and ranked among the great powers in the United Nations, but in reality her position as a power was a fiction not commensurate at all with the reality of the situation, with the practical effect of only aggravating the people's sense of mistrust toward the state and toward any policy which it would choose to follow.

I already have spoken of Italy. Although, as was said, she had fallen, she was better off and even more prosperous, since she had been forced to abandon the burdens of her imperial dreams, and there was a growing mistrust of military action as a means to gain success. To this it should be added that the division of the world into two blocs had repercussions in Italian internal politics, even more than in other countries. Italian states, since surviving the catastrophe of the Renaissance, had grown used to taking the part of France and Spain, making it almost natural in Italy to be open to the influence of foreign domination. As a result, the citizens did not feel obligated, on principle, to follow the orientation of the Italian state toward this or that power.

Neutralism also had arrived in Germany, chiefly because the second attempt to dominate the world had been more disastrous than the first, causing collapse of the state, destruction of a great part of German territory, uprooting of citizens, and, more important this time, charges of the perpetration of crimes against humanity. This great moral bankruptcy seemed to imply the failure of all German history, of all the efforts of the German people to band together as a national state, and, at the least, failure of the state as a military organization. *"Ohne mich, ohne uns"* was the spontaneous reaction to the first attempts to bring the German people back within a framework of politico-military obligations. Was not the loss of her "status" due to her having pursued too persistently the phantom of power? And now the other states were asking her to return to this road.

This profound sense of neutralism spread throughout Europe following the last war. It is deep-rooted and very strongly felt, and it defies any attempt at utilization for any purpose of state policy. It would be a grave error to neglect this as a factor in European politics, even if it has been possible on occasion for a state to adhere to this or that treaty, to this or that alliance. One should never forget that Europeans, with all the best intentions in the world of fulfilling loyally these accords, *have little faith in the capacity and ability of their states to operate in the field of foreign policy.* This does not mean that Europeans are not attached to their liberties or that they are not prepared to defend them. I am not sure that, in the event of an invasion, the large vote given today to the Italian and French Communist parties would necessarily mean that the vast majority of these populations would not take arms against the invaders. The dilemma, however, would not be so clear-cut, as it was in the case of France in 1939, if it were a question not simply of defending one's frontiers, but of having to fight for a political position, a principle, or something beyond one's borders. It seems a paradox, and indeed it is, that the loss of trust in the political capacity of one's state takes almost the form of a nationalistic revival or, at least, a return to national positions. European people are averse to supporting policies that go beyond the defense of their own frontiers, because alliances imply a policy of action and also the belief that through alliances it is possible to achieve some practical goals and the fruition of some common ideals. This cannot be guaranteed by the states which, after two great wars, whether won or lost, have shown their inability to carry through their policies of action and expansion. Hence they believe that the sacrifices needed to support these policies are wasted.

Here we have neutralism at its elemental stage, alive even though not expressed. In France political neutralism has found a voice in periodicals, in great organs of public opinion, even outside Communist circles. Certainly the gentlemen of *Le Monde, Esprit, Temps Modernes,* and *La Vie Intellectuelle,* even if their reasonings may be obnoxious, do not all reflect Communist influence. In Italy, this has not happened, or if it has, it has gained a voice only after the failure of the EDC. But does this mean that the basic elements of neutralism are less widespread in Italy than in France? If by neutralism we mean essentially a mistrust of the ruling class of a country and of its capacity to conduct an efficient foreign policy, then we can observe neutralist influence in the difficulty which its enemies encounter in having the population accept what, under normal circumstances, are the basic attributes of a state, i.e., the conduct of foreign policy. To understand how much the supporters of the Atlantic Pact feared the effects of neutralism, it is enough to note the many efforts which have been necessary in Italy, France, and Germany since the war for the conclusion of this and other alliances.[5]

For example, how can the chain of events which have taken place in eastern Europe since the war be characterized other than as an expansion of neutralism? It could be described as the reluctance on the part of some organs of the state, conscious of their extreme weakness in the field of internal and international policy, to get involved in any policy that would require burdens or risks for the country and binding international obligations. Although, on the other hand, the conditions of extreme weakness of these countries required urgent conclusions of alliances on the part of organs of these states, it is natural for the business of alliance-making and the development of neutralism to be tied together with the reorganization of the social and political structures. It is as if a different type of neutralism characterized each successive ring of a spiral.

Now let us go back to the beginning, to the Brussels Pact and the Marshall Plan. The Brussels Pact, which followed the typical pattern of defensive alliances, with clauses devoted to economic and cultural collaboration, permanent councils, etc., proposed a system of alliances and succeeded in having them adopted by a group of

[5] A lively example of this widespread feeling is illustrated by Alberto Tarchiani, former Italian Ambassador in Washington: "The meeting with Saragat was very enjoyable, especially since he had been described to me as the leader of the friendly neutralists. Actually he is clearly on the side of the United States, but he could not say so in public, and he would have denied it if I had quoted him, because many would have misunderstood his reasoning . . . but he remained decidedly and clearly on the side of the United States." Alberto Tarchiani, *Dieci Anni tra Roma e Washington* (Milano: Mondadori, 1955), p. 51. See also p. 169.

states in the midst of a moral and military crisis, but it tried to disguise the traditional elements in the alliances by appealing to the energies and new traditions of national liberation. Let us not forget that, formally, the Brussels Pact was a pact among victors, intended to prevent the resurgence of the German danger. This was quite evident during the debates over Italian accession, when the power which had initiated the pact was opposed to Italy's entree. Actually, there was opposition to it also in Italy, in spite of the fact that politicians believed it advantageous to be associated with the victors.

The Marshall Plan was conceived from the assumption that before being able to return to the international political arena with the necessary responsibility, the European countries had to be rehabilitated. This was considered necessary in order to restore to these nations a sense of self-reliance and renewed well-being which would provide a rational basis for the conduct of foreign relations together with a sense of responsibility for the risks involved if a reorganization of the political structure were deemed desirable. Therefore the Marshall Plan offered generous aid for the reconstruction of the European economies, not forgetting, however, that a reconstruction along national lines would necessarily restrict the results. This was a fundamental and just understanding of the plan, and it was not by chance, nor due solely to the sordid wish to receive aid, that arguments against the plan were never popular and that even the Communist attack upon it not only failed (as it had failed in the fight against the Atlantic Pact), but also failed to rally popular opposition to it. Moreover, the supporters of the plan never had to apologize for their position, as had been the case with supporters of other non-neutralistic plans.

It had been assumed that the necessity for economic co-operation, together with the obvious pressure that could be exerted by the United States, would per se be sufficient to channel the efforts of the receiving countries, in the natural development of events, toward a reconstruction above national levels. American aid would be given to reconstruct a united western European economy, and not to resurrect the old anachronistic and restricted structures. At least this was the hope. Instead, hardly had the organs for economic co-operation as envisaged by the plan come into operation, than all the old forces of national egoism and protectionism arose in their midst, and it became obvious that the American "experts" could do no more than write threatening reports and warn that unless the situation changed, American aid would be terminated. These threats were clearly in vain, because the same political necessity which had led the United States to propose the Marshall Plan continued to exist and, in fact, was even more urgent after the conclusion of the agreement. Moreover, reconstruction of western Europe in any form seemed preferable, once the plan had been inaugurated, to the abandonment of the initiative. With the ever-increasing tempo of Russian aggressiveness, plans and hopes for a military alliance gave added significance to the plan. How else can one explain the inclusion of England in a plan for aid to Europe, when England had not even negotiated, nor had any intention of negotiating the integration of the entire Continent in the sterling bloc? This combination of circumstances was responsible for the ambiguous results of the Marshall Plan with regard to the struggle against neutralism.

Actually, the Marshall Plan did bolster the political structures of the nations of western Europe and put an end to the danger of internal political collapse and the possible destruction of democracy through the necessity of adopting extreme restrictive measures, which would have been possible only by a coalition of extremist elements at both ends of the political spectrum. It was only through the Marshall Plan that the Atlantic Pact was made possible, not because as beneficiaries of American aid, these nations were pressured to adhere to the pact, but because the plan had steadied and strengthened the respective political structures of the states involved and so enabled them to enter the alliance. The states benefiting from the Marshall Plan, however, especially France, Germany, and Italy, were in no position, due to the lack of a concerted policy and common goals, to do anything more than concentrate on the immediate needs for reconstruction. It may be said also that the limited success of the Marshall Plan to bring about a degree of economic co-operation, which resulted in the creation of partially integrated economies, almost a timid return to the situation of 1914, contributed to the elimination of economic blocs which are the characteristic of autarchic states, strong or weak as they may be, and also helped to awaken in the officials responsible for the formulation of policy the feeling of "sacred egoism," and to strengthen popular mistrust toward any active policy.

Since the implementation of the Marshall Plan, and more clearly since the ratification of the Atlantic Pact, there has emerged in addition to the basic feeling of neutralism described above a professional neutralism reflecting the views of political leaders. On occasions, due to specific activities within the Atlantic Pact and to initiatives for economic integration, such neutralists have worked hand in hand, as in the fight against EDC, conducted at the same time by pacifists, Communists, and nationalists. The pacifists opposed German rearmament; the Communists wanted to prevent the creation of any European force which would stand in the way of action by the Soviet bloc; the nationalists were averse to relinquishing any rights of the state, especially now that it had been bolstered by the Marshall Plan. Here we have a repetition of the situation which existed before World War II, when popular opposition to any policies was channeled through propaganda media, and neutralism was against any broadly conceived foreign policy and any policy which would predicate action at a level higher than that of the state. At that time, this action of the neutralists was taken to oppose fascism; today the target is the political unification of Europe.

It must be said, however, that then, as now, this deviation from the original spirit of neutralism—in itself a simple psychological reaction to a practical situation, which would have disappeared once the ideal premises contained in it had been achieved—has assured some successes to neutralism, such as rendering less sure and putting on the defensive the supporters of alliances. A help to this deviation was the fact that no positive steps were taken to dispel it, and only psychological approaches were used to fight it. In other words, to take the critical period from 1933 to 1939, we had in the free countries the anti-Fascist position and pronouncements of some political leaders on one hand and vacillation, compromise, and even capitulation on the other. Similarly, in the period from 1945 to 1955 there was, outside the Marshall Plan, no concrete policy which expressed the psychological desire to put an end to the divisions plaguing western Europe by scrapping the system of national states. The very timid efforts of the European Coal and Steel Community and the implications of the EDC (especially in the ad hoc constituent assembly) really could not be expected to dispel neutralism, because they lacked the following and the drive necessary for the success of such attempts, as well as the potentials to assure the establishment of a supranational organization. This was due to the fact that they were devoid of political and constitutional content. For reasons of urgency (which, incidentally, were not shared by military experts), it was agreed to attempt a one-blow resolution of the problems of German rearmament and sovereignty, the inclusion of West Germany in the Atlantic Alliance, and the creation of a common European army and a common constitution to justify it.

This was obviously playing directly into the hands of neutralism, because it was possible to adopt against the treaty, simultaneously, the theme of sacred egoism and the argument that the only concrete points in the treaty were the creation of a new sovereignty and a partial return to the military formula which had proved so inefficient in the past. EDC did provide for action at the European level, and it embodied some ideas regarding the method for pursuing this goal. On a last analysis, the defeat of the treaty was not due to the opposition of the pure neutralists, those opposed to any type of alliance, but was brought about by the action of the neutralists of the sacred egoism type. For instance, Bidault did not present the treaty to the French Parliament as an ideal goal, but, especially with reference to the European aspects, as a sum of sacrifices which had to be made because of dire necessity and which eventually could be modified.

With the failure of EDC and the acceptance of WEU, devoid as it is of any concrete formula which could bring about a resolution of the crisis affecting Italy, France, and Germany, the opposition and fight against European neutralism is reduced to a mere psychological counterplay, lacking any concreteness. To understand the success of neutralistic offensives in Italy, France, and Germany, one should take note of the growing feeling that the new methods of warfare, implying the almost certain destruction of all belligerents, will be the decisive factors in tomorrow's war; the fact that Europe, which as yet does not possess atomic weapons, would be extremely vulnerable to atomic attack because of its geographical position; and the policy of distention inaugurated by the Soviet Union following the death of Stalin.

Due to the strengthening political cohesiveness of these European states, as well as to the situation in which they find themselves, European neutralism in 1956 has lost the elementary form which it assumed in 1947. Nowhere do responsible people speak of abandoning the bountiful ties of the Atlantic Alliance. Of course, the solidarity of an alliance can be measured best on the eve of a war. In general now alliances are no longer denounced, mainly because they have become rather negligible factors in the policy of a state, and also because, as Hamilton observed, if one partner fails to fulfill his obligations, the other will do likewise, thus eliminating the use of sanctions. For instance, America's policy toward the Arab world is repaid by French "forgetfulness" to fulfill her NATO obligations with respect to troops to be kept in Europe; British policy toward Cyprus is equated by a Greek policy; to French proposals concerning the eventual separation of the problem of disarmament from that of German reunification correspond the advances of Bonn for an eventual direct understanding. In Italy, where the Atlantic policy clearly interferes with internal policies, we have Nenni's declaration regarding the diminished importance of NATO and its military obligations, within the new framework of coexistence. For this reason as well the psychological efforts to combat neutralism which are still present fall short, as does also the almost routine device to label as European every agreement, even of a technical nature, every new point of view, and even the feeble propaganda efforts.

Alliances are reached, when they appear necessary, between interested partners and along lines of mutual necessity. There is always a sizable percentage of neutralistic feeling in every country, but this does not mean that if a war comes, as in France in 1939, it is not fought, nor if a defensive alliance is necessary as a deterrent, like the Atlantic Pact, it is not ratified. But we must not think that all alliances are made under the same conditions, or that there can be expected from weak and divided countries the same compliance as from countries more politically sound, where the state represents the people, countries which can set for themselves high and concrete goals in the field of foreign policy. If we want the nations of the European Continent to assume the burdens and risks of alliances, of a policy of co-operation with the United States and England, (and fortunately, although sacrifices will always be necessary, the risks will diminish), then we must provide them with an organization which can bear these risks and these sacrifices.

I am convinced that there is no serious possibility of creating these conditions within the framework of the national states in Europe, and this conviction is strengthened by the fact that there is still so much talk about building up Europe after the failure of EDC, the abandonment of a common European policy, and the abandonment of the hope to set up a United States of Europe through diplomatic pourparlers. The basic point of discussion, however, is the necessity of outlining clearly the policy to be followed. But it should certainly be questioned whether it is possible to follow this policy through the system of national states, or whether it is necessary to scrap these old political formulas, and once agreement is reached on this, then forcefully implement the policy. Psychological offensives have a short life span. Like drugs, they may exhilarate the body for a period of time, but then leave it weaker than before.

While the more immediate and stronger form of neutralism, the refusal to support any proposal or policy because of a lack of faith in the capabilities of the state, is today partially receding, the second form of neutralism, indifference and general popular mistrust toward governmental decisions on foreign policy, is more alive than ever, and thus more difficult to fight, because it is grounded on concrete reasons. This second type of neutralism can be combated only with facts, which will also result in time in the partial elimination of its psychological effects, as happened also to the first form of neutralism.

In Search of a Political Framework for an Integrated Europe

HANS NORD / *Secretary General of the Netherlands Council of the European Movement*

SINCE THE END of the last war, many European governments have written European integration into their national programs. It was widely felt that Europe's position in the world had undergone a fundamental change and that instead of struggling against each other, and at best preserving an uneasy balance, the nations of Europe should work together and inaugurate a new era. Mindful of Napoleon's dictum that men alone cannot direct the destinies of nations, but that institutions are needed to safeguard them, the statesmen of western Europe collaborated in setting up many European organizations. Some serve a specific, others a more general, purpose. They are the prefiguration of the institutional pattern for a united Europe. The pattern is not yet clearly visible; the lasting political framework for an integrated Europe has not yet been hammered out. This makes it all the more important that the problem of European political institutions should be considered. Without these institutions, European integration will remain a dream. With the wrong institutions, the dream might well become a nightmare.

The necessity for European integration is sufficiently well known. On the Continent of western Europe most of the leading personalities in public affairs are very much conscious of it. But, on the whole, this consciousness has only reached the heads, and not the hearts, of men. The European masses, though by no means unresponsive to the European idea when it is put clearly before them, have not yet developed any definite sense of European solidarity or unity. Nor have they yet been given any true leadership toward that end.

We are faced, therefore, with something very much like a vicious circle. European integration, the need of which is generally recognized, presupposes certain common institutions. Such institutions, in order to be effective, must command the loyalty of the citizens of the countries concerned. The feeling of unity, however, the sense of belonging together, on which any system of government by consent must needs be based, is insufficiently developed.

We must look for a way out of this dilemma. And we shall only find such a way out if we keep in mind certain facts and considerations. In the clash of opinions about European integration and the forms it should take, the ends it is supposed to serve are often forgotten. Terms like *unity, solidarity, integration,* and even *federation* are glibly used, but their meaning is seldom clearly defined. The first question is, therefore, what do we mean when we speak of integration? What do we expect or hope it to achieve?

Present-day Europe, seen as a whole, presents the spectacle of a society threatened with stagnation. We want to produce more and better things, in order to raise the standard of living of our populations, but the markets of our separate national economies are too small to allow us to reap the full benefits of modern production and distribution methods.

We want to safeguard ourselves against possible attack, but we find ourselves incapable of effectively organizing our own defense. Even a military alliance of the classical type with our European neighbors leaves the resulting chain no stronger than its weakest link. We want to preserve our democratic way of life, all the more precious to us after the terrible experience of tyranny and oppression we have recently undergone, but we find that the most important decisions have become more than national and escape our national democratic processes.

In short, we find that in the exercise of three most fundamental tasks of our national communities, namely the pursuit of prosperity, defense, and foreign policy, our national sovereignty has become largely fictitious. We are hampered and choked by the very frontiers which, in an earlier age, were formed to protect and safeguard our national existence. This is the sickness for which integration recommends itself as a remedy. The walls dividing the nations of western Europe must disappear, for they no longer serve the true interests of our citizens. A free flow of men, capital, and services throughout the area must be made possible.

That is what integration must mean, if it is to mean anything. Perhaps it would be better to speak of re-integration, for, in a very fundamental sense, the movement toward European unity represents an attempt to draw new inspiration from the past in which "Europe" did indeed exist. Today, all we can say is that events have forced the people of free Europe to face common dangers and common possibilities. It will be the task of the present generation of Europeans to avert the dangers and to realize the possibilities. To that end common institutions are indispensable. There must be set up a suitable framework which, without putting too much strain on the capacity of peoples to develop new loyalties, will make it possible to carry on the process of integration gradually and effectively.

This brings us to an all-important question. Can European integration be effected by voluntary co-operation between national governments, or do we need independent European institutions with authority of their own? In other words, is the framework we seek to be intergovernmental or supranational?

This question, which to many of us seemed solved conclusively some years ago, has become topical again since the fall of the European Defense Community Treaty and the attempt, inaugurated at the Conference of Messina in June, 1955, to relaunch the movement toward integration. Since then, it has become fashionable not to mention the word *supranational*. Does this mean that the concept of a European community, with common institutions endowed with powers of their own within their designated fields, has to be given up? I do not think so. A real alternative has not been given and the basic facts and requirements of our situation have not changed.

If one accepts the aims of integration as I have indicated them, one cannot escape the conclusion that the supranational community is the only possible political framework for European integration.

In any permanent alliance or community of states, the problem of power is paramount. There are, generally speaking, three ways of dealing with this problem. First, the structure of the community may be so weak that no real power is exercised in common. Famous examples of this can be seen in the associations of the city-states of ancient Greece. With this type of community, the problem of authority is not really solved, it is merely shelved. If the aim of the alliance is strictly ad hoc and temporary, it may be able to afford such a weak structure. But it will never lead a life of its own, nor achieve more than is acceptable to the immediate and separate interests of all its members.

The second way of settling the problem of authority is found in communities of nations where one of the partners is so much stronger than the others that the leading power imposes its will upon the group, carrying as it does, most of the common burden and responsibility. Even though the structure of the alliance may be weak, the presence of a hegemonist may render it effective. In the history of my own country, such a situation has existed for a time. The Republic of the United Netherlands was strongly dominated by the province of Holland and this made it possible to make and carry out decisions which might not have been accepted by all if the distribution of power within the confederation had been more even. Finally, the problem of authority may be solved by the setting up of joint institutions in which real powers are vested. These powers may be limited to strictly defined fields, but they must be real, in the sense that they are exercised independently of those who originally transferred them.

Which of these three types of association would be suitable and possible to serve as a framework for an integrated Europe? When we survey the European scene, the answer is obvious.

It is sometimes advocated that the political pattern of a united Europe should be modeled on that of the British Commonwealth. But it is seldom stated what advantages such a form of association would bring. What would be the difference between a European commonwealth and the situation we have now, with its many—perhaps too many—institutions and treaties? The problem of Europe is essentially that it cannot begin to solve its difficulties without going beyond its present structural pattern. True, the existing intergovernmental institutions have done a great deal of good work and, no doubt, will continue to do so. But their possibilities are limited by their very nature. If one accepts integration as Europe's present need, a European commonwealth would, in fact, mean the giving up of the attempt to integrate our Continent.

I can be even more brief about the possibility of Europe being united and led by a strong hegemonist. Many times in the past, this solution of Europe's divisions has been tried. It has always failed. The European spirit, of which love of freedom, nationality, and cultural diversity are an essential part, has always refused to accept one member of the European family as master of our common destiny. I often think that, immediately after the last war, a liberated Continent would have welcomed a strong lead from Great Britain, if Britain had been disposed to assume great responsibility in guiding Europe toward unity. But it was not to be. Although Britain participated in the creation of the Council of Europe in 1949, it soon became clear that integration, as I have defined it, had to be begun on the Continent. On the basis of a new understanding between France and Germany, for which Sir Winston Churchill had pleaded as early as 1947, an integrated European community would have to be built. And such a community, in view of the aims and essence of integration, could only be of supranational character.

No society can function effectively without the exercise of authority. Without such authority European integration cannot be brought about. No measure of integration achieved can be safeguarded without it. The common European interest which integration seeks to create and serve is not a simple sum of the various interests of the member states. It will and must exist on its own level and in its own right. The joint exercise of sovereignty which European integration implies must, therefore, rest with organs possessing the power to discharge their task. And, at the same time, these bodies must be subject to a public opinion functioning in the European community as a whole. As I said before, the term *supranational* seems to be rather under a cloud at the present time. If I were not afraid that the word *federal* would cause even more raising of eyebrows, I would prefer to use the latter term. For the concept of supranationality as the political framework of an integrated Europe is rather abstruse and already has led to misunderstandings.

It would be futile to attempt to draw a precise blueprint for a European political structure at the present stage. The making of Europe resembles the work of the gardener rather than that of the engineer. The European Community, which must embody unity while respecting, and even honoring, diversity, will have to grow. But its growth will depend primarily on the nature of the seed that has been planted. This simple truth is too often forgotten. The illusion persists that institutions without powers will somehow automatically evolve into institutions with powers. Although it would be useless to indulge in the drafting of a full-blown European constitution, the experience of recent years and the requirements of European integration itself make it possible and highly necessary to define more clearly and systematically the principles according to which a supranational European community should be brought into being. There are a number of points which, in this connection, are essential. First, we should not try to copy forms evolved, however successfully, in other parts of the world. To the minds of many Europeans, the North American federation shines as a glowing example to be followed, and who indeed would not be moved by the memory of the founding fathers? But Europe is not America. We shall have to find and develop our own forms of association and however much we may be inspired by what others achieved before us, we must remember that twentieth-century Europe presents problems for which new solutions, suitable to our own surroundings and political traditions, will have to be worked out.

This brings me to my second point, the concept of supranationality itself. We are living in the age of nationalism. The identification of the idea of the state with that of the nation has become, especially in Europe, almost complete. The nation has conquered the state and become its sovereign master and jealous guard. The concept of a supranational community—or, in other words, of a multinational state—therefore implies a fundamental re-thinking of political and constitutional theory in Europe. It means that the idea of the state itself is questioned.

To many people in Europe, accustomed as they are to identifying state and nation, and to regarding the unitary nation-state as the only possible one, because it is the only one they know, a united Europe means a unitary European state. A great deal of resistance to European integration stems from this fallacy. It cannot be repeated too often that the European Community is something quite different from the new Leviathan some people seem to fear. But, at the same time, it should be stressed that the European Community cannot be built solely with the existing national states as basic units. This danger is very real. It must be averted if European integration is to succeed.

Let us imagine for a moment what would happen if we chose the easy way and, using the present European pattern as a basis, completed our political framework by giving authority and powers of decision to bodies composed of representatives of the various national sovereignties. Such bodies would be supranational in the sense that their decisions would be binding. In order to reach these decisions, votes would have to be taken by majority, simple or qualified as the case might be. Every question would inevitably become more, not less, national. For instance, Benelux would be beaten by France, Germany, and Italy, or France would be outvoted by a combination of Germany and Benelux, with Italy abstaining. Many combinations are possible. It is clear that such a framework would only irritate and at the same time strengthen political nationalism in Europe. The European Community would become a battlefield for national interests, seeking majority positions within the organs of the community. Such a construction would be both a mockery and a tragedy. Also, it would not be able to withstand for long the terrible strain of conflicting national interests, for these, instead of being sublimated on a higher European level, would be, as it were, institutionalized and thereby artificially kept alive.

This, then, is what our supranational community should not become. No superstate, no authority giving orders to member governments and acting on and through them. The only sane framework for an integrated Europe is that which recognizes that the European and the national interests are both valid and have to be organized separately. There can be no subordination of national governments to a European government. They are both independent within their designated fields. In other words, the European Community cannot be built on the existing member nations alone—it must rest on a European citizenry. That is the only way to serve the interests of Europe and also that of its nations and their peoples. Every European must know that he is a citizen of his nation and also of the European Community. Only in that way can the conflict between nationalism and European integration be resolved. This is the new idea of the state which will have to be brought home to Europeans.

My third point is a logical corollary from what has preceded. It concerns the democratic control of the process of integration and of the European Community which will emerge from it.

The rise of democracy, of government by consent, has been a long process requiring constant effort and vigilance. In Europe, democracy is now being threatened not only by the forces of totalitarianism but also by the very insufficiency of the national states to perform the functions which are theirs. We can no longer afford to determine our national policies independently, or even at the expense of our neighbors. That being so, our governments conclude treaties which sometimes greatly influence the conduct of our national affairs. But are our parliaments really free to accept, reject, or amend such treaties and their applications? Quite naturally they are not. Even though they may not be happy with what is put before them, they have to keep in mind that it is the result of long and often difficult negotiations and that any modification, however minor, might endanger the whole. Parliamentary freedom is thus curtailed considerably and the people, without perhaps realizing the cause, observe the effect and lose interest in our parliamentary democracy.

If one accepts the concept of supranationality as the only valid one for European integration, the necessity for a common European parliament is obvious. It is obvious for three reasons: first, because integration cannot be achieved without the consent of the peoples expressing themselves through their representatives; second, because a European executive authority needs the complementary partner which only a parliamentary body can provide; and third, because integration without democratic control would lead to the progressive decay of democracy in Europe.

One cannot speak of a European parliament without broaching the question of European elections. This is a much debated matter, and many arguments are put forward on both sides. What should our decision be?

History has known many parliaments not based on direct and universal suffrage. In fact, our present-day type of election is fairly recent. In itself, therefore, a European parliamentary body chosen, for instance, by national parliaments, might be excellent. But it would lack an element which has come to be essential in our age, the feeling of our people that it would be truly their own parliament. Madame de Staël's word that the nation attaches itself to its representatives if it has chosen them itself is even more valid today. To present-day Europeans, a parliament with authority is a parliament which has been directly elected. That is a reality which we cannot afford to overlook.

It is often said that our people are not ripe for European elections because European problems are too far removed from their daily lives. There is certainly truth in this. But do we honestly believe that our national electorates are so well versed in the problems with which their national representatives have to deal? The argument about ripeness is a two-edged sword.

A great deal depends, of course, on the electoral system that would be used. It is natural to assume that, in the beginning, a system would be selected which would change very little the existing national political parties presenting their own "European" candidates to a national electorate. Strangely enough, this is sometimes used as an argument against European elections by its opponents. One would think that it would set their minds at rest! However, it may be regarded as certain that the first European elections would not produce any startling or revolutionary change. But they would open up new possibilities for the future. European problems are going to present new issues which no longer correspond to existing party political labels or to national points of view.

Gradually, therefore, European programs will come into being and a fresh breeze will blow through the political life of our Continent. Something resembling European parties, bound together by common European objectives, will play its part in reinforcing popular loyalty to the new community and in creating a new interest in public affairs.

The fourth point concerns the protection of our free way of life and our fundamental liberties. Modern history has seen the rise of the criminal state. It has been painfully brought home to us that the protection of our liberties transcends national boundaries and that common measures are indispensable to safeguard our freedom. In Europe, the Convention of Human Rights, with its Human Rights Commission and its Court, represents an important step in this direction. If we had had such an institution twenty-five years ago, the rise of Hitler might not have been possible.

The European Community must be so constructed that the fundamental liberties of its citizens can be effectively protected and preserved. Not only member states as such, but also individuals and groups of individuals, must be able to appeal when human rights are alleged to have been violated. I stress the importance of this aspect of the European Community. For it may become of the greatest value in dealing with those countries in Europe which at present cannot participate in our joint efforts.

My last point deals with the tension which will inevitably exist between the nations of Europe and the European Community. In the concept of two independent spheres of government, this tension should not be unbearable. It may even act for the common good. But it is essential that the rights of our national communities, however small, be respected. Uniformity is the mortal enemy of European civilization. Tolerance and love of diversity should be our guiding virtues. As our friends from Luxembourg have often put it: "Wir wollen bleiben was wir sind."

In the European Community all peoples will be in a minority. Our political framework should be based upon this fact. A balance must be found between national and European rights, duties, and interests. Without entering into details, it can be said that both the executive and the parliamentary bodies of the community must reflect this dual character. Some form of bicameral system will be indispensable.

These, then, are five principles which should be regarded as basic for a real and organic European Community. Let us now consider their practical application in the European situation of today. After it became clear that the Council of Europe could not provide a framework for integration, the Coal and Steel Community was set up to provide a new stimulus and an example. It was never intended that it should remain alone. Other communities would follow and through a process of interlocking and merging institutions, a supranational Europe would continue to grow.

The Coal and Steel Community with its High Authority, Parliamentary Assembly, and Court of Justice, introduced the supranational principle for the first time in European affairs. The next sectional institution for integration, the European Defense Community, was closely modeled on its predecessor and it was generally recognized that an over-all political structure would soon be needed. Using a clause in the EDC Treaty, the foreign ministers requested a European parliamentary body to draft a statute for a European Community.

The history of the EDC Treaty and of the work of the ad hoc assembly need not be gone into here. It is sufficient to note that with the fall of EDC our whole concept of how the European Community would have to be built had not been considered. The draft statute of the ad hoc assembly, however valuable in itself, was no longer in the range of possibility. The political approach toward European integration had become unusable for the time being.

At Messina, therefore, a different approach was made. The creation of a common economic market and the joint development of the power of the atom were to be our immediate aims. The framework needed to achieve this was only vaguely indicated. The studies of the Brussels Committee would reveal what institutions would be necessary and what powers they would have to possess. Not theoretical notions, but practical necessity would decide.

Recently, the Brussels report was completed and released for publication. I believe that it contains possibilities for the application of the principles I have indicated.

Economic unity and political unity, though they may be separately discussed, are nonetheless two sides of the same coin. It is true that a political structure without an integrated economy is no more than a façade—one cannot have a community without having something in common. But it is equally true that, under present-day conditions, an integrated economy cannot exist without a political structure.

Economic integration is more than just the liberation of trade. The whole pattern of the economy will have to change if integration is to bring the benefits expected from it. And this will happen only if there is a guarantee that, in times of difficulty, the integrated market will not fall apart again. This guarantee can only be given by a political body, responsible for the creation and maintenance of the common economy.

But there is more to it. In our times, economic matters are handled not only on their own merits, but also with an eye to social and political considerations. In other words, the static concept of a common market does not exist. We shall be faced with the dynamic concept of a common economic policy which implies a responsible political body charged with the task of conducting it.

Therefore, what I said about a European political structure in general is highly applicable to the present stage of European integration. The European Commission for the Common Market, the leading organs of Euratom, the High Authority of the Coal and Steel Community, must be closely interrelated and function as a general executive, acting independently within the sphere of its power and competence. A parliamentary assembly, directly elected as soon as possible, must assume its proper role. A common court of justice must guard over the correct application of the treaties.

The Brussels report, of course, if carried into execution, provides no more than a point of departure. But, as I said before, it is the nature of the seed which will determine the growth of the tree. The economic approach to integration may lead to a true European Community if the necessary conditions regarding its institutional framework are fulfilled.

I have not tried to define in detail the powers and responsibilities of the various European institutions we need at the present time. I repeat, such a task would be in vain. The draft statute of the ad hoc assembly contains much that will remain valuable in that respect. For the moment, our main chance is to begin organizing the common market and Euratom. The treaties will define most carefully the various spheres of competence. As we succeed in our efforts, we shall begin to have a common European interest which must be served and defended. In this manner, starting from modest beginnings, the European Community will grow in stature and authority.

So far, we have only considered the efforts toward integration of the six countries of the Coal and Steel Community. But these six are not Europe. Their integration should proceed within a framework which must be suitable for a larger area. The European Community cannot be a closed fortress—it must be an open society.

What are the natural frontiers of Europe? It is impossible to say. Europe has never been and never can be a mere geographical concept. One thing, however, is certain—all European peoples must have the right to decide freely whether they want to join the European Community. The present dividing line between freedom and slavery cannot last forever. A permanent relaxation of tension can only be achieved if all the peoples of Europe obtain the right to choose their destiny. While building what can be only a nucleus and a beginning, we must prepare ourselves for the wider community we desire. It is here that the importance of the joint protection of human rights and liberties becomes particularly clear. All members of the European family can take part in the process of integration. But they will have to accept the common discipline and democratic way of life.

Among the nations of western Europe, also, there are those who have so far stood apart from the attempt at integration. In this respect, Great Britain occupies a special position. While it is clear that the process of integration must go on, even without full British participation, it is of the utmost importance that Britain should be associated as closely as possible with the Continent. Her treaty of association with the Coal and Steel Community provides a valuable precedent in this connection. It should also be a pointer toward future developments and possibilities.

Here, we pass beyond the strictly European theater and enter into a wider world, the Atlantic Alliance, in which the free democracies of the West have united to defend themselves against aggression and preserve and develop their free institutions. It cannot be repeated too often that European integration is in no way an alternative to Atlantic co-operation. The unity of Europe will strengthen the central sector of NATO and it will also promote the internal stability of the Atlantic Alliance.

Twice within a generation, the New World has been called in to redress the balance of the Old. To separate America from Europe would be an act of criminal folly. The unity of Europe is essential to keep them together. Then, the Western world will be strong enough to counter the common danger.

The European Community must be ready to assume its responsibility in an ever-widening measure of Atlantic co-operation. The very structure of the European Community must be seen against this background. The effort to integrate Europe is, essentially, an effort to pass beyond the age of nationalism. And it is fitting that Europe, which gave political nationalism to the world, should be the first to take a step forward, as Professor Kohn has put it so well, on the road to deeper liberty and to higher forms of integration.

Does the Old World still possess the will and creative energies to achieve this victory over itself and effect a peaceful but profound political revolution? We cannot tell. We can but continue our efforts, remembering the words of the poet:

> Knowledge we ask not—knowledge Thou has lent,
> But, Lord, the will—there lies our bitter need,
> Grant us to build, above the deep intent,
> The deed, the deed.

5

*European Integration
and the Non-Communist World*

Asian Views of an Integrated Europe

CHARLES MALIK / *Former Ambassador of Lebanon to the United States*

FROM THE point of view of a man like myself coming from the Near East and, indeed, from Lebanon itself, nothing can serve as a better guide or a more pregnant point of departure for his attitude toward and his reflections upon the question of European integration than the European myth of the rape of Europa by mighty Zeus. You will recall how, according to your own mythology, fairest and loveliest among all maidens was Europa, the daughter of the King of Sidon, or of the King of Tyre, or perhaps of a mighty king farther north in the very region near Tripoli where I come from, but by all accounts certainly daughter of some Phoenician prince.

One spring morning Europa awoke early, troubled by a strange dream, not indeed of some god or hero who sought her favors, "but of two Continents who each in the shape of a woman tried to possess her, Asia saying that she had given her birth and therefore owned her, and the other, as yet nameless, declaring that Zeus would give the maiden to her." Once awake, Europa could not go to sleep again. She summoned her companions, "girls born in the same year as herself and all of noble birth, to go out with her to the lovely blooming meadow near the sea . . . each one a maiden fairest among the fair; yet even so, Europa shone out among them as the Goddess of Love outshines the sister Graces. . . . As Zeus in heaven watched the pretty scene . . . Cupid shot one of his shafts into his heart, and that very instant he fell madly in love with Europa." He transformed himself into a beautiful bull, appeared to the girls as they were gathering flowers on that meadow, induced Europa to ride on his back and then rushed, not into, but over the wide sea until he landed in Crete. There Europa would bear Zeus "Glorious sons whose sceptres shall hold sway/Over all men on earth." And Zeus named the dark and hitherto nameless Continent, Europa.[1]

There is, of course, a sequel to this story. The father of Europa sent her brothers to search for her, and one of them, Cadmus by name, when Apollo at Delphi told him he would not find her, founded the Royal House of Thebes. He first had to fight and kill a terrible dragon, whereupon Athena appeared to him and bade him sow the earth with the dragon's teeth. "He obeyed with no idea what was to happen, and to his terror saw armed men spring up from the furrows. However, they paid no attention to him, but turned upon each other until all were killed except five, whom Cadmus induced to become his helpers." With their assistance he made "Thebes a glorious city and ruled over it in great prosperity and with great wisdom." And Herodotus says that Cadmus introduced the alphabet into Hellas.[2]

The myth of Europa and Cadmus is something very deep. It contains a measure of truth beyond what the myth-makers themselves knew or suspected. It illustrates four salient points in the historical relationships between Europe and the Near East.

The first point is the eternal interaction between these two regions. Through the Egyptians and Phoenicians, Ionia, Alexander and Rome, through Christianity, the fecund Hellenistic era, and Byzantium, through the Crusades, the wars with the Ottoman Empire, and the political, economic, and intellectual penetration of the Near East by the West since Napoleon, throughout all history, there has been under one aegis or another close interaction, interpenetration, and interstimulation between the Near East and Europe. Whether in war or in peace, whether in receiving from or in giving to each other, Europe and the Near East have not been able and probably never will be able to let each other go.

It is this great Mediterranean Sea which really gave birth to

---

[1] This account of the myth of Europa is taken from Edith Hamilton, *Mythology* (New York: The New American Library, Mentor Books, 1953), p. 78.

[2] *Ibid.*, p. 254.

everything, together with the fact that *ex oriente lux,* that has bound, apparently eternally, their fates together. Take away the original impregnation of Europe by what was first seen, suffered, known, and enacted on our shores, and you will certainly take away the very soul of European civilization. Apart from any narrow political considerations, which certainly have their place and their relative validity, and despite periodic historical misunderstandings and often estrangements and wars, the Near East, while certainly not a territorial part of Europe, nevertheless forms with Europe, from the point of view of culture and inevitable interaction, an indissoluble union. Zeus, it seems, had to fall in love with a Phoenician maiden and had to transport her to the dark lands beyond the sea, for otherwise how could these lands have been started on the road to light, truth, and being? To be is at least to have a name, and the Western Continent had to receive its very name from the East.

The second point which the myth of Europa and Cadmus brings out is that although *ex oriente lux,* this light shines not in the East, but in the West. The loveliest of maidens was born and brought up on our shores, and none other than Zeus himself fell prostrate before her. But he could not live with her in Sidon or Tyre or Beirut; he had to carry her westward, where they gave birth to those glorious sons. This has been our historical fate from the beginning. One vision after another, one creation after another, one truth after another, one being after another, arose in the Near East; but it only arose there, it did not take root there, or at least its root did not last long. We gave, but we did not retain; we created, but we did not perfect; we dreamed and longed for, but we did not achieve. The loveliest products of the Near East (for example, Christianity) were always destined to be appreciated more in the West than in the Near East. The naturalistic explanation of this strange phenomenon on the grounds of geography, race, and the ravages of wars and conquests neither affords any comfort to us nor alters the stark and tragic fact. Today in practically every facet of human existence we stand to learn from Europe or from Asia, and we have nothing to teach them. Even what Europe first learned from the Near East we have to re-learn ourselves from Europe. This whole point raises the questions of how much the Near East can really hope to enjoy the highest and deepest things in isolation.

The departure of Europe from our shores, as also the departure of Paul when he set his face to go west, as also many other departures before and since, raises radical issues about the destiny of the Near East in its relations to Europe.

Thirdly, Europa was deeply troubled by her dream. Asia claimed her, but the god prepared for her a different destiny. This same concern Europa carried over with her to the new land on which Zeus conferred her name. For the history of Europe when Europe had to face and decide its destiny as a whole, ever since Thermopylae and even earlier, consists largely in the actual, historical enactment of this nightmare of Europa the anxious question whether Europe was to run its own independent course or whether it was to be assimilated into Asia. This tribulation has time and again visited and tormented Europe, and the present form of its visitation, in the double sense of the Communist and Asian challenge, is neither the least so far, nor in all probability the last. Thus Europa's dream was prophetic both for the land of her origin and the land of her adoption. For with us in the Near East, and especially with us in Lebanon, this dialectic between Asia and the West is our perennial preoccupation. Lebanon, the very land of Princess Europa, is at once in the East and in the West, in Asia and in a deep sense Europe, and both the Parisian or New Yorker and the Iranian or Pakistani can feel perfectly and equally at home in our midst. Even physically Lebanon is so different from the surrounding arid region that you can actually ski six months of the year in our mountains. We understand and appreciate at the same time the deepest things both of the East and the West. All of this, taken together, is much more than can be said of any country in the Middle East, if not of the world. To be Asian or to be European, this is the question of our existence, and while Europe was always somehow able to resolve it in its favor, the poignancy of this question in our case consists precisely in the tragic fact that we have never been able nor are we likely ever to be able to resolve it one way or the other. Our being, therefore, appears to be essentially questionable.

Last, Cadmus searched for his sister, but did not find her, and finally, after an awful struggle with the dragon and in obedience to the god, had to settle and prosper abroad. If we search for all the lovely things that have gone out of the Near East, in order to bring them back home as though they belonged to us alone, we will never find them. If we try to close ourselves upon ourselves as though we were apart from the rest of the world, we will always come to grief. The Near East is at the heart of the world in space; the three ancient continents meet there. The Near East is at the heart of the world in time; history begins there. The Near East is at the heart of the world in the final things; the God of the West and the God of a goodly portion of the East chose to reveal themselves there. The Near East is today at the heart of the world economically; the fantastic oil deposits of the Near East are the most important prerequisite for the industry of Europe and one of the prime considerations in any calculation for war or peace or survival in the world today.

Thus, whatever of value we have produced in the past, or we possess today, can never be enjoyed by us alone, but must have universal significance. We live as much for others as for ourselves, and to rebel against this fate is to live a most miserable life. Commenting upon this aspect of our life, Professor William Ernest Hocking, of Harvard, says: "Of the Near East in general we may say that it is fated by its geography to live more than its own life, to become world-conscious, to add to its local genius a general sophistication."[3] This fate could be either tragic or glorious, depending upon whether we accept it cleverly or responsibly; depending even more deeply upon whether we pitch our tent for this world alone or for something beyond this world. But Cadmus must obey the god rather than his natural father. He must cease seeking to retrieve his sister. He must settle down in humble co-operation with others in the building of culture and peace, even if he should have to fight the most terrible of dragons for his life. Better to settle and build than to wander over the face of the earth, or over the face of one's own soul, in quest of the irretrievable.

It follows from all this that a man from the Near East, and especially a man from Lebanon, and more especially a man like myself, cannot discuss the problem of European integration as though it did not concern him at all. He is not a pure Asian and therefore he cannot view the issues involved in a spirit of indifference or of hostility. He is already Europeanly engaged. He is just enough removed to see things in some detachment and some perspective,

[3] William Ernest Hocking, *The Spirit of World Politics* (New York: The Macmillan Co., 1932), p. 432.

but he is not so removed as not to see them at all, or to see them without emotion and interest. The fate of Europe decisively affects our fate in the Near East, and I well remember how in August of 1944 there was as much rejoicing—I will not say more—in Lebanon upon the liberation of Paris as I believe there was anywhere else in the world.

I followed the events of the last decade with intense interest by reason both of my official activity and my responsibilities in Washington and at the United Nations. I took part in the United Nations deliberations which liquidated UNRRA, established machinery for the reconstruction of the war-devastated areas, set up the Economic Commission for Europe, established the International Refugee Organization, dealt with the Greek civil war, debated the developing situation in North Africa, and, in the case of the former Italian colonies, settled the fate of those territories, elaborated the Universal Declaration of Human Rights, bore upon the Indonesian problem, recommended human rights provisions that were later incorporated into the peace treaties with the eastern European and Balkan countries, and discussed disarmament and the international control of atomic energy. But above all, I watched and actively debated on three movements of the utmost importance at the United Nations which brought home to me the realities of the European situation. The first was the Communist reaction to and condemnation of the developing united front among the European and Western powers; the second was the dominant role played by the United States; and the third was the rise of the variously called Arab-Asian or Asian-African or anti-colonial bloc.

More than anything else, perhaps, the Communist pressure brought about a conscious sense of common destiny to the peoples of western Europe. The establishment of the Communist frontier at the heart of Europe, the Greek civil war, the growth of the Communist parties in western Europe, the Czechoslovak coup, the Berlin blockade all forced western Europe to consider its fate and to take steps to safeguard its independence. The movement for integration is the reaction of whatever was left of Europe to the immense and multiform Communist onslaught.

But action and reaction quickly exchange roles. The reaction to the Communist menace itself called forth a Communist reaction. At every point in the growth of the European movement the Communists reacted violently, by intimidation, by direct pressure, by attempts at subversion, by propaganda, by the utilization of the puppet Communist parties and front organizations in the Western world, and by the incitement of the dependent peoples of Asia and Africa to rebellion.

And yet it was Sir Winston Churchill, that father of the European movement, who at its beginning in 1947 assured the Russians that they stood to gain everything and to lose nothing from a more integrated Europe. This is how Sir Winston put it:

> It is alleged that advocacy of the ideal of a United Europe is nothing but a manoeuvre in the game of power politics, and that it is a sinister plot against Soviet Russia. There is no truth in this. The whole purpose of a united democratic Europe is to give decisive guarantees against aggression. Looking out from the ruins of their famous cities and from amidst the cruel devastation of their lands, the Russian people should surely realise how much they stand to gain by the elimination of the causes of war and the fear of war on the European continent. The creation of a healthy and contented Europe is the first and truest interest of the Soviet Union.[4]

The European movement, then, is a defensive movement against aggressive communism. And it is for this reason that communism will always actively combat it. But even apart from that, the living deposit of the history of Europe is rich in differences, antagonisms, and diversities which this movement cannot overcome easily. There is European nationalism, there are conflicts of interest in the economic sphere, there are diversities of culture and race, there are the age-old hostilities and rivalries, and there is the special position of the United Kingdom as at once European, English-speaking, and the mother country of the Commonwealth. It follows that any simple, idealistic concept of European unity, even in the face of the Communist menace, is excessively naive.

And yet the steps that have been taken in the last decade, the Brussels Pact, the Council of Europe, the organizations that arose in the wake of the Marshall Plan, the North Atlantic Treaty Organization and all the defense and other matters that grew from it, the Schuman Plan, all have been most remarkable, especially if

[4] Winston Churchill, Speech at the Royal Albert Hall, London, on May 14, 1947. *Keesing's Contemporary Archives,* vi (1946–48), 8606–8607.

viewed in the light of the tensions from within and the pressures from without to which every one of these arrangements has been subjected and which it has had to withstand. In the words of Chancellor Adenauer: "In Europe the answer is integration. The process of integration, which in my opinion is the great movement of our time, is also a process of regeneration."[5]

It is impossible for Europe to be united in any shape or form without Germany playing a central and positive role. Germany is not only a chief bulwark at the heart of the Continent and has been such for centuries; it is not only, in the words of Chancellor Adenauer, "the West's eastern bulwark." German industry, thought, inventiveness, and sense of duty, when wedded to the humane and democratic ideal, constitute a fountain of untold blessings, not only to Europeans, but to the whole world. It can be shown that the nuclear weapons may have conditioned, but did not in the least obliterate, the strategic importance of Germany or the value of German manpower. The functioning of the German people as peaceful, democratic, and productive members of the European community, playing their full part in honor, equality, and justice, and dedicated to the ideals of freedom, is the key to the whole problem of European integration. The mighty strides that have been taken by the German Federal Republic toward that end under the matchless leadership of Dr. Adenauer and with the statesman-like understanding and active support and foresight of France, England, and the United States, are among the primordial phenomena of this era.

But a peaceful, happy, and productive Germany at the heart of Europe necessarily means a unified Germany. If, then, the right integration of Germany into the European family is the heart of the problem of European unity, the problem of German unification is the core of the heart. There can be no United Europe without Germany and there can be no Germany without a unified German nation. But since the Federal Republic has already cast its lot with the West, since it constitutes the overwhelming majority of the German nation, and since all evidence seems to indicate that even East Germany, if permitted to make a free choice, would throw off the Communist rule and join West Germany, a Germany unified

[5] Konrad Adenauer, *World Indivisible* (New York: Harper & Brothers, 1955), p. 7.

peacefully and freely would mean a retreat of communism from the heart of Europe.

Would communism be prepared to make such a retreat in order to allow Germany and therefore Europe to be united? Obviously aggressive communism, Stalinist communism, classical communism, would not. But there are three possibilities under any one of which such a retreat is conceivable. It is conceivable if communism has radically changed its character so as to cease to think of itself as destined to dominate Europe and the world. It is conceivable under the Soviet concept of an integrated Europe which they have been putting forward during the last year or two, that is, if the Soviet Union itself becomes an integral part of the United Europe. Finally, it is conceivable that if adequate guarantees can be devised which would be entirely satisfactory to the Soviet Union, when communism retreats to its proper domain it will be entirely secure and safe there so far as external attack is concerned. It is partly the character of communism, then, partly the legitimate desire of Russia to be a responsible part of Europe, and partly Soviet fears of a strong and united Europe that externally and ultimately stand in the way of a genuine European integration.

The lifting of the Iron Curtain cannot be confined to Germany. East and southeast Europe are still part of Europe. Poland, Czechoslovakia, Hungary, the Baltic and Balkan states, all have had the most intimate political, economic, and especially cultural relations with western Europe, notably with France. Is it to be allowed that these are to be forever cut off from the West? The problem of European unity is not only how western Europe must unite in order to defend itself against aggressive communism or perish; it is not only how Germany must first integrate itself and then be integrated with western Europe, or conversely; it is also and equally how the original cultural and economic unity of the whole Continent, east and west, may be restored. When western Europe first awoke to its nakedness just after the war, it could not but start with itself. But as the European movement gained momentum, the original claims of the whole upon the part became more and more manifest. Any conception of European integration that does not include such profoundly European people as the Czechs and Poles is politically shortsighted and essentially false. But this again raises the ultimate question of the conditions under which communism and the Soviet armies may be peacefully induced to withdraw eastward. The effective lifting of the Iron Curtain from the whole of Europe at least back to the Russian frontiers, so as to permit the rise of democratic systems based on free elections, and so as to enable the energies and aspirations of the peoples of eastern Europe to complement and be complemented by the energies and aspirations of the peoples of the West, appears to be the ultimate aim of any genuine European movement, for the necessary realization of which every honorable and peaceful means is both legitimate and urgent.

The question arises at this point whether the new Soviet policy of coexistence makes a difference to this whole matter. Tension evidently has relaxed, Stalinism appears to be in the process of liquidation, fresh approaches to problems keep originating from Moscow, fruitful visits, official and unofficial, have taken place back and forth across the Communist frontier, and the atomic stalemate may have reduced the chances of aggression and of general war, so that both the Russians and the West may now feel more secure. The impulse for European integration need not therefore persist as far as any threat from the East is concerned, and a new phase of peaceful coexistence and competition may therefore be inaugurated in international relations, especially between communism and the rest of the world, and most especially in Europe itself. Let Europe then relax and enjoy peace of mind.

The bearing of coexistence on European unity could be disastrous. Unless there is absolute proof of a change of mind and heart on the part of communism, the lulling effect of coexistence may prove the deadliest weapon yet used to combat or undermine, neutralize or disintegrate, the European movement. And the required proof of a genuine change in the theory and practice of communism is precisely the lifting of the Iron Curtain to which we referred—the allowing of Europe, east and west, to unite in freedom and justice; some progress in the negotiations on disarmament; the production of unmistakable evidence that the Communist view of man, history, truth, freedom, government, and law, as taught in Communist textbooks, has fundamentally changed; the development of genuine freedom of thought, conscience, and religion in the Communist realm. These things have not happened, and since the European movement exists in part in order to induce these things, the European movement must continue. In fact it must now be intensified, precisely because the seductions and soothing of coexistence are so great. A whole civilization absolutely at stake cannot coexist in peace with its mortal enemy without first making absolutely sure that this enemy has really become its friend.

On May 10, 1956, Sir Winston Churchill said in Aachen that the principle of NATO was simple and majestic:

> We all join hands together in our wish to avoid the aggressor, whoever he may be.
> A new question has been raised by the recent Russian repudiation of Stalin. If it is sincere we have a new Russia to deal with, and I do not see why, if this is so, the new Russia should not join in support of this solemn agreement. We must realise how deep and sincere are Russia's anxieties about the safety of her homeland from foreign invasion. In a true unity of Europe, Russia must have her part.[6]

These are the words of a great statesman. Nothing would be better than if the Soviet outlook were so changed as to make it possible for Russia and the West to come to a sincere agreement on the security of Europe even in addition to the forswearing of aggression in the United Nations Charter. Nothing would be better than if Russia could organically complement the unity of Europe on a European, free, and non-Communist basis. Two things, however, are also clear from Sir Winston's speech: NATO was to be preserved and strengthened because it was "the main theme of salvation"; and the change hoped for in the repudiation of Stalin included the peaceful liberation of eastern Europe, including the unification of a free Germany.

But even if all the conditions for coexistence were completely satisfied, would that be a reason for Europe to cease to become one? The European Community antedates communism, and whether or not communism existed, the Europeans would reach for their unity. Again I quote from Dr. Adenauer:

> It is quite wrong to consider the European agreements primarily or even exclusively in terms of defense against Soviet aggression. I am convinced that these tensions between East and West will

---

[6] Winston Churchill, Speech at Aachen on May 10, 1956. *Keesing's Contemporary Archives*, x (1955–56), 14875.

pass in time. But the European agreements look forward toward a far more distant future. They will be in force for fifty years, and are intended to make a war among the European nations impossible in the future . . . the integration of Europe, as the Washington Foreign Ministers Conference recognized, is important and useful in itself, quite aside from a threat or lack of threat to Europe on the part of the Soviet Union.[7]

Sir Winston Churchill, in his advocacy of the cause of a united Europe, has always stressed the essential rightness and naturalness of this cause entirely independent of relations with the Soviet Union. In 1947 Sir Winston said:

> We accept, without question, the world supremacy of the United Nations Organisation. In the constitution agreed at San Francisco direct provision is made for regional organisations to be formed. United Europe will form one major regional entity. There is the United States, with all its dependencies. There is the Soviet Union. There is the British Empire and Commonwealth. And there is Europe, with which Great Britain is profoundly blended. Here are the four main pillars of the world temple of peace.[8]

The whole view here is that of the essential naturalness of regional and cultural groupings precisely in the service of order, stability, and peace.

Europe is provoked toward unification as much by its community of interests with America as by the Communist challenge. From the moment General Marshall launched his idea at Harvard in 1947 until today, the one persistent theme in United States policy has been the strengthening of Europe economically, politically, and militarily, and the promoting of as much integration among the members of the European family as possible. In fact, one reason for the collapse of China and the deterioration of conditions in the Middle East has been the fact that, because the resources, economic, military, and moral, of even the largest nation are limited, the United States shortly after the war decided to concentrate practically all her attention on Europe, letting matters in these other areas take their own course for the time being. The price of saving Europe

[7] Konrad Adenauer, *op. cit.*, pp. 10, 95.
[8] Winston Churchill, Speech at the Royal Albert Hall, London, on May 14, 1947. *Keesing's Contemporary Archives*, vi (1946–48), 8606.

was to neglect Asia, and considering the concrete issues at stake and the strategic and industrial importance of Europe, if a choice had to be made, this undoubtedly was the right one.

Since 1914 one thing has been unmistakably proven in international relations, and that is that Europe needed America both economically and in its own defense in time of war or peace. Without the shield of the American atom after the war who can be sure now that Europe would not have been overrun by the Communists? Without the sustenance of the Marshall Plan who can be sure that Europe would have recovered? But beyond economics and defense, the Atlantic Community, despite its manifold richness, is nevertheless culturally one. There is more creative interaction and interstimulation within it than between it and any other community in the world. It faces the world as one cultural whole, rooted in Greece, Rome, Western Christianity, Western science, Western humanism, and Western political-democratic experience. In every way, then, European integration is set within, presupposes, depends upon, merges into, is completed by, Atlantic integration.

American leadership in and for Europe, as indicated by the testimony of those who have worked with the United States, including Churchill, Eden, Bevin, Schuman, Adenauer, and Spaak, has been at once generous, understanding, unselfish, and farsighted. This is how Sir Winston expresses it:

> We must all be thankful that the nation called to the summit of the world by its mass, its energies, and its power, has not been found lacking in those qualities of greatness and nobility upon which the record of famous States depends. Far from resenting the creation of United Europe, the American people welcome and ardently sustain the resurrection of what was called the Old World, now found in full partnership with the New.[9]

The statements of United States presidents, United States secretaries of state, United States Congressional leaders, and the concrete economic, political, and military decisions and acts of the United States during the past decade all bear witness to the highmindedness of the American spirit.

The deeper roots of community in the Atlantic world are brought

---

[9] Winston Churchill, Address at The Hague Congress of Europe in May, 1948. *Loc. cit.,* p. 9317.

out in the Preamble to the North Atlantic Treaty. It is there stated that the parties to the treaty "are determined to safeguard the freedom, common heritage and civilization of their peoples, founded on the principles of democracy, individual liberty and the rule of law."[10] There is thus an absolute self-consciousness with respect to the "common heritage and civilization" of the Western peoples. European and Atlantic unity is ultimately grounded in this self-consciousness. In the modern contracted world, where every culture is awakened to self-consciousness, there is one segment of humanity enjoying "a common heritage and civilization" and compromising the European world, including its overseas offshoots, which proposes to integrate and develop itself in unison and "to live in peace with all peoples and all governments"[11] in conformity with the purposes and principles of the United Nations Charter. In the modern world, Europe, if it is to survive and shine and to remain faithful to its deepest insights and values, is unthinkable apart from the closest ties with the United States. Beyond the human—all-too-human—irritations and annoyances, carpings and nostalgias, arising on either side of the Atlantic as a result of this inevitable development, and despite the Communist liberal sowing of suspicion and estrangement, there is among the nations of the Atlantic world the overriding sense of a common destiny in this cold and dangerous world. As Barbara Ward aptly put it:

> Again, if the appeal of a European federation is the union of all nations of a common culture, it is purest arrogance to exclude the countrymen of Jefferson and Lincoln and deny to the Americas—or to the English-speaking Dominions—their essential attribute of having recreated the great traditions of the West in new continents overseas. It is an impoverishment, not an enrichment, of Europe to say that it ceased to recreate itself at some point in the middle of the eighteenth century. From the cultural standpoint, the Atlantic is as much the 'closed sea' of the West as was the Mediterranean in the heyday of the Roman Empire.[12]

The European Community appears in its distinctiveness not so

[10] Halford L. Hoskins, *The Atlantic Pact* (Washington, D. C.: Public Affairs Press, 1949), p. 77.
[11] *Ibid.*
[12] Barbara Ward, *Policy for the West* (New York: W. W. Norton and Co., 1951), p. 282.

much, as we have seen, vis-à-vis the Slavic world, nor certainly vis-à-vis the New World, but vis-à-vis Asia and Africa. The developments in Asia and Africa at once condition and are conditioned by the evolution of the European movement.

The European empires in Asia and Africa have crumbled for a number of reasons—the natural maturation of the peoples concerned, the weakening of Europe as a result of its internecine wars, the increasing potency in those territories of the European ideas of freedom and self-reliance, Communist agitation to expel western European influence from Asia and Africa, the United States example and philosophy of independence. It is the natural right of every people and culture to determine itself freely, independently, justly, and without endangering international peace and security. Such sincere self-determination can only serve the cause of peace. This applies as much to the countries behind the Iron Curtain as to the peoples and cultures of Asia and Africa.

As a result of this variously-caused self-determination of Asia and Africa, Europe has had to fall back upon its own distinctive resources. First it must compensate for its economic losses in Asia and Africa by economic co-operation and intensive industrialization among its peoples. Then it must work out new relations of friendship and co-operation with the new Asia and Africa, and this requires some prior understanding among the European nations themselves as to the broad principles of the new European posture in the world. The deterioration of many an overseas relationship could have been avoided, or at least arrested, if at the right moment the Europeans had been able to rise above their own bickerings. Europe cannot afford to see Asia and Africa developing a hostile bloc against it. Nor can it sit by unconcerned if country after country in the two continents should slip, whether actually or potentially, behind the Iron Curtain. European integration, then, both for mutual self-help and collective self defense, is a direct outcome of the lessening of European influence abroad. When people are thrown back upon themselves, two contradictory processes set in. First they irritate each other, but then they are forced to seek a deeper community among themselves. If the first tendency prevails, they are doomed; but the realization of the European Community already demonstrates that when it comes to a decision in a moment of danger there are infinite resources of wisdom, vitality, imaginativeness, and accommodation in the European soul.

The Asian and African peoples are becoming increasingly responsible for their own fate. It is one thing to close your eyes for the time being to your real problems while concentrating all your energies upon the struggle for independence, blaming foreign rule for all your ills; it is another thing entirely to find yourself suddenly responsible for your own situation and to have to face and live with your problems alone, year in and year out. Some Europeans have a way of bewailing their lot in the modern world. But let it be said that the challenges facing Europe are nothing compared to those facing the leaders of Asia and Africa. The new Asian and African leadership requires and deserves every understanding, every sympathy, every assistance, nay every love, from its more experienced brethren in the old Continent of Europe.

The problems of Asia and Africa are absolutely legion. They can never be faced without two kinds of wisdom, neither of which abounds in Asia and Africa—the wisdom and welfare that science and technology alone provide, and the wisdom that enables fellow citizens to live and prosper together in peace. Scientific wisdom and political wisdom will be two of the most pre-eminent needs of Asia and Africa for the next one hundred years.

The struggle in the political field will be between ideas of free democracy and ideas of totalitarian control. Europe can only stand in its impact on independent Asia and Africa upon free democracy. This does not at all mean that the West may naively expect its own view of man and government to take root unchanged in the cultures of Asia and Africa. Asia and Africa are very sensitive to success. So long as communism receives no serious setback anywhere, but, on the contrary, moves from triumph to triumph, the Asian and African people will continue to be profoundly impressed by it.

Concerning science and technology, there are only three significant sources of these goods in the world today—the Soviet Union, western Europe, and North America. Some of the most radical issues facing Asia and Africa, especially in the economic and social fields, require for their solution a type of wisdom existing outside Asia and Africa. It follows that in science and technology the independence of Asia and Africa is a myth. The question, therefore, for Europe and the West in general is how far they can establish friendly political and moral relations with Asia and Africa, either in co-operation or competition with the Communist realm, or to its exclusion, in order to enable the West to help the East on honorable and mutually beneficial terms with the skills and methods which the East desperately needs.

Not by lording it over the East nor infringing on its dignity, not by endeavoring again to exploit it nor reimposing Western rule over it, not by being callous and indifferent to its woes or hostile to its interests, nor by forming a Western bloc against it, can the West help and work together with the East. But the West can do so by treating the East on equal terms, by being humble before it while remaining sure of its grounds, by entering into a creative partnership with it for the sake of freedom and human welfare, and by being worthy of the West's own deepest spiritual, intellectual, and moral convictions, convictions which spring from a wonderful religion of love, justice, beauty, truth, respect for man, and mutual helpfulness, and which in their universal intent most certainly embrace East and West alike.

European integration is a necessity for the West. When Europe achieves its unity and feels its strength, it might then be tempted to reconquer the East. But there are better relations between East and West than those of conquest, even when the West is strong. There is the relation of partnership between equals in the interest of man and of all that is noble and high and good. And man and what is true and noble and good certainly reside in the depths of the Western conscience. Thus the fall into the temptation of force and conquest is not a fated event—and certainly not for the European soul.

It is also possible that when Europe achieves a sense of security through strength in unity it will be far more relaxed in its dealings with the East. The secure is less nervous and more human than the insecure. A strong and happy Europe under the rule of its better self may therefore prove a wonderful neighbor to Asia and Africa.

The problem of European unity is not only an economic or political, military or social, problem. Europe is or is not one by reason of its spirit and its mind. The grounds of European integration must first be sought in the depths of the spirit, and if there are problems in these other realms, it is because the spirit is in trouble. May it not be that if you meet the spirit on its own terms, namely, if you dispel fear, conquer selfishness, overcome narrowness of vision, soften national pride, instill trust, promote a common positive purpose, develop an overriding message drawn not from the accidents of the moment but from the abiding roots of the European experience for the last two thousand years, you will then move more than half way toward resolving the economic and political difficulties? Is the spirit so impotent, so secondary, so derivative that it must wait helplessly upon the economic and political before it can speak and make itself felt? May it not be that at the heart of the entire crisis lie precisely this original weakening of the spiritual sense of independence and creativity, this overwhelming of the spirit by the material, the economic, and the political, this inability of the spirit to assert its dominion over them all? May it not be that what cannot be achieved by human design may at least be and is in fact being approximated by prayer and by faith

I do not believe the Europe of the church, the Europe of the wonderful humane tradition, can possibly fail to rise to the challenge of the moment. But above the din of the economic and political you need the ringing voice of the saint, the philosopher, and the poet. These men have vision and faith and can and do rise above cynicism and weariness. One Saint Francis, one Saint Augustine, and one Goethe, fully understanding the concrete character of the times and given the widest artistic access to the minds of the masses, will put to shame the forebodings of all the Marxes, all the Spenglers, and all the weary statesmen.

It is not enough to be on the defensive nor to reject the false and the demonic nor to seek strength through unity in order to survive. It is not enough to be a good neighbor to Asia and Africa. All this is necessary and legitimate, but it is not sufficient. What is needed above all is active faith in the ultimate values of Europe.

Europe is rooted in Greek reason and love of beauty, in Roman law and sense of order, in Christian charity and faith in God and the infinite worth of the individual human soul, in the practice of democratic government based upon free elections, and in the conviction that without genuine freedom of thought, of conscience, and of being, life is not worth living. The basis of the possibility of European integration is the sharing by all the European peoples in these things.

More than anything else, it is weakness in or unfaithfulness to one or another of these elements in the existential constitution of Europe that has brought about the present bewilderment of the European mind.

What is therefore needed is a vigorous reaffirmation of the authentic European conception of man and the good life. On the basis of this living conception alone can Europe not only integrate itself, but also face and answer the Communist and Eastern challenge. Europe must rediscover and reaffirm its own soul. For it can be shown that the multiform challenge now facing Europe is a point-by-point contradiction of its cumulative positive heritage for three thousand years. I do not believe there is anything comparable to the richness and certainty of this heritage. When Europe knows what it believes, when it is not ashamed of what it believes, and when it rises above the compulsions of economics, politics, and power to the vision of God and of the creative spirit of man, then not only the distant cousins of Princess Europa, but the whole world, will bless Europa's name, and not only Cadmus, but everyone, will end his doubts and searchings and settle down in order to build.

The North Atlantic Community
and Western Europe

L. D. WILGRESS / *Canadian Ambassador to NATO*

THE PLACE of western Europe, whether further integrated or not, in the world today should be considered in connection with that larger association which has come to be known as the North Atlantic Community. Unlike the proposal for a United States of Europe, this is a very new conception. It emerged when the consequences of the last war became clear to all and we were confronted with a marked change in the balance of forces. The disappearance of German and Japanese power had left the Soviet Union as the dominant military force of Europe and Asia. West of the Soviet sphere of power, there was a group of nations which were unable to defend themselves against the Soviet Union without the help of the other dominant military force that had emerged as a result of the war, the United States of America.

It was of vital importance to the security of the United States that Soviet power should not be extended over the countries of western Europe with their collectively large population and their highly developed industries. It was of still more vital importance to these countries that they should not become subject to Soviet power. Besides this community of security interests, there were other interests that the North Atlantic countries had in common. Most of the population of both the United States and Canada are descended from people who emigrated from the countries of western Europe. It was they who carried across the Atlantic the civilization that had been developed in Europe. Later on, this civilization was developed further on both sides of the Atlantic into what we now describe as modern civilization, a civilization distinguished by three characteristics—democracy, individual liberty, and the rule of law. All three would be extinguished if Soviet power penetrated into any part of the North Atlantic Community.

The wealthiest and most highly developed countries of the world are included in the North Atlantic Community. Together they account for approximately two-thirds of total world trade. In a very real sense the Atlantic region represents the mainspring of the world. Political and economic developments within the region have repercussions far beyond the scope of similar developments elsewhere. The concept of the North Atlantic Community, therefore, is founded on something more than the security needs of the moment. Yet it was those security needs which gave birth to the instrument through which the community is now finding expression. That instrument is the North Atlantic Treaty Organization, generally known as NATO.

So far as I am aware, the concept of the North Atlantic Community was first described by Walter Lippmann in a book which he wrote during the last war. In doing so he showed remarkable prescience. It was some years after the war, however, before the North Atlantic Alliance came into being. Even then the process was hastened by a series of events which brought home forcibly to the North Atlantic people the imperative need for co-operative efforts. These events all stemmed from Soviet actions. It is true to say, therefore, that Stalin was the chief originator of the North Atlantic Alliance. The strenuous attempts now being made by the Russians to disrupt the alliance are the measure of its success. The concept of the North Atlantic Community is so real, however, that it is probable that the alliance would have materialized irrespective of the form taken by postwar Soviet policy. Stalin hastened the process, but the basis of the alliance is the genuine community of interests between its members.

The alliance at the start took the form primarily of a defensive military pact. After the war, it soon became evident that the wartime co-operation between the allies, which had led them to victory, was not being carried on in peacetime. The Western powers disarmed while the Russians remained armed. Gradually it dawned on Western opinion that the destruction of German power had left a vacuum in Europe. This vacuum was likely to be filled by the Soviet Union unless some counterweight could be found to maintain the balance.

This led at first to a groping for the realization of a United States of Europe, an idea which had evoked much sympathy and intellectual support in the period between the two world wars. Opinion in Great Britain, however, was cool. Looking across the seas at their world-wide interests, particularly those in the Commonwealth, the British were doubtful about the effect on these wider commitments of their participation in European unity. Bevin, then British Foreign Secretary, took the initiative in proposing, as an alternative to a united Europe, a defensive pact with France and then, after this had been concluded in the Treaty of Dunkirk, a broader pact embracing the United Kingdom, France, and the three Benelux countries. The result was the Brussels Treaty. Both the Dunkirk and Brussels treaties were designed in theory as a protection against the resurgence of German militarism, but in reality they were the first steps toward the restoration of a balance of power.

It soon became evident that the Brussels Treaty countries were not strong enough to serve as a counterweight to Soviet power. The assistance of the United States was necessary if a proper balance was to be restored. Three actions by the Soviet Union brought home the urgent necessity for such a restoration of the balance of forces. The first of these actions was the Soviet Union's rejection in 1947 of the Marshall Plan and of the curt order to the satellite countries to follow suit. The second action was the Communist seizure of power in Czechoslovakia in 1948. The third was the blockade of Berlin in the winter of 1948–1949. This was the Soviet answer to the successful efforts of the Western powers to rehabilitate West Germany.

Even before this third hammer blow fell, events had begun to take shape. St. Laurent, the present Canadian Prime Minister, had shown the way in a speech he delivered before the United Nations General Assembly in November, 1947. He indicated that the failure of the United Nations to provide security would make it necessary for likeminded countries to organize collective self-defense in accordance with article 51 of the United Nations Charter. About the same time that the Brussels Treaty was concluded in 1948, Senator Vandenberg introduced his resolution into the United States Senate, where it received overwhelming support. This showed that both parties in Congress were willing to effectuate the Truman Doctrine, which had been declared a year before when the United States took over the responsibility of protecting Greece and Turkey from Communist infiltration.

These developments made the next step very obvious. During the latter part of 1948 and the first few months of 1949, negotiations took place for the conclusion of the North Atlantic Treaty, which was signed on April 4, 1949. In the preamble to the treaty, the parties declared their determination to safeguard the freedom, common heritage, and civilization of their peoples, founded on the principles of democracy, individual liberty, and the rule of law. Thus we see that a movement which began by groping for a European solution ended up with a North Atlantic one.

Because it was designed to fill an urgent need for collective self-defense, the North Atlantic Treaty was primarily a defensive military pact. Each of the parties agreed to consider an armed attack against any one as an attack against all. In support of this agreement the members of the alliance undertook by self-help and mutual aid to strengthen their military capacity to resist aggression. Rearmament was to be on a collective and co-operative basis.

At first, progress on this military front was painfully slow. Then came the event which profoundly altered the whole tempo of activities. This was the sudden attack on South Korea by Communist forces in the summer of 1950. This showed that the Communist powers were not above using force to accomplish their aims of territorial expansion. It was a clear indication that the outbreak of another world war could be regarded as an immediate, rather than a remote, possibility. From that time onward the individual rearmament programs of the member countries were greatly accelerated. In September, 1950, the important decision was taken to establish an "integrated military force, adequate for the defense of freedom in Europe." This meant that from an organization concerned with planning and co-ordinating a collective defense program, NATO became a body to which the member countries transferred a considerable part of the direct responsibility for their own security. This was a remarkable surrender of sovereignty to be made in peacetime.

Thus it was that events, particularly Communist actions, tended to emphasize the primarily military character of the North Atlantic Alliance. But this was not intended to be merely a military alliance. Before the treaty began to take shape, the late Mr. Bevin of the United Kingdom referred to the need of establishing "some form of union, formal or informal in character, in Western Europe, backed by the United States and the dominions." He further stated that what was necessary was "such a mobilization of moral and material force as would inspire confidence and energy within and respect elsewhere." St. Laurent of Canada stressed the importance of developing "the dynamic counter-attraction to communism of a free, prosperous and progressive society." The reasons for this emphasis on something more positive and more constructive than a mere military alliance are not difficult to find. When plans were being drawn up during the war for a security system that would minimize the possibility of future wars, it was realized that there would have to be much more attention paid to economic and social betterment than had been the case in the past. Plans were made, therefore, for an economic and social council as part of the machinery of the United Nations and for a whole series of specialized agencies covering the economic and social fields. The great increase in the number of independent sovereign nations, the narrowing of the world through the progressive improvement of rapid transportation, and the growing complexity of relations between nations all served to make imperative much closer international co-operation. Unfortunately, many of the hopes held out for the intergovernmental agencies set up after the war were frustrated by the obstructive tactics of the Russians. This led to the tendency to set up complementary agencies, particularly in the economic field, where like-minded countries could pursue some of these aims on a narrower, but more effective, front.

Canada took the lead in insisting that there should be a provision in the North Atlantic Treaty to serve as a focal point for these aspirations. The concept of the North Atlantic Community greatly appealed to the imagination of Canadians. For the first time we saw the possibility of our close participation in an international association which would appeal equally to all sections of our population. Included in the community was our great and powerful neighbor to the south, with whom we had intimate relations. The community also included the United Kingdom, with whom we had close historical ties and with whom we shared participation in the British Commonwealth of Nations. Nearly half of our population were descended from ancestors born in the British Isles. The community embraced France, to which country 30 per cent of our population could trace their ancestry. The great bulk of the remainder of our population traced their origins back to the other countries of the North Atlantic Community.

Moreover, Canada had only recently grown up to be a nation. While we have been completely self-governing for nearly ninety years, it is only in my lifetime that our sense of nationhood has matured and that we have begun to play an important part on the world stage. We are most anxious to preserve our national identity and our newly acquired sense of nationhood. At the same time, surveying the world scene we see clearly the need for restraint on the exercise of individual national sovereignty. We realize the importance of developing the closest possible co-operation between nations. To us it is self-evident that this co-operation should be particularly close between countries having a community of interests. Our partnership in the British Commonwealth of Nations, which like Canada has evolved slowly into its present workman-like arrangement, makes us familiar with the possibilities of such close co-operation, where ability to agree upon fundamentals is not vitiated by agreement to disagree on less essential matters. At the same time, having trade interests of a world-wide character, we realize that closer co-operation with some nations should not exclude co-operation with others.

Thus it was that on the insistence of Canada, but with support from other countries, the North Atlantic Treaty became something broader than a mere military alliance. It is set forth in the preamble that the parties "seek to promote stability and well-being in the North Atlantic area." The means for effecting this are covered by article 2 of the treaty. This provides that the parties contribute toward the further development of peaceful and friendly international relations by strengthening their free institutions, by bringing about a better understanding of the principles upon which these institutions are founded, and by promoting conditions of stability and well-being. The article then goes on to provide that the parties shall seek to eliminate conflict in their international economic policies and shall encourage economic collaboration between any and all of them.

Not a great deal has been done directly by NATO to carry out the provisions of article 2 of the treaty. An information policy has been developed to keep the peoples of the North Atlantic Community informed not only about the progress in building up defense, but also about the links that bind them together. While not falling within the scope of article 2, the progress made in the development of political consultation has been most encouraging and is a means of increasing the general realization of the existence of a North Atlantic Community. It is in the economic sphere that NATO has found the most difficulty in giving direct expression to the mandate conferred upon the alliance by article 2 of the treaty. This is because the field was pretty well pre-empted by other international organizations set up before NATO came into existence.

It was not considered wise for NATO to duplicate work that already was being done effectively elsewhere. The members of the North Atlantic Community, moreover, have been giving concrete expression to the provisions of article 2 of the treaty through their co-operation within the framework of the other international organizations. These bodies have a membership wider than that of NATO. In most cases economic co-operation is more effective if extended over a broader base than the members of the North Atlantic Alliance provide. The international economic organizations that are important from the point of view of article 2 of the North Atlantic Treaty are the International Monetary Fund, the International Bank for Reconstruction and Development, the General Agreement on Tariffs and Trade, and most important of all, the Organization for European Economic Co-operation, better known as the OEEC.

The OEEC is often spoken of as the most successful of the many postwar experiments in international organization. It has behind it a remarkable eight-year record of constructive achievement and effective close co-operation between nations. It is in no sense a supra-national institution. It is an intergovernmental body. Its decisions are subject to the unanimity rule. All of the European members of NATO are full members of OEEC and the United States and Canada are associate members. From the point of view of article 2 of the treaty, therefore, OEEC goes very far to fulfill the requirements of an agency through which the members of the North Atlantic Community can co-operate closely together in the economic field. Its disadvantages for that purpose arise from the fact that it was set up as a western European regional organization and not as one covering the whole of the North Atlantic Community. Although the United States and Canada participate in its work, they do so as associate and not as full members. The membership of OEEC being wider than that of NATO, moreover, there can be no formal link between the two organizations, and a NATO country cannot invoke article 2 of the North Atlantic Treaty in any discussions that take place in the OEEC forum.

Because of these disadvantages of working through other bodies, it is now being proposed that the NATO countries discuss economic questions from time to time as they arise. Such discussions would be concerned primarily with the broad political implications of these questions and would, therefore, represent a further extension of the present practice of regular political consultation. In this manner NATO could be developed as an agency for organizing common policy in fields other than the military, that is, in the fields covered by article 2 of the Treaty. Due care would have to be taken not to give the impression to non-NATO countries that there was to be a rigid common front of the NATO countries in other international organizations. Subject to this precaution, it should be possible to find a means of organizing a common political and economic approach to world problems and of co-ordinating the views of the member governments as to how they should meet threats which are other than military.

Western Europe is an essential part of the North Atlantic Community. The concept of that community grew out of the realization that the destinies of western Europe and North America are inextricably linked. Any steps taken to strengthen the defensive capacity and stability of a part of the community is of benefit to the whole community. The only thing we have to be careful about is that any steps taken to increase the unity of some of the nations comprising the community will not jeopardize the unity of the community as a whole. Proposals for European integration have to be judged from their conformity to these criteria. When a purely European solution to a problem confronting western Europe is not found to be feasible, a North Atlantic solution can often provide the right answer.

This has already been the experience in the defense field. We have seen that the first stage in the evolution of the North Altantic Treaty was an effort to bolster the common defense of western Europe. There was a similar experience in connection with the perplexing question of German rearmament. The first approach was for the creation of a European Defense Community, but after four years of acrimonious debate it was finally decided to scrap this European solution in favor of a North Atlantic one. The admittance of Germany into the Western European Union can now be seen in retrospect as merely providing a European bridge across which the Federal Republic could enter the North Atlantic Community.

It is possible that the experience may be repeated in connection with the development of nuclear energy for peaceful purposes. The proposal has been made for the integration of national efforts with supranational features. There is much to be said in favor of this approach. Here we have a brand-new industry with great potentialities for the future and without those well-entrenched vested national interests that make progress in other fields so difficult. Special efforts are necessary if the countries on the Continent are to catch up with developments in the nuclear energy field. The proponents of integration have been pointing in particular to the great cost and the enormous technical difficulties involved in the construction of an isotope-separation plant for the production of enriched uranium. President Eisenhower, however, recently announced that the United States would offer twenty metric tons of enriched uranium to be used by other countries for peaceful purposes under appropriate safeguards. This offer requires the European countries to think carefully before embarking on a costly and technically difficult enterprise, which the advance of scientific knowledge could render obsolete before it has been very long in operation. An isotope-separation plant is a heavy consumer of power and is best located at a place where there is a minimum of other demands for power. It may be, therefore, that the European countries will conclude that for the time being it might be better to rely on supplies of enriched uranium from North Africa.

The alternative to integration with supranational features is close co-operation. Both involve the relinquishment of national sovereignty, although to a less degree in the case of close co-operation. Whenever there is an agreement between two or more countries the sovereignty of the parties is diminished to the extent that they agree to abide by its terms. The formal renunciation of sovereignty is not necessary. The advantage of close co-operation over integration with supranational features is that it encourages the participation of a greater number of countries.

The outstanding example of successful integration has been the creation of the European Coal and Steel Community. Remarkable progress has been made in the elimination of tariffs and other barriers to the trade in coal and steel within the community. Freight discrimination among the members of the community has been reduced. All of this has led to an expansion of trade in the products concerned. It is conceivable, but doubtful, that the same results could have been attained by the conclusion of an agreement without the supranational features. The impetus for the creation of the community, however, came at a time when there was a strong drive in western Europe for the supranational approach.

It is now proposed to capitalize on the success of the experiment in the coal and steel sector by a frontal attack on all sectors simultaneously. This is the proposal for a common market. While the gains from the creation of a common market will be enormous, it is one which will be very difficult to attain. The differences in cost structures present formidable problems of an economic character. The breaking down of the resistance of the vested interests in national protectionism can give rise to sharp political repercussions. There is also the danger that, instead of achieving a genuine customs union in twelve or fifteen years' time, the proposal would be carried out only a quarter or half way toward a full customs union. We would then be left with a new preferential system, the members of which would be discriminating in favor of each other against the rest of the world. This could have prejudicial effects on the unity of the North Atlantic Community and could also operate against the real interests of the six countries contemplating a common market.

The economies of these countries, although to some extent complementary, are all dependent to varying degrees upon trade outside Europe for their essential requirements of raw materials and foodstuffs. Probably few countries have more to gain from the continued strict application of the most-favored-nation clause. It would deal a severe blow to the maintenance of the European standard of living if the six countries should find themselves the least-favored nations in other parts of the world. Yet this could happen because the formation of a discriminatory group among countries so important in world trade could lead to the formation elsewhere of other discriminatory groups or preferential systems.

It would not be in the interests of the western European countries to start a stampede in the direction of discriminatory agreements, bilateral trade balancing, encouragement of inefficient production, and lower standards of living. A new preferential group could start such a stampede. This would not be the case with a genuine customs union or a free-trade area in sectors other than coal and steel, since these are generally recognized as exceptions to the principles of nondiscrimination. These exceptions are consistent with the trade rules embodied in the General Agreement on Tariffs and Trade. The interests of the western European countries could be served best of all if the United States at some appropriate time in the near future could take the lead in a renewed drive for the convertibility of currencies and the multilateral approach to freer trade and payments. This would be a truly North Atlantic solution in full keeping with the spirit of article 2 of the treaty.

History as well as geography inclines western Europe to trade contacts with the outside world. With the rapid expansion of consumer goods industries in other continents, intra-European trade has taken on a new significance. The character, however, rather than the volume, of trade with other continents is apt to change, because as these countries outside of the North Atlantic Community develop economically, the standards of living of their peoples will rise and so will the demand for imported goods. The extraordinary resurgence of the western European economy in the past few years and the expansion of European exports to third countries belie the allegation that European industry cannot compete with North American industry. Much still remains to be done to bring stability to the economies and commercial relations of western Europe as well as of other countries of the free world, but the future economic potential of the western European countries can hardly be in doubt.

There is little possibility of creating in western Europe another political group to match the economic power of the United States and the Soviet Union, the two super-states that have emerged as a result of the last war. Each of these two super-states is characterized by a large population, a great expanse of territory, abundant natural resources, and only minor dependence upon foreign trade.

Western Europe has a large population, but it lacks the compact territory and the natural resources necessary to match the United States and the Soviet Union. It is much more dependent upon imports for essential requirements than either of these two states.

To avoid the risk of becoming subject to Communist domination, the nations of Western Europe require the opportunity to develop further their national or regional identities in close co-operation with American power. Whether they do this by continuing as separate nations closely co-operating with one another, or by progressive integration between some of them leading eventually to political union, depends upon the free choice of the majority of their peoples. Either course is consistent with the concept of the North Atlantic Community. Seen in this light as a flexible league of freedom, the North Atlantic Community is an idea which, I am confident, will win increasing support among the peoples of all our nations.

The United States and the Integration of Europe

HENRY STEELE COMMAGER / *Professor of American History, Amherst College*

My theme is not so much America *and* the Union of Europe, but America *as* the Union of Europe. For in the perspective of distance and of time perhaps the most remarkable thing about America is precisely this, that it does vindicate in so many ways the promise of the motto first contrived by Benjamin Franklin, John Adams, and Thomas Jefferson: *E Pluribus Unum*. It is many in one; it is all Europe in one. More, it is all mankind in one. The fact is elementary, but its very obviousness sometimes prevents us from appreciating it, for we all tend to be chary of the obvious. It has furnished the theme for a hundred novels, plays, songs, and a thousand learned monographs. Europeans are doubtless most familiar with what might be called their part of the story, with the fact that the Irish in America outnumber the Irish in Ireland, that New York and Chicago are among the largest of Italian cities, Cleveland and Buffalo of Polish, Minneapolis and Omaha of Scandinavian. It is, perhaps appropriate to remind you that the process of assimilation has embraced non-Europeans as well. We boast a million or more French-Canadians, over a million Mexicans, more than a million Puerto Ricans, hundreds of thousands of Orientals, to say nothing of the sixteen to seventeen million Americans of African origins whose presence confronts Americans with that dilemma so perspicuously explored by a great European, Gunnar Myrdal.

What we have here is a vast and continuous unification of Europe.

The "American Farmer," Hector St. John Crèvecoeur, described the process (he called it Americanization) in the third of his remarkable *Letters*. The European, he said, when he finds himself an independent farmer, becomes an American almost overnight. He throws off his Old World allegiance, and with this he throws off, too, his Old World habits of thought, his Old World prejudices and hostilities and antagonisms. This description, written about 1780, is wonderfully prophetic. For what is most remarkable about European unification in America is that it has come about so easily and so peaceably, that it has come from within rather than from without, that it has come voluntarily and by democratic processes. Unification of Europe in America has been achieved without religious wars, without racial wars, and without even that class war so confidently predicted by Marxist dialecticians. And for the overwhelming majority it has come not as a series of sacrifices, but as a fulfillment, not as a traumatic experience, but as a creative experience.

It is not only in the obvious physical—almost physiological—sense that America unified Europe. In the cultural and intellectual sense, too, the United States achieved and is still in process of achieving a sort of amalgamation or synthesis of European civilization. It is not merely that America inherited (as a matter of nature and of right) the whole of European civilization—the ancient traditions from Judea and Greece and Rome, the modern contributions from England and France and Germany and Italy—but that in a characteristically energetic fashion Americans undertook to acquire the best of each current European culture and to assimilate it to American culture. It is an instructive story and a moving one, too, and although it sometimes had vulgar aspects (as in the bodily transplanting of European castles to America), it is fair to say that if a great power is to display imperialism, it is well that that imperialism should be concentrated on the aggrandizement of culture rather than on its destruction.

At the end of the eighteenth century it was to London that the American artists went for study, and for patronage. Early in the new century the sculptors descended on Florence and Rome—at one time there were over fifty American sculptors with studios in Italy—and some lingered on. The philosophers turned to the Germany of Kant and Fichte, but happily transformed and Americanized their doctrines; the theologians levied on Tübingen and later on Marburg and Basle; the painters shifted from London to Paris, to Barbizon, and some went to Dusseldorf (which gave us "Washington Crossing the Delaware"). America led the world in popular education, but in the 1840's educators like Horace Mann and Henry Barnard were studying the educational systems of Prussia, and a little later it was Switzerland that inspired the American kindergarten. American doctors and surgeons studied in Edinburgh and Leyden and Paris. Architects levied, almost indiscriminately, on every country: on classical Greece and Rome, on Georgian England, and, alas, on Victorian, on Gothic, on Renaissance France, and even on medieval Germany. And American men of letters levied, similarly, on every country for the content and style of literature—classical, romantic, and naturalistic, imaginative and critical and scholarly.

Perhaps the ultimately important thing about all this is not that Washington Irving drew on Granada for romanticism and Longfellow took the meter of Kalevala for "Hiawatha;" that Hiram Powers and Horatio Greenough studied sculpture in Rome and Allston and Page painted in that same center of art; that the jurist Joseph Story drew on Mansfield and Eldon for the law merchant and William Livingstone on Beccaria for a more humane penal system; that theologians like Theodore Parker could rejoice in Strauss and translate De Wette, and philosophers like Ripley and Hedge bathed themselves in Kantian idealism, and anti-slavery reformers like Garrison found inspiration and support from a Wilberforce or a Granville Sharp. Perhaps the important thing, is rather, that these and others were able to carry their findings back with them to America without embarrassment or difficulty, and fitted them to American needs and put them to American work without suspicion or opposition.

Canada and Australia offer analogous rather than comparable histories. Both countries have fused disparate elements into a national unity, although it is proper to add that the fusion between the French and the British north of the Canadian-American boundary is rather less complete than the fusion to the south, and that Australian immigration policy has been less hospitable than American in the last century or so. Yet who can doubt that in both of these vast and rapidly growing nations, as in the United States, we are witnessing the process of European unification.

There is, needless to add, one other nation which has successfully organized a European union. When Sir Winston Churchill gave that great speech which, in a sense, inspired the present movement for European unity, it was to this state that he referred as an example and a model for the whole of Europe. "All the while," he reminded us, "there is a remedy which, if it were generally and spontaneously adopted, would, as if by a miracle, transform the whole scene and would, in a few years, make all Europe . . . as free and as happy as Switzerland is today." Here, in this remarkable Swiss laboratory, we have a European microcosm of the American macrocosm—a small country with two faiths, three languages, and a score of separate histories and traditions, all bound together in a common nation and a common loyalty. And, although Switzerland is far and away the most encouraging example of what Europeans can do when they have the will to harmonize their differences in larger unity, it is not the only example; there is Belgium with its Walloon and Flemish elements, and Finland with Finnish and Swedish, and Britain herself with the Scots, the Welsh, and at least some of the Irish living happily together under a single flag and crown.

There have been, of course, ambitious efforts to unify Europe, or efforts to unite it on an ambitious scale. The achievements of the Universal Church of the Holy Roman Empire, and of the all-European Crusades come to mind, but we can dismiss them as largely irrelevant to our problem because they flourished before the rise of modern nationalism. There was something of a union, or at least a community, in the eighteenth century, too. During the era we call the Enlightenment it was possible for philosophers and scholars and artists and scientists, and for the aristocracy, too, to move freely from country to country. It was an age when the claims of learning and science and art, and even of class (if the upper) took precedence over the claims of the nation, when Frederick the Great could use French as the language of his court while fighting the French; when George III could retain the American, Benjamin West, as painter to his court while fighting the Americans; when Turgot and Franklin could decree that no harm should come to Captain Cook because he was engaged in work useful to humanity; when the American-born Benjamin Thompson could emerge as Count Rumford of the Holy Roman Empire, organize the Royal Society, reorganize the kingdom of Bavaria, and leave his fortune to create the Rumford chairs of physics and chemistry at Harvard College; when Napoleon's mother could, with impunity, invest her money in British securities; when during the height of war Jefferson could remind his compatriot, the scientist David Rittenhouse, that it was never the intention of Providence to waste the genius of a Newton on the affairs of state, and urge that he give up public service and go back to his experiments! It was a very real community, this empire of reason, but it was one that functioned on a small stage and for but a brief moment, and whose benefits were limited to a narrow circle of the elect. It was not an international community strong enough to resist the rough impact of nationalism.

The era of nationalism itself has witnessed three major attempts at unification: Napoleon's effort to establish a European imperium; Hitler's attempt to impose Nazi rule on the Western world; and the current drive of the Communists to establish not only a European, but a global, hegemony. These three enterprises have two things in common: they are imposed from without and not from within, and they are imposed by force and not by reason. Perhaps we may already say that they have a third thing in common—that they are unsuccessful. The only really successful unifications remain, then, on a small scale Switzerland and on a large scale the United States. Can Europe unify on a small scale only in Switzerland, or can Europe unify on a large scale only outside Europe?

If we look at this problem from the perspective of the United States, the difficulties seem to be not so much economic or military, or even political, as historical, cultural, and psychological. It is, apparently, easier for Europeans to achieve at least partial unity in the economic, military, and political realms than in the social and cultural. It is easier to reduce tariff barriers than to reduce the barriers between universities; easier to do away with visas than to do away with the hurdles that get in the way of recognition of professional degrees or certificates; easier to arrange monetary agreements than to standardize library classification or practices. Belgium joins cheerfully in a program of economic and military co-operation, but the ancient university at Louvain must maintain in effect two faculties to satisfy the demands of the Walloons and the Flemings, although each student group knows well the language of the other. Skane was for centuries part of Denmark, but now Danish books have to be translated into Swedish if they are to be read ten miles from Elsinore, and though Norway and Denmark have had a common language for some centuries, the Norse seem as eager as the Irish to encourage a language, or languages, of their own. Or, to turn from the particular to the general, UNESCO seems to have done less to mitigate nationalist misunderstanding than OEEC, and European intellectuals have, in the past decade, contributed rather more than their normal share to accentuating and exacerbating differences within the community of Western civilization, especially the differences between the European and American branches of that community.[1]

How have Europeans in America managed to avoid so many of the misunderstandings, prejudices, enmities, and wars that afflicted them in Europe? How did it happen that Europeans, who repudiated or shattered their very genuine community of culture in the Old World, nevertheless carried that community with them and reconstructed it in the New? How did it happen that Europeans, unable to avoid religious conflicts in Europe, achieved religious tolerance in America; unable to mitigate the ravages of chauvinistic nationalism and aggressive imperialism in Europe, built up in America a nation free of nationalism, a colonial power that abjured colonialism, and a world power that is not yet imperialistic?

There is no pat set of reasons that I can submit for the success of European unification in America, but there are historical processes, habits, and institutions which help to explain it.

One of the elementary and most important of these is the federal system. The great Dutch historian, Pieter Geyl, recently said, with understandable impatience:

> I may seem dangerously near the conclusion that only trained historians are fit to rule the world. In all sincerity that is not what I mean, although I can't deny that I have sometimes wished that, for instance, American statesmen who now exercise so direct and profound an influence on the destinies of the world, knew more about the history of Europe. They might not, in that case, talk so lightly about European federation.

True enough, but one might express the wish, too, that European statesmen knew more about American history. They might not in that case talk so desperately about European federation. It is not by chance that the great European statesman who knows most about history, including American history (I mean, of course, Winston

[1] See any issue of *Le Monde* or *The New Statesman and Nation*.

Churchill), is also the one who is the inspiration of the movement for European union.

It is, of course, folly to suggest American federalism as a pattern for Europe. The situations are profoundly different. But the important thing about federalism is not so much the particular form of organization, but rather the techniques for reconciling and balancing general with local interests. American history represents the triumph of the general over the particular, whereas in Europe the particular triumphed over the general. But this triumph has not come, in America, through the creation of a highly centralized or militarized state, nor through the sacrifice of local cultural or economic interests. It has come through a distribution of authority among governments which, in the end, has strengthened rather than weakened the constituent parts of the union. While it is unlikely that a scheme like the American could be adapted to the needs of western Europe, it is not at all difficult to imagine a number of small federations—Benelux, the Scandinavian countries, the Iberian peninsula, the Balkans—which may some day furnish the ingredients for a larger federation.

And if the familiar and traditional methods will not do, we must invent new ones. The last fifteen years have been among the most inventive in modern history. In these years we invented Lend-Lease, a unified army and an integrated high command, the United Nations, Marshall Plan, OEEC, Benelux, the Coal and Steel Community, NATO, technological assistance, international atomic research, and a host of other international organizations and devices. There is no reason to suppose that these remarkable inventions have exhausted European or American ingenuity. As Arthur MacMahon has written, "Europe, while conserving the beauty of the past, must invent and is inventing forms of organization and economic policies novel in the world." The age of invention is but in its infancy.

American federalism may not, in itself, serve as a pattern for Europe, but what I call the reserve side of federalism is not without interest to Europeans looking for a pattern. For federalism is, in a sense, the repudiation of a statism. Although the tradition of the state is relatively new in Europe, it is immensely powerful, and nowhere more so than in those central bastions of European civilization, France and Germany. Americans have never known statism, never known the state as a mystical entity, a religious symbol, a brooding omniscience in history. Our attitude toward government was, from the beginning, disrespectful and almost supercilious. "Government, like dress," said Tom Paine, "is the badge of lost innocence." They made a state—by contract—and determined to keep it in its place, which was a subordinate one. They devised a constitution designed to make sure that government could not become too strong. They created neither army nor navy in any real sense. They did not put their officials in uniforms or give them titles or honors—or even pay them very well; they created no *droit administratif;* they established no national system of education and no national university; they scarcely had a national capital, until the twentieth century, and still lack, in a sense, a national name!

Because they do not worship and scarcely respect the state, it is not difficult for Americans to concede equality to all other states, even the smallest and weakest; and since the adoption of the Northwest Ordinance in 1787 they have stitched the principle of the coordinate state into the fabric of their governmental and philosophical system. Federalism here is both cause and effect. Because the Americans did not want a powerful state, they created a federal system; because they started with a federal system—started indeed with thirteen states that thought themselves sovereign and independent—they looked with suspicion upon a powerful national state, and the terrible question, who shall curb behemoth, who shall bridle leviathan?, has never had any real meaning in America.

There is one analogy between the American experience and the current European problem that is not without interest. Whereas in the Old World nationalism customarily developed long before the organization of the political state—as in Italy, Germany, Norway, Greece, Finland, Bohemia, Poland, and so forth—in America the political organization of the nation came first, and the other ingredients of nationalism were added afterward. In this respect present-day Europe is closer to the United States of 1787 than to its own constituent parts. The political organization of Europe can be completed by acts of federation and of union. It will still remain to fill in the cultural and the emotional ingredients, to create a sense and a sentiment of union. That the task is difficult will be readily conceded, but it should be no more difficult for Europeans to recapture and reanimate a cultural unity that once flourished than it was for Americans to create one out of miscellaneous ingredients of history and experience.

An important part of American history has been what might be called a series of exercises in avoidance. One thing that the United States has avoided until now is clearly relevant to our problem. We have avoided dependence on the military, on wars, on the nursing of national antipathies. We have never had, in the United States, a military class, a class that played a political and social as well as a professional role; and we certainly have never had an officer class, nor even a permanent general staff which has influenced the conduct of foreign policy. During the whole of the nineteenth century our army was smaller than that of Switzerland or Sweden. When it was enlarged to fight wars, as in 1861, it was enlarged as a citizen, not a professional, army, and speedily disbanded.

We were fortunate, perhaps, rather than wise, in not having, or nursing, national antipathies. Every Frenchman, every Italian, every Irishman, every Finn knows who is the traditional enemy of his people, but the Americans would be hard put to it to think of any candidate for that post. Britain was a candidate for a short time, but it is always easy for the victors to forgive the vanquished, and the British, on their part, were inclined to apologize for the War of Independence and to forget entirely the War of 1812. Aside from Britain there were no other national enemies, and the inability of Americans to think of the Germans as enemies after two wars, or to treat them the way victors in the past treated the vanquished, has been something of an embarrassment to America's erstwhile allies! What this meant was that in the United States nationalism could flourish without resort to war, without the glorification of the military, or the creation of a military class. The greatest of American heroes are not military; the greatest American military hero is the leader of an unsuccessful rebellion against the United States, Robert E. Lee! American literature has no military tradition. The only American battle songs come from the Civil War and are heavily sentimental. American painting is almost as innocent of battle scenes as of nudes. We need only contemplate the role played by the military and by war in the development of European nationalism, or the role of antipathies in the nationalism of newer nations like Ireland, China, or the Arab States, to appreciate how fortunate the American experience has been in this realm.

National enmities are a product of history, as indeed the fragmentation of Europe is a product of history, and history cannot be exorcised by devout incantations. But national enmities and the fragmentation of Europe are also, in a sense, the product of historians. All through the nineteenth century, and in almost every country of Europe, historians were the willing and zealous apologists for the most parochial and chauvinistic nationalism. The German historians, from Dahlmann and Droysen to Von Sybel and the egregious Treitschke, were doubtless the worst offenders, but they were not alone in the sorry business of forcing Clio to speak in the vulgar accents of nationalism. Michelet and Thiers and Masson in France, Arneth and Klopp in Austria, Botta in Italy, Lafuente in Spain, Geijer in Sweden, Palacký in Bohemia, Paparrhegopoulos in Greece—all these displayed the same enthusiasm for nationalism and confessed the same confusion in distinguishing between patriotism and history.

And not only did historians celebrate nationalism for the most part uncritically. Even quantitatively they concentrated on a national and parochial version of history. Instead of instructing their readers that nationalism was a new and in many respects an artificial thing; that all nations had much the same origins and each was but a part of European society; that the whole notion of national character was something of a myth and the notion of the natural superiority of any one people or nation a pernicious myth; and that every citizen was a citizen not only of a state but of the larger community of Western Christendom, historians did their utmost to inflame nationalism and chauvinism.

Although the worst excesses of nationalist historiography are happily a thing of the past, historians still tend to force history into a national framework, and to concentrate attention upon the history of one individual nation. Thus to this day historians of Denmark are preoccupied with the problems of Danish history, and those of Holland with Dutch history, and so forth. If this preoccupation were merely a matter of the study it would not be so serious, but it carries over into the university, and from the university it percolates down to the secondary and the elementary schools, so that in almost every country of Europe the young are trained, from childhood, to an astigmatic view of history.

The United States has been singularly fortunate in almost wholly escaping this nationalistic preoccupation with, and interpretation of, history. We have never had a nationalist school of historians in the United States, nor have our historians concentrated upon the history of the United States. Of the leading historians of the nineteenth century only Bancroft is an exception to this generalization, and even Bancroft was more concerned with vindicating democracy than with celebrating nationalism, and did not in any event carry his studies past 1789. Prescott wrote of the Aztecs and the Incas and of the Spain of Philip II; Motley celebrated the rise of the Dutch Republic; Parkman described the struggle between Spain, France, and England for North America; and Admiral Mahan traced the influence of sea upon history; while Henry Adams, who did write nine brilliant volumes on the administrations of Jefferson and Madison, began and ended his literary career as a medievalist. Nor has the twentieth century brought a reversal of this tradition of interest in the history of other peoples and times.

It is not only the absence of nationalism in American historical writing that is noteworthy, but the early, continuous, and pervasive interest in history outside America. It is only recently, indeed, that American history has made its way into the curriculum of the schools, and in some states it has required legislation to assure some study of American history in the secondary schools. Our universities, too, address themselves assiduously to the history of other nations and civilizations. Thus Columbia University maintains not only professorships in American history, but professors who specialize in the history of Britain, Canada, Latin America, Scandinavia, Germany, Italy, Spain, France, Russia, China, Japan, and India!

Perhaps the New World historian can say what it seems difficult for Old World historians to admit—that history is too often a refuge for and an enticement to nationalist sentiment. Where it emphasizes the particular rather than the general, where it teaches the superiority of each national state and culture, it blinds rather than enlightens. The sense of the past is always with us, but we may become prisoners of the past to a degree where we are not masters of the future. It was a great historian, perhaps the greatest of our time, who reminded us just a decade ago at Zurich that "there must be a blessed act of oblivion." He had in mind oblivion of the cruelties and wickedness of the immediate past, but may we not say there must be an act of oblivion for the long heritage of national egocentricity and vanity as well?

One other feature of American life has made it easy for Europeans to live together in America without rivalry or hostility—the historic separation of church and state. The United States was the first Western nation to try the bold experiment of separating church and state and ordaining complete equality in religion, and almost the only modern nation to have escaped religious wars and conflicts. We have in America today some thirty-five million Catholics, perhaps seventy million Protestants subdivided into over a hundred different denominations, and perhaps five million people of Jewish faith. All these live happily side by side and, except for minor lapses, they have always done so. Had the United States attempted to guarantee one religion a privileged position, the consequences would have been fatal. Had Europeans been encouraged or permitted to indulge in religious rivalries and animosities in the New World, the consequences would have been fatal. What is most interesting, however, is not that the fathers made the right decision in 1787—they could scarcely have made any other—but that the decision has been accepted and implemented so effortlessly. Europeans, accustomed for centuries to religious conflicts, persecutions, and wars, found it the easiest and most natural thing in the world to live with rival religions. There has been some anti-Catholicism in the United States, but it evaporated very early. There has been some anti-Semitism in the United States, but it has never been allowed to take overt or vulgar form. Even the *kulturkampf* came to have little meaning in a society where each denomination was free to establish its own churches and maintain its own schools and colleges, and where those who were not devout could be as independent as they pleased.

Separation of church and state in America not only made it possible for Europeans to abandon age-old religious rivalries; it also broke that historic connection between religion and the state which has done so much to inflame aggressive nationalism elsewhere in the world. It is difficult to imagine the national states of Ireland, of Pakistan, of Israel, even of Spain, without the religious ingredient, and it is tempting to speculate on the dazzling possibilities of economic and social progress in the Near East which technology makes available, but religion vetoes. It is not irrelevant to ask why men and women of different religious faiths can live together in Ohio and Pennsylvania, but not in Ireland, Spain, Egypt, or Pakistan and their neighbors. Are religious conflicts unavoidable? If they are, there can be no European union, but the experience of the United States, and of some other nations as well, suggests a happier answer.

When Alexis de Tocqueville wrote his magisterial analysis of democracy in America, he devoted two chapters to what he considered the most remarkable of American characteristics, the practice of voluntary association. He saw clearly the role of the voluntary association in stimulating self-government and dispersing the power of the state, but even he did not fully appreciate one of the major functions of the voluntary association—its harmonizing and unifying function. Voluntary association is the institution that has done most to cut across the boundary lines of state, race, religion, class, and interest, and bind together by a thousand strong though invisible ties a numerous and heterogeneous people.

I need not remind you of the elementary, indeed the faintly absurd, fact that the United States is a nation of joiners. We join together for the serious task of making a church, a political party, a labor union, a college, and we join together for all other conceivable and some inconceivable purposes. Veterans of wars unite; alumni of colleges unite; doctors and lawyers, the teachers of the young and the parents of the young who are taught, advertisers and automobile salesmen, Rotarians and Elks, the Daughters of the American Revolution and the Minute Women of America all unite. Vegetarians cannot enjoy their diet alone, but must form a national organization; stamp collectors join happily in a nation-wide orgy of philately; and even those who read books feel happier if they belong to a club of readers.

Most organizations are nation-wide; some, like the Rotary or the Boy Scouts or the Red Cross, transcend national boundaries. Almost all of them are unifying rather than nationalizing. They cut across boundaries to form an intricate network of new and highly personal unions. Lawyers can compare cases from state to state; fishermen of Vermont tell fish stories to fishermen of Oregon; Rotarians and Lions find friends and companions in every town in the country.

In short, Americans have formed, over the years, this wonderful system to fragment government and to superimpose social and professional loyalties upon political and class and religious loyalties. These new associational loyalties are nowhere strong enough to threaten the state (as some of the class or religious loyalties of nineteenth- and twentieth-century Europe have done), but they are strong enough to create or enlarge bonds of interest and affection. They mitigate nationalism without impairing it; they fragment the leviathan state without undermining it; they stimulate social and economic democracy without discouraging political democracy. Because they are so many and so diverse, they unify without standardizing.

Americans do not have a monopoly on the habit of voluntary associations. The English are almost as adept as the Americans in this practice, and every European nation boasts its scores and hundreds of private organizations. Two factors, however, should be considered. First, the tradition of state direction of religion, education, medicine, social services, and many other things has tended to give less scope to the practice of voluntary association in European nations than in the United States. And second, precisely because so many of these activities are directed by the state, it is difficult to organize across national boundaries, and the habit of forming European, as distinct from Danish or Italian, organizations is therefore still weak. Nothing, I suggest, would contribute more to creating a spirit of unity among Europeans than a vigorous growth of this practice. Scholars, men of letters, and scientists now commonly enjoy their European congresses, but the habit of meeting together has not percolated down to the average man and woman. When rose-growers of England organize with those of Switzerland, when the school teachers of Sweden join with those of Italy, when veterans of the Resistance movements can meet together and know each other, they will discover that the things that unite them are stronger than the things that divide them. After all, if enthusiasm for Grace Kelly or passion for Coca Cola can give an evanescent harmony to European tastes, think what might be done if the men and women of Europe generally could unite on more enduring interests.

Mention of Coca Cola suggests that this is as good a place as any to touch on that bogey of the European intellectual, standardization. I say a bogey, because as far as it affects the problem of European union it is largely a figment of the imagination; I say European intellectual, because we are not so standardized in the United States as to have any group who can be called intellectuals.

The very term *standardization* is a semantic trap, for it conjures up a sort of Orwellian nightmare. But some standardization is a very good thing, even in the cultural realm. We do not want a standardized literary style, but a standardized typewriter keyboard facilitates creative writing. We do not want standardized music, but we do need standardized scales and terminology. I need not elaborate on what is so obvious; you can supply additional examples for yourselves. The notion of a peculiarly American standardization is, too, a somewhat exaggerated one, for American society is less standardized and European society more so than most Europeans realize. Compare the monolithic religious landscape of Sweden and Italy with the diversity of the American religious scene, or the uniformity of higher education in France or Spain with the diversity in the United States.

What is important, however, is to keep in mind that there is no necessary connection between European union and European cultural standardization. Not only can union be achieved without standardization—after all, there is as much variety in the literature of the English-speaking world as in the literature of twenty European countries—but standardization can and will advance without union. Indeed, I am not being merely paradoxical if I suggest that cultural standardization may advance faster without European union than with it. Standardization within a single nation is potentially much more dangerous than over a large area embracing many countries. Witness what happened in Germany under the Nazi regime. And this kind of standardization is a product of those forces that are generated by chauvinistic nationalism—of the leviathan state, or the monolothic and intolerant church, of war and preparation for war, or a rigidly controlled economy. The chances are far less of any of these forces operating on a united Europe than on single states—especially if they are hostile states.

Finally I return to the point I raised at the very beginning, that because (by good fortune, it now appears) America started without a culture of its own to protect and exalt, it largely escaped the ravages of cultural chauvinism and could serve therefore as a cultural clearinghouse for the Old World.

In the tiny square of Bellosguardo, Italy, looking down on the gleaming domes of Florence, stands a granite shaft with the simple inscription:

JAMES FENIMORE COOPER
NATHANIEL HAWTHORNE
LOUISA MAY ALCOTT
HENRY JAMES
Loved this Place

For well over a century now Americans have been making that declaration of love not to Florence alone, but to the hundreds of centers of art and learning and beauty which constitute, in Hawthorne's phrase, "our old home." They have done so, however, with no sense of unfaithfulness to their own country. For over a century America has accumulated the culture, art, architecture, music, science and scholarship of the Old World and welcomed and assimilated, at the same time, each successive generation of European artists, scientists, and scholars. The process has gone so far that we can almost say that while French culture flourishes only in France and Italian culture only in Italy and Irish culture only in Ireland, European culture flourishes best in America. This is what Lewis Mumford had in mind when he wrote that the uprooting of Europe was the settlement of America. It is what Professor Panofsky has in mind when he argues that European historians of art are so circumscribed by national prepossessions that the artistic history of Europe can best be studied and written in the United States. Certainly our formal institutions of culture, universities and libraries and museums, represent not the loot of the European past, but a genuine assimilation and continuation and enrichment of that past.

One form of the continuation and enrichment is of immediate interest—the colleges and seminars devoted to the study of the unity of the West. President Eisenhower has recently called upon American universities to redouble their efforts to assist a program of scientific and cultural unity for the free world. There is no reason why Europe should not create and maintain a dozen flourishing centers of study devoted to the recovery of the cultural unity of this "noble continent."

It is useless to say that European union *cannot* be achieved, because it *has,* in a very real sense, been achieved in America. What is impressive about the achievement is how readily the peoples of the Old World adapted themselves to it, how cheerfully they abandoned the nationalist and religious antagonisms, the class consciousness, the cultural vanity, even the linguistic commitments, which had been second nature to them in the Old World. What is impressive is how easily they accepted a common language, common education, common practices of voluntary association, common social habits and standards, and a common culture. It is granted that the situation in the Old World is different from that in the New, and that the boundary which separates France from Germany is not like that which separates Indiana from Illinois; it is granted, too, that a common language and a single government immensely facilitate understanding. But some of the boundaries of the Old World seem quite as artificial as those of the New; a common language has not yet reunited Norway with Denmark or Belgium with Holland and France; and racial heterogeneity is greater in the United States than in all Europe. The explanation of the unification of Europe in America and the fragmentation of Europe in Europe does not lie so much in these hard facts of language or race or politics as in the realms of history, philosophy, religion, and psychology.

It is here that the scholars, the artists, the men of letters, the moral leaders, can play a decisive role in the mitigation of those historical and psychological factors that so powerfully inhibit cultural and moral unification. So far, over a period of a century or more, they have not done so. So far they have contributed more to the cult of the particular than to the religion of the general, more to fragmentation than to unity. So far they have seemed more sensitive to what President Eisenhower has called "the intense fear of losing cherished local traditions and cultural and political institutions," than to the values inherent in the enlargement of cultural horizons for hundreds of millions of men and women. They have been, many of them, like secular priests so determined to cultivate the dogma of their particular denomination that they ignore the common moral values of all religion. The prison in which so many Europeans, even European intellectuals, live is one of their own making. It is a prison fabricated from the fears, the disappointments, the suspicions, the vanities, and the timidities of the past. Let us say what the venerable Justice Holmes wrote to one of his younger disciples—that it would be well if we were to consult our hopes and not our fears.

The British Commonwealth and Western Europe

CHARLES E. CARRINGTON / *Professor at the Royal Institute of International Affairs, London*

A Nation of Shopkeepers

The British are no less a nation of shopkeepers today than they were when Adam Smith so described them nearly two centuries ago. Overseas trade is their livelihood and its value has increased steadily. Fifty or a hundred years ago, Britain was, of course, by far the greatest trader among the nations, and although that is no longer the case, Britain's decline has been relative, not absolute. It is not that she has gone down; other nations have come up. As De Tocqueville pointed out, the United States would inevitably surpass its mother country in material wealth. The British have long been accustomed to this prospect, which was clearly demonstrated to them in 1883 by J. R. Seeley in his *Expansion of England,* a book regularly prescribed to university students for many years. He foretold a time "which many here present may live to see," when "Russia and the United States will surpass in power the states now called great as much as the great country-states of the sixteenth century surpassed Florence." This, he said, was a serious consideration for a state like England. "Can we cancel the growth of centuries," he asked, "for a whim, or because, when we throw a hasty glance at it, it does not suit our fancies?"

British trading strength was built up largely although not entirely, by the formation of colonial settlements in America and Australia, and by the simultaneous development of colonial possessions in Asia and Africa. This trading strength was never expected to decline when these colonies took their natural course toward self-government; nor did British trade ever depend upon coercion. During all the years of British supremacy in sea-borne commerce, from the 1840's to the 1930's, Great Britain and her dependent colonies enjoyed free trade, and, in advancing the process of self-government, Britain granted her colonial territories the right to control their own external commerce at an early stage, even if it implied their right to discriminate against Great Britain. Free trade brought its own reward in the establishment of mutual trading links which were to last, to the benefit of all parties. Apart from that, colonial trade had no advantage over foreign trade until the 1920's.

The United States and Russia have now surpassed Britain in population, in strategic power, in industrial production, even perhaps in external trade, and Britain no longer rules the waves. It would, however, be a false conclusion to assume that British trade has decayed. Not only has its absolute value increased, but it follows much the same lines as it did fifty years ago and, with respect to long-distance oceanic commerce, Britain is still probably the world's greatest trading power. We are accustomed to thinking of North Americans as the wealthiest of peoples, certainly much wealthier than the British, but in 1953 the export trade of the United States averaged $98 per head of the population, while the export trade of Great Britain averaged $150 per head.[1] Overseas trade is a marginal activity for Americans, accounting for less than 3 per cent of their gross national income, while they normally live upon their home market. Overseas trade is a necessity for the British.

Britain and France

It may be more to the point to compare Britain with France in this respect since France also is a trading nation with great overseas possessions. The estimated gross national income of the two countries for 1953 (the last year of which there are comparative statistics) is

[1] Note on sources: statistics from *Annuaire Statistique de la France,* 1953 (Paris: Imprimerie Nationale, 1954); *Annual Abstract of Statistics,* No. 92, 1955 (London: H.M.S.O., 1955). All figures are approximations calculated at the rate: Fr. 960 French; £1 sterling; $2.80 U. S. Unless otherwise stated, the year taken is 1953.

not dissimilar: France, about £12,400 million sterling; and Britain, £14,800 million sterling. This works out, in each case, at more than $800 per head of the population.[2] But in Britain, 18 per cent of this income is earned directly from the export of British goods, 9 per cent from the export of British goods to the Commonwealth. In France, on the other hand, less than 12 per cent of the gross national income is derived from exports, and less than 5 per cent from exports to French territories overseas.[3]

The contrast is made stronger if we consider the geographical distribution of the trade and arrange the best customers of the two countries in order of importance. The largest buyers of British goods are Australia, the USA, South Africa, Canada, New Zealand, and India, five of them Commonwealth countries and all of them far distant from Europe. The six best customers of France are Algeria, Switzerland, West Germany, Indo-China (1953 figures), Belgium with Luxembourg, and Morocco, all but one of them France's near neighbors.[4]

In 1953 New Zealand, with a population of two million people, bought British goods valued at about $281 million;[5] France, with a population of 42 million, bought British goods valued at abut $184 million. The economy of New Zealand is complementary to that of Britain, while our trade relations with France are of marginal importance. Of all countries in the world, in language, religion, political constitution, laws, administration, and social system, New Zealand is the most like England, while France is profoundly different in every one of these respects. But, geographically, France is the nearest country to Britain, and New Zealand the farthest away. If New Zealand lay twenty miles away from Dover, we should not federate with her, but form a political union; if France lay in the Pacific Ocean, what point of contact should we have? That question will be dealt with later.

---

[2] Since the method of calculation is not identical in the two countries, these comparisons are to be regarded only as general approximations.
[3] In 1953 Great Britain received 49 per cent of her total imports from Commonwealth countries; France received 25 per cent of her imports from French territories overseas.
[4] See the appendix to this article.
[5] The percentage was much higher in 1954, nearly $350 million.

The Complex of British Commerce

The fraction of our gross national income derived from the export of British goods does not represent the whole advantage of our overseas commerce. In the year 1953 the British trade figures showed a nominal adverse balance of $2.1 billion, most of which was covered by our "invisible earnings" from shipping (not less than $350 million net), from overseas investments (not less than $170 million net), etc. No adequate analysis of these earnings is available in simple statistical form, but it is generally believed that published estimates fall well below the real totals. At any rate the greater part of this sum is earned somewhere, and mostly earned by financial services to the Commonwealth members. That is to say, the crude annual figures of exports and imports are merely the current trading account of an immense and highly organized administration with world-wide connections. If the whole balance sheet could be presented with its stock, good will, and overheads, the total turnover would exceed the trading account by a huge, incalculable sum. This is the Commonwealth business, the real activity of the nation of shopkeepers, and, so far is it from declining as colonies attain self-government that in the past it has always continued to grow to the mutual advantage of all parties. Britain has retained her place as the banker to the sterling area and, like other bankers, lives on the principle of mutual indebtedness. If the customers all chose to withdraw their balances together, they could break the bank—but they do not want to. Three of the four states which have left the Commonwealth altogether (Ireland, Burma, and the Sudan) still have chosen to retain membership in the sterling area group.

Trade routes follow natural geographic lines by sea as well as by land and, unless they are interrupted by faction and folly, they are longer-lived than political constitutions. To the British (as to the Norwegians and the Dutch) the sea has always been a pathway and never a frontier. Our concept of our geographical situation is oceanic. We consider ourselves a North Atlantic power rather than a European power and just as deeply engaged in the affairs of Canada as in the affairs of Germany. Nor do our concerns end with the NATO region. Ours has never been a closed, exclusive trade with certain particular colonies where we enjoyed a political monopoly, but always a natural, spontaneous growth, which has been the secret of its vitality. It has, however, been fostered and maintained in no way more remarkably than by the cable communications which formed the nervous system of the British Empire. Good communications, by British-owned cables, created the great seaports of Bombay, Singapore, and Hong-Kong; they enabled the Commonwealth to conduct a world-wide strategy in two world wars; they gave importance to lonely places like Bermuda, Ascension, the Seychelles, the Cocos Islands, and Fiji; they imposed upon the British the necessity of watching the line through the Mediterranean from Aden to Gibraltar. Cheap rates for press telegrams have maintained common news services over the whole Commonwealth and in recent years the similar extension of radio stations has followed the same routes. The network of communications, the trade that uses them, the commercial centers at the nodal points, the messages conveyed by the English language—these factors made the old Empire and have survived substantially as the new Commonwealth after the superstate, to use Lenin's celebrated phrase, withered away. If we are weakened today, it is the threat to these services that weakens us, not the loss of imperial authority.

The Sterling Area

The sterling area is, as its name implies, an area and not an institution. It means no more than the region within which countries make use of the London banking system in order to discharge their international balance of payments. The banking system in turn makes use of the communications; the shipping companies follow the same routes; and trade follows the movement of sterling currency. Almost 50 per cent of British exports are sent to sterling countries and another 12 per cent to the USA and Canada, while the proportion sent to the OEEC countries of western Europe is about 27 per cent. The other sterling countries send varying proportions of their exports to Britain (Australia, 40 per cent; India, 21 per cent), but all keep their accounts with banks which in turn keep their accounts with the Bank of England. In the case of Commonwealth members, they are under no obligation, legal or moral, but do so for the advantage of access to the London money market where loans to dominions and colonies are given favorable terms under government guarantee. The whole commercial system of the city of London, although without legal or formal organization, has grown over the years into a permanent trading machine with branches, contacts, and "good will" everywhere.

If we turn to that sector of British trade which lies outside the sterling area, the most significant case will be Canada, the senior of the dominions, the nearest geographically, the one with which we are most closely bound by strategic necessities. Canada is a dollar country and has been for a hundred years. It would be difficult for Britain to live without Canadian wheat and, although the sale of wheat to Britain is no longer Canada's staple of commerce, the Canadian economy could hardly survive without the market in Britain plus the complex of railways, shipping, banking, and investment which has been built up during the last hundred years to maintain that trade in wheat. About three-quarters of Canada's external trade is with the United States, but the loss of the other quarter, her sterling-area trade, would be disastrous to her. Canada, then, is the bridge between the two halves of the English-speaking world, between the dollar area and the sterling area. On balance the sterling area pays more dollars for Canadian wheat than it receives by selling British goods in Canada. The dollars are earned by other parts of the Commonwealth which sell more to the dollar area, but buy more from Britain for pounds sterling. Gold Coast cocoa and Malayan rubber are great dollar-earners, and both these colonies hold large balances in the London banks. It is not impossible that when they gain self-government they may propose to withdraw their balances and set up in business on their own. This would be a sore blow to the sterling area and to the British commercial system, but it would also involve the new nations in financial hardship. They would have to secure the backing of their own currencies, borrow on their own credit, build up their own trading organization, and find their own markets in a world not always sympathetic to primary producers. It was the strength of the British financial system that made Canada a great power; that system, if allowed to go on with its beneficent work, might do as much for Malaya.

Commonwealth Strategy

Since the island of Britain would be starved out in a few weeks if deprived of its overseas trade, British strategy has long been and must still be concerned with defending its trade routes more than with defending its coasts. Total nuclear warfare breaks all precedents and defies all means of passive defense; but in a partial or local war the defense of Britain will mean, in the future as in the past, the defense of the North Atlantic region. It will always be an advantage to hold our foes (if we have them) at a distance, but even if they come as close as possible by land, as they did in 1940, we can still survive if we have sea and air power. Our first strategic priority is the general preservation of world peace; our second is the defense of the North Atlantic; our third is the defense of western Europe.

Since the fall of Singapore there has been no single strategic plan for the defense of the whole Commonwealth from its own resources, and it seems unlikely that there will be such a plan again. Whatever it may be, the Commonwealth is not a strategic unit; it cannot make war or peace. Ireland (then still a dominion) stood neutral in World War II; India stood neutral in the Korean War. But even after making this admission we can learn from the Korean War what the moral unity of the Commonwealth implies. In that arduous campaign there was a large American contingent and a number of small contingents from other United Nations members, which presented problems of military organization. Those contingents which came from Commonwealth countries fell together spontaneously, formed themselves into an infantry division (not the least worthy division in the army), and acted with complete mutual confidence, an integration which was easy because all had the same administration, discipline, military education, and code of conduct, not because any superior authority compelled them to combine.

As in the case of the sterling area, a voluntary grouping of some, but not all, Commonwealth members for their mutual convenience, so in the case of strategical planning we prefer to combine into groups for appropriate purposes. The defense of the North Atlantic (NATO), which includes Britain, is a matter for Britain, Canada, and their neighbors, but not for Australia; the defense of the South Pacific (ANZUS) is a matter for Australia, New Zealand, and the United States, but not for Canada or Britain. Needless to say, however, no one doubts after the experience of two world wars, that Commonwealth members will do far more for one another, in a great emergency, than they are bound to do by treaty.

In addition to her general obligations under the United Nations

Charter and her particular obligations to Portugal and other old allies, Britain is bound by four general treaties of military alliance: NATO, the Brussels Pact, the Baghdad Pact, and SEATO. If all these should hold good (and since the Pacific is covered by the ANZUS treaty), the whole Commonwealth, its trade routes, and the numerous underdeveloped colonies for which the British are still responsible should be secured, in principle, so far as abstract planning is a security. The Baghdad Pact and the future status of Singapore are the problems which show the greatest urgency at this time, but they lie outside the scope of this article. NATO, which particularly concerns us, has two military aspects: (1) air and sea defense in a war fought over the polar regions; (2) air and land defense in a war fought over western Europe. Either would be equally damaging to Britain, and against both threats we have taken precautions on a far greater scale than any British government ever has taken before in time of peace. In addition to our traditional air and sea defenses we have repudiated the old English tradition by maintaining conscription (with a longer period of military service than any other NATO member) and we have undertaken by the Paris Agreements to station four infantry divisions on the Continent, under international command. What more can we do? What further concession could we make to western European defense if we were politically integrated with the western European countries? On the contrary, we might call on them to contribute more to the defense of the seaways which are vital to us.

The Commonwealth and the United Nations

As in our internal relations with the other Commonwealth members, so in our external relations with the countries of western Europe we prefer appropriate groupings for functional purposes, not formal political ties. We join with one European group (NATO) for strategic planning, with another (EPU) to arrange the balance of payments, and with another (GATT) to reduce tariff barriers. We draw no line here, and are prepared to go with ECSC, or any other body which may arise, as far as it may be useful for its particular function.[6] It is precisely because we have found this form of

[6] The field in which a greater degree of co-operation between Britain and her neighbors (France, Belgium, and Portugal) seems most desirable is colonial

international co-operation so effective in the Commonwealth that we recommend it outside the Commonwealth. It is no question of *mystique;* it is merely the way that all the business of the human race is carried on, except the limited range of activities which usurp the name of politics. A nation of shopkeepers must attempt to please its customers. It need not impose its will upon them; it desires that they should be prosperous, friendly, and closely associated for the mutual benefit of all. The method is no trade secret; it is continuous consultation at all levels in order to obtain the greatest possible measure of agreement. It requires no uniformity, no coercion of minorities; it rejects the notion of sovereignty. It concerns itself in arranging co-operation between those who are willing to co-operate for particular ends, but it allows those who disagree on a particular issue to stand aside. It could make little progress by the stereotyped methods of diplomacy, and still less by reference of practical problems to political factions. The Commonwealth method produces spontaneous action with good will. How unlike the Assembly of the United Nations, where, in an atmosphere of the strictest protocol, the delegates meet to exploit and prosecute their quarrels!

We have our failures, of course, like all institutions of human beings. We make lamentable mistakes, but on the whole our Commonwealth holds together and even those states which resign their membership have remained on terms of friendship and association.

The Assembly of the United Nations has failed to realize the hopes of its founders because it was constructed on the obsolescent model of a world consisting of sovereign states. National sovereignty is no longer relevant in the mid-twentieth century and self-determination is a slogan from the past. These are the pathetic fancies of the small, the backward, and the self-conscious racial groups who suppose that they can do in this century what Cavour and Bismarck did in the last. The great progressive nations are concerned with quite different plans which accord better with the spirit of the age. In every department of their national life they are engaged in making partial surrenders of sovereignty in the forming of new combinations which have small regard to national frontiers and historic prejudices, but which look to world-wide social obligations. If we are to search for hopeful projects, for the modest successes of world

---

administration. They have more obvious common problems in Africa than in Europe.

organization, we shall find them in the nonpolitical activities of the United Nations, in the commissions controlled by the Economic and Social Council, in such bodies as the Food and Agriculture Organization, the World Health Organization, the International Monetary Fund, the Universal Postal Union, or the International Telecommunications Union. These are concerned with the real business of life and not with arid national disputes.

The Commonwealth Relations Office

The political relations between Great Britain and other countries are conducted through one of three channels. There are foreign nations with whom we correspond through the Foreign Office by means of the formal process of diplomacy. There are the colonies, all now moving toward self-government, but all for the present under the authority of the Colonial Office, which retains residual sovereignty. In an intermediate state there are the Commonwealth members, with whom we correspond through the Commonwealth Relations Office. When a colony achieves full self-government, it is released from the control of the Colonial Office and is placed in quite a different relationship with the Commonwealth Relations Office, which has no residual sovereignty and gives no orders. It is a liaison office which organizes conferences on many subjects at all levels— not only the occasional publicity-winning meetings of prime ministers. It is not much bound by protocol, so that innumerable friendly contacts are made between its officers and their "opposite numbers" overseas. It freely exchanges confidential information between members, on a scale that professional diplomats of even the most friendly states rarely achieve. But, even more important than these functions is the long list of advisory and co-operative activities (their description occupies twenty-eight pages in the annual Commonwealth list) which are sponsored and encouraged, though never dominated, by the Commonwealth Relations Office. If I mention the Association of Universities of the Commonwealth, the Commonwealth Scientific Conference, the Commonwealth Agricultural Council, the Air Transport Council, the Commonwealth Economic Committee, the Commonwealth Parliamentary Association, the Commonwealth Press Union, the Commonwealth Shipping Committee, the Commonwealth Telecommunication Board, and the Institute of Commonwealth Studies, it will serve to show that the true and best function of the Commonwealth resembles the nonpolitical function of the United Nations.

Imperial Federation Rejected

If it may now be granted that our mode of thought inclines us toward sea power rather than landpower, toward a loose-knit trading Commonwealth and not to a political super-state, it may be useful to glance back at the historical process which brought us to this way of thinking. Broadly speaking, it derives from enlightened thinkers in the dominions rather than from the considered policy of any government at Westminster. Colonial nationalism, to give it its older name, was freely discussed, a hundred years ago, in Canada and Australia, by politicians who had no wish or intention to separate themselves from the mother country. They still looked to Britain for markets, for emigrants, and for supplies of capital. It was in Britain that a contrary view emerged when some political theorists of the 1870's began to assert that this illogical situation could not last. The Empire must "either federate or separate." But three generations have passed since this theory was propounded and the Empire has neither federated nor separated. No political party has ever attained power in Britain or in any dominion with a declared policy of imperial federation, and the theory may now be described as moribund.

Here we differ profoundly from the Americans. Close as we are to them in many aspects of our social organization, far closer than to any European nation, we are a world away from them in our political system. The American republic, with its rigid constitution, balanced powers, and traditional origin in a union between thirteen distinct colonies, is conceived to have been founded by an act of federation, so that federation is part of the American legend. Not so with us! Our political tradition, our vitalizing myth, is the final supremacy of the House of Commons, which, in the last resort, can alter fundamental laws and dethrone kings. When planting new houses of commons overseas, it is our intention to raise them eventually to similar plenary powers, hoping that they, like the mother of parliaments, will use these powers with moderation. The long-established tradition of the British Empire is the decentralization of political power. Long ago we abandoned the notion of federating our own group of associated nations into a super-state, and, whatever we may have to regret in British history, it is certainly not the process of our relations with Australia and Canada.

It is not that we renounce the constitutional device of federalism where it will be useful. Three of our eight Commonwealth members have federal constitutions and it may be remembered that the federation of Canada, ninety years ago, was a task of appalling difficulty, brilliantly accomplished. At this very time, the Colonial Secretary is engaged upon providing federal constitutions for two groups of colonies, with the approval of their representatives. But these are questions (as was the question of federating the thirteen colonies in America) of building up small ineffective groups into larger, "viable" units, questions of practical utility and immediate urgency. The British Parliament does not concern itself much with political theory; utility and urgency are necessary to spur it to action.

Notions of Integration

If there were in Britain any strong sense of the desirability of integrating our country into a larger political group, even if we felt ruefully that such a course would be useful though distasteful, it is to our Commonwealth members that we should turn first. But nothing is more unlikely, because no one can suggest any more effective form of co-operation than already exists. We believe that we already have found a more practical solution than federation for our own imperial problems, and a federal legislature, at best, could do nothing but interpose bureaucratic delays.

Co-operation suits us very well and, looking outside the Commonwealth, the North Atlantic powers are the group with which we co-operate most fully. A federal union between Britain, Canada, and the United States is not inconceivable, but since we have decided, with the greatest good will, against a federal union with Canada, a federal union with the United States is, *a fortiori,* much more unlikely. Compared with these, how difficult would be a political integration with Benelux, with the Scandinavian countries, with West Germany, or with France.

If we were to apply our minds to the problem, we should first consider our traditional relations with France, our nearest neighbor, our ancient enemy and rival, our ally and friend for the last fifty years. In generation after generation, France and Britain have reacted upon one another. To France we have looked, and still look, for primacy in many of the modes of art, letters, and philosophy. The old saying that every civilized man has two fatherlands, his own and France, was never more true, and perhaps I may be permitted the liberty of saying that it touches my heart. And yet the action and reaction between Britain and France gain their force from their differences, not from their resemblances. It is because they have so few points of mutual contact that the contrast is a perpetual stimulus. No two countries would be more difficult to integrate, and the artificial structure thus created would have little relevance to the pre-existent needs or wants of either. An Anglo-French union, now, would be unrelated to any of the commonplace facts of the workaday world, except perhaps to the development of tropical Africa.

The critics of our Commonwealth are often disposed to write it down as a mere thing of sentiment and emotionalism. Precisely the contrary is true. The Commonwealth relationship is concerned primarily with material advantages. The Commonwealth system has been hammered out in practice to meet immediate needs; it has been quick to shed juridical bonds which served no visible purpose. On the other hand, the integration of Britain with Europe is a romantic idea, derived from the heart, not from the head.

APPENDIX

Britain's Best Customers, 1954

Exports of British merchandise by value (£ 000)

The best customers in order of importance

1	Australia	277,812
	South Africa	156,245
	United States of America	149,309
	Canada	131,875

(CONTINUED OVERLEAF)

5	New Zealand	125,997
	India	114,907
	Irish Republic	100,621
	Netherlands	99,806
	Sweden	92,973
10	Denmark	82,511
	West Germany	70,532
	Norway	68,517
	Malaya and Singapore	65,414
	France	64,325
15	Italy	58,996
	British East Africa	54,634
	Belgium	54,612
	British West Indies	49,264
	Nigeria	48,810
20	The Rhodesias and Nyasaland	48,524
	Pakistan	45,852
	Gold Coast	33,876

Summary of British Exports, 1954 (£000)

To:		
	Sterling Area	1,329,900
	Non-Sterling OEEC Countries	723,600
	North America	281,200
	Soviet Eastern Europe	24,300
	Other	314,400
	Total	2,673,400

Index

A l'Échelle Humaine (Leon Blum): 201
Aachen: 241
Actes du Congrès Historique du Centenaire de la Révolution de 1848 (Renouvin): 19
Action Committee for a European Constituent Assembly: 59–60
Action Committee for the United States of Europe: 62, 78
Ad hoc assembly (on political integration): 60, 61, 115, 211, 225, 226
Adams, Henry: 272
Adams, John: 262
Aden: 283
Adenauer, Konrad: 7, 45, 178, 190, 191, 193, 194, 195, 238, 238n., 241–42, 242n., 243
Africa: 1, 2, 4, 11–12, 21, 27, 30–31, 52, 155, 156, 161, 191, 237, 247, 248, 262, 279–80, 287n., 291; and Asia, nationalism, 27; problems of, 245–46
Agriculture, in a united Europe: imports and exports, 155–56; production, 154; protection by high tariffs, 152; self-sufficiency, 157
Air Transport Council: 288
Alcott, Louisa May: 276
Alexander the Great: 11, 232
Algeria: 195, 281
Allston, Washington: 264
Alsace: 14, 202
Anarchy: 163–64
André, Pierre: 180
Anti-Americanism, as consequence of European decay: 170
ANZUS: members of, 285, 286
Arab world: 157, 202, 270
Arab-Asian bloc: 236
Arneth, Alfred von: 271
Asia: 1, 2, 4, 11, 21, 27, 30–31, 34, 66, 125, 155, 156, 157, 191, 233, 234, 237, 243, 247, 248, 279; and Africa, nationalism, 27; problems of, 245–46
Assemblée Nationale: 179, 180
Association: spirit of, in America, 274–75; way of (*see also* Co-operation), 115, 116
Association of Universities of the Commonwealth: 288
Atlantic Council: 59
Atlantic Ocean: 1, 125, 127, 244
Atlantic Pact, The (Halford L. Hoskins): 244n.
Atlantic Pact. *See* North Atlantic Security Pact
Atlantic solidarity: 170, 171
Atomic energy (*see also* European Atomic Community): and common market, 78; Europe of the Six and Europe of the Fifteen, 106, 118; integrated approach to, 94–95, 161, 258; and Messina Conference, 94, 225; revolution, consequences of, 66; and sectoral integration, 146, 148; stalemate, and reduction of chances of aggression, 240; weapons, effect on strategic importance of Germany, 238
Aumeran, General: 179
Australia: 2, 39, 264, 279, 281, 283, 285, 289, 290
Austria: 14, 15, 17, 18, 28, 106, 109, 135–36, 271
Austrian treaty: 189
Automation, term: 98

Baghdad Pact: 286
Balance of power: 3, 5, 6, 13, 89, 250; Dunkirk and Brussels treaties as steps to restore, 252; French revolutionaries' rejection of, 16; and principles of international law, 15; in reign of Louis XIV, 14; Wilson's view of, 17; World War I, effect on, 18
Balkan Pact: 33
Balkans: 24, 62, 66, 169, 236, 239, 268
Baltic states: 29, 239
Bancroft, George: 272
Bank of England: 283
Bank for International Settlements: 130
Barnard, Henry: 264

INDEX

Basle: 130, 263
Battaglia, Felice: vii
Beccaria, Cesare Bonesana di: 264
Belgium (*see also* Benelux, Low Countries): 32, 93, 162, 163, 278, 281, 286n.–287n.; coal and steel, 141–43; integration of Walloon and Flemish elements, 265; and Luxembourg, frontier taxes, 121; patriotism in, during world wars, 172–73; Social Democrats, 45
Bellosguardo: 276
Benelux (*see also* Belgium, Luxembourg, Netherlands): v, 84; and American initiative, 268; and Brussels Treaty, 252; and customs tariffs, 92; and customs union, 135; defense of, 174; and economic integration, 116; and Europe of the Six, 106; and free-trade area, 133; and Great Britain, political integration difficulty, 290; and joint marketing, 120; *malaise* in, 162; political federation, 126; and trade increase, 95; and voting in supranational bodies, 221
Berlin blockade: 236, 252
Berlin Indemnity Bank: 152
Bevin, Ernest: 83, 243, 252, 254
Beyen, J. W.: 125, 130
Beyen Plan: 130, 130n.
Bidault, Georges: 212
Big Europe and Little Europe (*see also* Europe of the Fifteen, Europe of the Six): choice between, 105; distinction between, 103
Bigiavi, Walter: vii
Bismarck, Otto von: 17, 202, 287
Blum, Leon: 201
Bohemia: 269, 271
Bologna: v, xii, 100; University of, vii, xii
Bonnefous, Edouard: 101, 101n.
Botta, Carlo Giuseppe Guglielmo: 271
Bracher, Karl Dietrich: 185n.
Brecht, Bertolt: 199
Bretton Woods Conference: 130
Briand, Aristide: 38, 82
British Commonwealth: 25–26, 85, 88, 119, 252, 254–55; committees, councils, etc., 288; Commonwealth Relations Office, 288–89; and complex of commerce, 282–83; defense strategy, 284–86; and imperial federation, 289–90; integration, notions of, 290–91; protectionism and new industries, 153; sterling area, 283–84; system of, as model for a united Europe, 218; and United Nations, 286–88; and western Europe, 279–91
Bruderrat: 188
Brussels Committee: vi, 83, 133n., 226; atom, report on, 118, 225; and common market, 73, 74, 76, 77, 79, 122, 123, 225; on sector-by-sector integration, 120; and Spaak, 65, 71
Brussels Pact: 208–209, 237, 252, 286
Bulganin, N. A.: 166, 193
Bundesjugendring: 188
Burritt, Elihu: 20
Byrnes, James: 186
Byzantium: 5, 232

Cadmus, in myth of Europa: 232, 233, 234, 235, 249
Caillaux, Joseph: 199
Canada (*see also* British Commonwealth): 31, 39, 81, 84, 102, 250, 254–55, 256, 257, 264, 281–85 *passim*, 289, 290
Capitalism: 27, 129
Carnot, Lazare Nicolas: 16
Cartels, and common market: 129
Catherine II, Czarina of Russia: 13
Catholic political parties, rise of: 44–45
Catholicism: 44, 45, 187, 273; French and German, differences, 187
Cattaneo, Carlo: 19, 20, 37
Cavour, Camillo Benso di: 163, 287
Central Europe: 13, 28–29, 34, 88, 196, 204
Cerularius, Michael: 12
Chabod, Federico: 197, 197n.
Charlemagne: 107
Charles II, of Hapsburg: 14
Charles V, Holy Roman Emperor: 3, 13, 14
Chevalier, Michel: 19, 19n.
China: 84, 85, 102, 111, 156, 242, 270, 272
Christian Democratic party (Germany): 182
Christianity: 1, 3, 5, 12, 13, 232, 233, 243, 271
Churchill, Winston: 7, 40–41, 53, 54, 58, 83, 219, 237, 237n., 241, 242, 242n., 243, 243n., 264–65, 267–68
Civil War: 270
Civilization: common, 34, 53, 244, 253; Western, ix, 4, 26, 27, 28, 29, 32, 34, 83, 138, 165, 233, 250–51
Clemenceau, Georges: 174, 185
Coal and Steel Community. *See* European Coal and Steel Community
Coal and steel industries (*see also* European Coal and Steel Community): by-

INDEX

products, demand for, 147; consumption, 64–65; and economic expansion, 141–44; economic and political problems, 81; and Europe of the Six, 108–109; free trade in, 131; functional approach, 51; Korean boom, and steel prices, 72; protection of, in a united Europe, 153; and regression, 140–41; and sovereign powers, 69

Cobden, Richard: 19

Coexistence: 48–49, 170, 213, 240–42; term, 114

Cold war: 61, 177, 191, 192

Columbia University: 272

Colonialism: 158, 202, 267; Colonial Office, 288

Common market (*see also* Brussels Committee, Messina Conference, Spaak Report, Venice Conference): and *ad hoc* assembly, 60; and atomic energy, 78–79, 95, 121; benefits of, 71–72; benefits of, and a larger Europe, 110, 117, 135; Benelux, progress toward, 119–20; and J. W. Beyen, 130; and Britain, vi, 119; concept of, 101–102; Council of Ministers, power of, 76, 77; and customs problems, 122–23; dangers of, 259; economic and political significance of, xi, xii, 62, 66, 225, 226; establishment of, 132–34; and Europe of the Six, 70, 106, 107; and European Coal and Steel Community, 70, 140; "European Free Trade," 129n.; as example of horizontal integration, 90, 130–31; and exchange rates of the Six, 135; and free trade, 118, 127–29, 138; and French claim against customs union, 135; institutions of, 75–76, 76–78; labor and business problems as a result of, 135; labor and quotas, 73–74; as long-range objective, 70; monetary aspects, 123; and protective measures in a united Europe, 153; and restrictions, 129; Russian, 102; as "single large market" in Hoffman "Integration Speech," 126; and supranationality, 70, 122; term, 133; treaty, vi, xii

Communism (*see also* Russia): anti-, in Germany and the United States, 194; in Asia and Africa, 245, 246; Asian, as challenge to Europe, 234; Churchill on, 53; coming defeat of, 167; and conflict with West, 173; and East Germany, 238; and European capitalism, 129; and fascism, 30; and France, 55, 177, 186, 207–208; in Germany, 186–87; global hegemony, attempt at, 266; in Greece, 33, 253; and Hitler, 29; hot war and nonintervention, rejection of, 167n.; imperialism, and Europe, 111; and Marshall Plan, 57, 209, 243; Marxism, and messianic spirit of Russia, 87; Marxist dialecticians on class war, 263; and new relations with the West, 239–40; and North Atlantic Community, 209, 244, 254, 261; parties in Italy, 207; promise of, 83; propaganda against EDC, 181; in Russia, possible dying of, 166; Russian, as challenge to Europe, 26–27; and South Korea, attack on, 253; Stalinism, being liquidated, 240; threat of, and need for Western unification, 165–66, 171–72, 211, 236–37, 242, 249; in Turkey, 253; and World War I, 43

Competition: 150–53

Conseil Fraternel: 188

Constitution, European: 38, 212, 220

Constitution of the United States: 24, 39, 269

Convention for European Economic Co-operation: 84

Convention Nationale, decree of: 16n.

Convertibility of currency. See *under* Currency

Cook, Captain James: 265

Cooper, James Fenimore: 276

Co-operation (*see also* Organization for European Economic Co-operation): and Britain, 290–91; between Britain and Commonwealth, 286–87; and Council of Europe, 105; economic, and Marshall Plan, 210; and Europe of the Fifteen, 104, 110; and federalism, 100, 103, 105; and integration, 80, 89, 217, 258–59; and sovereignty, 105

Coray, Adamantios: 21

Coste-Floret, Alfred: 180, 181

Coudenhove-Kalergi, Count: 38, 82, 86

Council of Europe: 54, 55, 59, 67–68, 83, 84, 88, 103, 105, 116, 127n., 169, 170, 184, 219, 224, 237; reports of, on economic integration, 85–86, 86n., 90, 90n., 91

Coupland, Reginald: 31

Crèvecoeur, Hector St. John: 263

Crucé, Émeric: 82

Crusades: 232, 265

Currency: 102, 104, 123, 131, 150; convertibility, 118, 122, 123, 128, 132, 260; exchange rates, 135

Customs union. See *under* Trade

Cyprus: 33, 169, 213
Czechoslovakia: 17, 236, 239, 252

Dahlmann, Friedrich Christoph: 271
Daladier, Édouard: 182-83, 201
Danilevsky, N.: 27
Dante Alighieri: 7, 82
Das Parlament: 185
De recuperatione Terre Sancte (Pierre Dubois): 18
De Wette, Wilhelm Martin: 264
Defense (*see also* European Defense Community, North Atlantic Security Pact, North Atlantic Treaty Organization): armaments race, 189, 191; British Commonwealth, strategy of, 284-86; disarmament, 170, 236, 240; and East-West struggle, 5-6, 191; failure of approach, xi; forces, development of, 191; forces, lack of, 174-75; individual states, self-defense of, 85, 216; integrated approach to, 161; and NATO, 93, 253; necessity of, in view of failure of United Nations, 252; North Atlantic and European solutions, 257-58; problems of European, 58-59; protection of United States after World War II, 53; against Soviet aggression, 241; in a united Europe, 155, 157; of western European states, present status, 85
Democracy: in Asia, 34; in Asia and Africa, 246; Atlantic, little interest in, 170; as characteristic of modern civilization, 251; Christian, as a main current of European political life, 164; Christian, after World War II, 44; in eastern and Central Europe, 34; in Europe after World War II, 51; federal, of United States, 48; federalist organization as political force of, 164; in Germany, 165, 183, 194; and market economy, 146; in NATO Treaty, 253; principle of, and Atlantic Community, 244; and rearmament of Germany, 181; in Switzerland and among her neighbors, 24; systems, rise of, after Iron Curtain lifted, 240; de Tocqueville, 34, 274; totalitarianism, threat of, 222; tradition, national flag as symbol of, 164; in World War II, 29
Denis, André: 179
Denmark: 14, 44n., 162, 266, 271, 278
Depression of 1929: 40, 153
Deutsches Reich: 32
Dialectical materialism: 5

Diplomatic Revolution (Reversal of Alliances): 15
Disarmament: 170, 236, 240
Dobrovský, Josef: 21
Dreyfus Affair: 203
Droysen, Johann Gustav: 271
Dubois, Pierre: 18
Dulles, John Foster: 166n., 168, 191
Dunkirk, Treaty of: 252

East-West tension: 4-6, 189-90, 191
Eastern Europe: 13, 28-29, 34, 44n., 47, 52, 53, 99, 208, 236, 239, 241
Eckermann, Johann Peter: 22-23
Economic Co-operation Administration: 98
Economic integration: Beyen on, 130; considerations in, 100-101; and ECSC, 68-70, 147; ECSC, and disadvantages of sectoral arrangements, 128; and federal character of institutions, 77; and federal powers, 70; free-trade community, membership, 132-34; functional way, 116-19, 120; goal of, 138, 140, 148; and Great Britain, 119; Hoffman "Integration Speech," effects on, 126; and Little Europe, 127; and Marshall Plan, 67; members involved, 125-26; and neutralism among political leaders, 211; OEEC, future of, 119-20; prior to World War I, 131-32; term, 98, 125
  and political integration: x, 85-86, 95, 115, 134, 225-26; differences, 64; interrelation, 69; need of both, 89-90
ECSC. *See* European Coal and Steel Community
Eden, Anthony: 243
Egypt: 232, 273
Einaudi, Luigi: 37
Eisenhower, Dwight D.: 59, 184, 184n., 258, 277, 278
Elbe River: 18, 29, 30
Eldon, John Scott, first earl of: 264
Elizabeth, Queen of England (1533-1603): 15
Ellis, Howard S.: 184n.
England. *See* Great Britain
Enlightenment: 21, 25, 26, 98, 265-66
Entente of the Three Emperors: 17
Erasmus, Desiderius: 7, 82
Erhard, Ludwig: 115
Erler, Fritz: 194
Esprit, neutralist sentiment in: 207
Ethiopian war: 198
Euratom. *See* European Atomic Community
Europa, myth of: 231-32, 233, 234, 249

INDEX

Europe (*see also under* individual countries): anti-Americanism, 170; and Asia and Africa, challenge of, 4; balance of power (*see* Balance of power); boundaries of, 13, 21; citizenry of, necessary for European Community, 221; civic enthusiasm, lack of, 172–74; commerce commission, inter-European, 150; and communism, challenge of, 26–27; concepts of, 1–2, 11–12, 21–22; constituent assembly, 57; contributions of, to America, 263–64, 276–77; courts, in a united Europe, 152; decadence of, 48, 78 (*see also Malaise*); diplomacy, and nationality principle, 17; as distinct from Asia and Africa, 11; and Enlightenment, 21; fascism and communism, effects on, 29–30; federation (*see* Federation, Integration, Unification); of the Fifteen (*see* Europe of the Fifteen); free, Saint-Simon on, and Franco-British alliance, 23; geographical and ethnical constitution of, 1; heritage of liberty and peace, 29; ideologies, decline, in interwar period, 201–202; industry, 246, 260; modern, birth of, 13; and myth of Europa, 231–32, 233, 234, 249; and Near East, 231–36; neutralism in, 199–200, 207–208, 208n., 210–11; as one of four pillars of world, Churchill on, 242, 242n.; political structure, necessity for gradual growth, 219–20; political unity, breakdown of, 2–3; in relation to Russia and the United States, 30–31, 40, 58, 64–66, 78, 84–86, 87, 99–100, 101–102, 111, 138, 250, 260–61; in relation to the world, 111, 245; of the Six (*see* Europe of the Six); solidarity, lack of development, 215–16; of states, 13–18; supreme court of, 150; term, etymology, 11, 97–98, 100, 125, 126; union (*see also* Integration, Unification), 53, 83; as united, relation to world economy, 150–58; United States of, 37, 83, 214, 252; world position, 25–26, 27, 46, 215; World War II, cultural and economic effects, 30–31

Europe, Concert of: 19

Europe of the Fifteen: xi, 103, 104, 106, 110, 116

Europe of the Six: xi, 88, 103, 105–106, 109, 110, 127, 128; and Action Committee for the United States of Europe, 62; and atomic power, 109, 118, 121; Beyen on, 130; and Britain, 117, 119; Charlemagne, empire of, 107; coal and steel, 56, 108–109; and common market, 20, 129, 132, 259; common market and Euratom treaties, vi; ESCS, ratification of, 57; and European army, 60; and federal union pact, 57; as framework for European renewal, 118; and free trade, 130, 134; and German unity, 106–107; and hostility of French Catholics, 187; industrial production, 65; integration of, 57; joint market and Britain, 119; and limitations on in regard to rest of the world, 107–108; Messina, Conference of, 62; per capita income of, 65; political and economic commissions, 106; and steel consumption, 65; supranationalism, 61, 104, 110; and unions of electric power, transport community, and green pool, 109

European army: Churchill on, 58; and ECSC, 180; governments represented at conference for, 60; and neutralism, 212; and sovereignty, 59

European Atomic Community (*see also* Atomic energy): 154, 195, 226; Action Committee for the United States of Europe, 62, 78; and common market, 62, 78–79; and Europe of the Six, 109; as an immediate objective, 70; importance of, to European industrial structure, 121; and national economies of countries concerned, 131; responsibility for, 94–95; and "Spaak Report," 128n., 131; treaty, drafting of, vi, 133n.

European Coal and Steel Community: advantages of, 108; atomic power, discussion of, 118; and Brussels Committee, 74, 79, 123; coal and steel barriers, 259; Common Assembly, 56, 72n., 73, 81–82, 139; component parts, 76; Council of Ministers, 76, 95, 139; Court of Justice, 95, 139, 224; and customs duties, 92; and economic integration, 68–70, 81, 88, 90, 116, 125, 132–33, 137, 179; and EDC, 60, 224; establishment of, 56–57, 84, 126–27, 128; as Europe of the Six, 103, 106; evaluation, 144–45; as example of vertical (functional) integration, 56, 90, 115, 120, 128, 129, 145–46; expansion, reaction to, 141–44; as federal organization, 69–70; and Franco-German relations, 81, 186; free trade, proposal for, 130; and Great Britain, 108, 227, 286; High Authority, 56, 62, 70, 74, 76, 77, 131, 139, 142, 143, 144, 224, 226; industrial production of member states (1955), 65; Italian steel industry, 144–45; and labor, 73–74; and neutralism, 211; and OEEC, 116–17; organs of, and Euratom, 95; and power, 118; purpose of, 224; regression, reaction to, 140–41; results of, 140; and sovereign rights, 93; structure of, and common market, 76; as successful example of integration, 259; supranational character of, 51, 68, 70, 95, 138–40, 224; and trade policies, 131

common market of: 145–49; business fluctuation, periods of, 72; effects of, in period of regression, 141; and expansion of trade, 144; functioning of, 140; position of ECSC with respect to, 138; of raw materials, and Italian steel industry, 145; stabilizing influence of, 142

European Commission: functions and powers given to, 76, 77, 122; study on, by Brussels experts, 122

European Community. *See* Integration *and under* Sovereign state

European Defense Community: construction of, 59; debate over, 128; and Europe of the Six, 106; failure of, v–vi, x, 84, 106, 115, 214; and functional (sectional) approach, 118, 224, 225; and France, 174, 179–81, 182; and Germany, 174, 181, 182, 183, 258; and integration idea vs. co-operation, 217; and Monnet, 127; and neutralism, 208, 211, 212; predictions of, 108; provisional arrangement, 60; treaty, ratification of, 61

European green pool: 109, 127

European idea: x, 98–100, 177; Legaret on, 181

European movement (*see also* Federalist movement, Integration): and Churchill, 53, 237; and Spaak, 59; term, meaning of, 98; after World War II, 43n.–44n.

European Payments Union: 84, 117, 126, 286

European Recovery Program: 97–98

European Union and United States Foreign Policy (F. S. C. Northrop): 107, 107n.

Expansion of England (J. R. Seeley): 279

Fascism: 26, 27, 28, 29, 30, 40, 43, 44n., 45, 198–99, 201, 203, 204, 205, 211

Fatherland: 164, 175, 200, 205; word, 21–22

Federation (*see also* Integration): advantages of federated area, 89; American, European, and Swiss experiences, 50; Anglo-French conflict, resolving of, 109–10; Atlantic, with the United States, 40; Britain and the Commonwealth, 38–39, 40, 289–90; and Eisenhower and Atlantic Pact, 59; Europe of the Six and individual problems, 109; Fascist countries, 40; forerunners of, 37; formal, and OEEC, 109; as Latin or Cartesian idea, 38–39; meaning, 216; Monnet and EDC, 127; need for, 169–71; Pan-Europe, 38; Paris Agreements on, 192; and supranationality, uses of, 109

federal: character of institutions in economic integration, 77; experience, and British political spirit, 39; institutions, 50, 54, 68; integration, and Schuman Plan, 68; organization, 69–70, 78; principle, in United States, 25–26; projects, and United States sovereignty, 127; powers, to common market and Euratom, 70; society, and French federalists, 56; system, in America, 267; term, 219

federalism: American, as pattern for Europe, 268–69; and co-operation (*see under* Co-operation); criticism, and European army, 59; failure of attempts at political community, 61; vs. functional approach, 50–51, 57–58, 63; ideas on European political entity and European defense, 59–60; kinds of, 105; and opponents, 68; potential of, 164–65; and protection of liberties, 223–24; solution, for Europe, 37; success of, 59; or supranationality and co-operation, 105; and supranationality and sovereignty, 103; in United States, 31

federalist movement: advances, 162–64; and Churchill, 40–41, 53, 54; development of, 49–50, in England, 39–42; Federal Union movement, 38–39, 41; in France, 55–56; in Italy, 40; and left-wing and trade-union leaders, 163; limitation of, 52; and Schuman Plan, 57

Ferdinand of Aragon: 12

Ferdinand I, Holy Roman Emperor: 14

Feudalism: 16

Fichte, Johann Gottlieb: 82, 263

Finland: 265, 269, 270

Flanders: 172

Florence, Italy: 263, 276, 277, 279

Food and Agriculture Organization: 288

INDEX

Foreign Office (Great Britain): 69, 190, 288
Four Power Conference: 189, 190
France (*see also* Franco-German relations): army, lack of, 174; and birth of modern Europe, 14–16; British proposal for federal union, refusal of, 41; Canada, French in, 31, 255, 264; Catholic parties in, 45; choice, between French Union and European unity, 62; communism in, 129, 207; confidence in state, loss of after World War II, 206; Constitution, 178; currency, 135; the East, relations with, 191, 239; and EDC Treaty, 61; and European army, 58; federalist movement in, 55–56; Fourth Republic, politicians of, 55; and free-trade area, 133, 134, 135; and German rearmament, 179–84, 192; and German sovereignty, 56; and Great Britain, 23, 40–41, 109–10, 143, 280–81, 286n.–287n., 290–91; import policy, 68; and Italy, 55, 196–97, 204, 205, 206; and Marshall Plan, 210; and Napoleon bid for European hegemony, 28; nationalist sentiments of, 268, 270, 271; NATO obligations and United States policy toward Arab world, 213; neutralism in, 207, 208, 212; North African problem, 169, 195; and nuclear energy, 109; and overseas territories as joint market, 121; and de facto contacts with Pankow, 193; Paris Agreements, ratification of, 189; production in, 72; protectionism and new industries, 153; public opinion, and British pro-European attitude, 55; republican undercurrent in 1789, 163; Revolution of 1789, 15, 16, 22, 166, 175, 181; and Russia, 177, 191, 194; and Saar, 33–34; as sovereign state, 3, 12, 93; steel, increase in orders, 141; Third French Republic, as secular state, 45; and Treaty of Dunkirk, 252; weakening of moral leadership after World War I, 202–203; World War I, justification for, 201; writers, on European federation, 23; mentioned, 25, 30, 32, 40, 45, 62, 83, 88, 106, 109, 126, 127, 129, 199, 212, 221, 252, 263, 264, 272, 276, 277, 278
Franche-Comté: 14
Franco, Francisco: 29
Franco-German Fraternal Council: 188
Franco-German relations: 34, 38, 47, 53, 55–56, 57, 58, 69, 81, 109, 191–93, 202–203, 219; differences, 186–87; history, importance of, 184–86; links between, 187–88; political difficulties, 186
Franco-Italian Customs Union: 123
Franco-Russian alliance: 200
Franco-Soviet Treaty, effects of Paris Agreements on: 190
François I: 13, 14
Franklin, Benjamin: 262, 265
Frederick I, Holy Roman Emperor: 3
Frederick the Great: 3, 15, 265
Free trade: area, advantages or disadvantages of, 101, 260; Benelux, example of, 135; Beyen on, 130; in coal and steel, 131; and common market, 127–29; difficulties in establishing, 134–35; Dutch proposal for, 130; and economic integration, equating of, 131; and Europe of the Six, 132–35; free market, 138, 143, 144; and Great Britain, vi, 280; membership, 135–36; in nineteenth century, 122; and United States lead toward, 260
Freedom. *See* Liberty
French Council of Youth: 188
Front Party: 172
Frontiers: European, 13; natural, 16, 28; as tax frontiers, 121

Gablenz, Otto Heinrich von der: 167n.
Gama, Vasco da: 12
Garrison, William Lloyd: 264
Gasperi, Alcide de: 7, 45
Gaulle, Charles de: 55
Geijer, Erik Gustaf: 271
General Agreement on Tariffs and Trade (GATT). *See under* Trade
Geneva: 50, 116, 118, 175
Geneva Conference: 189
George of Podebrad: 18
George III, King of England: 265
Gerlach, Hellmuth von: 199
Germany (*see also* Franco-German relations): army in, 61; Atlantic Alliance, 212; and Brussels Pact, 209, 252; Catholic parties in, 45; choice of, between national unity and European community, 62; and coal and steel industry, 141, 142–43; confidence in state, loss of after World War II, 206–207; Constitution and conscientious objector, 182–83; Democratic party in, 34; diplomacy, present deadlock of, 191–92, 194–95; Dunkirk treaty and militarism of, 252; and Eastern bloc, 189–91, 192–94; and Europe of the Six, 106–107; and European integration, v, 24, 55–56, 58, 62, 83, 88, 106–107, 108, 109, 126,

178-79, 180, 221, 238-39; and free-trade area, 133; and Great Britain, 143, 282, 290; and Marshall aid, 58, 178, 210, 252; militarism, 174, 178, 181, 185; military power, rebirth of, 58; and national socialism, 29, 38; nationalism in, 34, 40, 61, 93, 108, 178, 268, 269, 271; and neutralism, 203, 208, 212; and nuclear energy, 109; production in, 72; protectionism and new industries, 153; quarrels between government and opposition, 165; rearmament of Federal Republic, 106, 108, 173-74, 179, 180-84, 211, 212, 258; reunification, 51, 181, 182, 184, 188, 190, 191, 192, 192n., 193, 195, 213, 238-39, 241; and Russia, 29, 171, 177, 191, 192, 194, 203; and Saar, 33, 34, 143; Socialists, 183, 194-95; sovereignty, 55, 56, 178-79; *mentioned,* 1, 5-6, 13, 17, 18, 25, 27-28, 30, 43, 45, 49, 57, 99, 152, 173, 177, 179, 180, 184, 193, 199, 200-201, 202, 250-51, 263, 264, 270, 272, 276
Geyl, Pieter: 267
Giolitti, Giovanni: 197
Giraudoux, Jean: 201
Glorious Revolution: 25
Goethe, Johann Wolfgang von: 22-23, 248
Gold standard, acceptance of, prior to World War I: 131
Goya Lucientes, Francisco José de: 175
Great Britain (*see also* British Commonwealth): attitude toward herself after World War II, 41; backgrounds in, differing, 31-32; Briand's European constitution, opposition to, 38; and Brussels Treaty, 83; and Canada, 31, 255, 264, 284; and common market, 133n., 135; and Council of Europe, 54, 219; constitution, idea of, 39; and co-operation with the Continent, 213; Cyprus and Greek policy, policy toward, 213; and ECSC, 56, 109, 227; and European army, 58; European movement, role in, 53, 54; in European politics, 40; federalist movement, 39-42; and Germany, 55, 238; and Greece, friendship with, 169; and Integration position, 41, 69, 88-89, 106, 227, 237, 252; and joint market, association in, 119; and Labour party, 41, 45, 53, 204-205; leadership after World War II, attitude toward assumption of, 219; and Marshall Plan aid, 54, 210; nationalism, 42; neutralism vs. will for self-sufficiency in in-terwar period, 204-205; and OEEC, 54, 117; Pankow, de facto contacts with, 193; Parliament, and political theory, 290; parliamentary government, 23; as part of Atlantic Community, 254; the press in, and German-Soviet relations, 191; pro-European attitudes of, 55; and reconciliation with Russia, 194; relations with East, and Germany, 191; role in world affairs, secondary, 46; and Russian imperialism, 53; and Schuman Plan, 69; and Socialist experience, 53; as sovereign state, attitude of, 42; traditional civics, importance of, 173; and United States, 54, 85, 89, 168, 263, 264, 270, 279-80; and Western European Union, 116; world status of, 40, 242, 242n.; and written legal texts, 88; *mentioned,* 12, 14, 15, 25, 30
  and France: collaboration with, Saint-Simon on, 23; comparison of trade of, 280-81; problems of integration, 290-91; union with, 40-41
  trade and commerce: Appendix, Britain's Best Customers, 1954, and Summary of British Exports (1954), 292; coal imports, 143; complex of commerce in, 282-83; decline in trade of, 279-80; and free-trade area, vi, 133n.; and steel consumption, 65; and sterling area, 283-84
Greece: 1, 2, 11, 21, 33, 99, 109, 169, 213, 218, 236, 243, 253, 263, 264, 269, 271
Greenough, Horatio: 264
Grotius, Hugo: 82

Hague, The: Congress (1948), 54, 81, 178
Hamilton, Alexander: 213
Hamilton, Edith: 232n.
Hapsburg monarchy: 14, 15, 24, 28, 42
Harvard University: 83, 235, 242, 265
Hawthorne, Nathaniel: 276, 277
Hedge, Frederic Henry: 264
Hegel, Georg Wilhelm Friedrich: 1, 5
Heilperin, Michael A.: 130n.
Henderson, Arthur: 205
Henri II, King of France: 14
Henry the Navigator: 12
Herder, Johann Gottfried von: 22
Herodotus, *History:* 11, 11n., 232
Herriot, Édouard: 82, 182, 183
Hesiod, *Theogony:* 11
History of International Relations (Renouvin): 17
Hitler, Adolf: 3, 29, 34, 41, 43, 165,

INDEX

171, 172–73, 183, 185–86, 193, 203, 223, 266
Hitlerism, rise of, and present German studies: 185
Hocking, William Ernest: 235, 235n.
Hoffman, Paul G.: 125, 126
Holmes, Oliver Wendell: 278
Holy Alliance: 19, 51, 52
Holy Roman Empire: 2, 265
Homer: 11
Hoskins, Halford L.: 244n.
House of Commons: 83, 289
Hugo, Victor: 19, 37
Human Rights, Convention on: 223
Hungary: 3, 18, 239; crisis in, vi, x

Idealism: 24; Kantian, 264
India: 39, 84, 85, 102, 111, 156, 272, 281, 283, 285
Indo-China War: 181
Industry (*see also* Coal and steel): automotive, in Europe, 65, 141; building, 141; competition, North American and European, 260; European, and dependence upon Near East oil, 235; French and German, differences, 187; imports and exports, in a united Europe, 155–56, 157; increase in Europe, as compensatory measure, 245; in Italy, after World War I, 204; protection of, in a united Europe, 152, 153; United States and Britain, contrasted, 280
Institute of Commonwealth Studies: 288–89
Integration (*see also* Europe of the Fifteen, Europe of the Six, European Coal and Steel Community, Federation, Supranationality, Unification): achievements after World War II, 83–84; as affected by United States, 47–48; America as example of, 262–63; in America, reasons for success, 267–68; Atlantic, 242–44; and Atlantic Alliance, 227; and atomic energy, 94–95; attempts, 82–83, 115–16; attitude toward, of Britain and northern countries, 88–89; and Britain, 69, 227, 252, 290–91; broad approach to, 6–7; Canada and Australia as examples of, 264; and coexistence, 240–41 and common European parliament, 222–23; common-market approach, 127, 130; common market as immediate goal of, 138; Commonwealth system, 218–19; and communism, 236–37; concept of, 137–38; as it concerns a Near Easterner, 235; and co-operation (*see under* Co-operation); and cultural standardization, 276; development of idea since World War II, 215; and East-West struggle, 4–5; economic (*see* Economic integration); and elections, European, 222, 223; Europe, danger of as "closed shop," 96; European Community, and the state, 220–21; examples, 224–25, 237–38, 259, 268, 277–78; functional approach, 49, 50–51, 57–58, 60, 62, 71, 90–91, 115, 116, 118, 145–46; or functionalism of ECSC vs. association of OEEC, 115; future growth of, 226–27; and future relations with Asia and Africa, 247; German sovereignty, means to gaining, 178; and Germany, 238–39; global, 120–21; gradual, 120–21; horizontal, Beyen on, 130; and Hungarian and Middle East crises, vi, x; idea, awareness of today, 215; impetus for, need of, 175–76; importance, as independent of East-West struggle, 5–6; 241–42; and individual state, 224; industrial, on racial lines, 158n.; and lessening of European influence in Asia and Africa, 244–45; Marshall Plan effect on, 53–54; method of, 114–15; monetary aspects of, 123; and national sovereignty, 3–4; and nationalism, 32–34, 266; necessity for, ix–x, 4; and necessity for proper institutions, 215, 216, 217; and North Atlantic Community (*see under* North Atlantic Community); objections to, 91–94, 95–96, 117; and OEEC and Council of Europe, 55, 67–68; political (*see* Political integration); positive approach to, 161–62; power of, and ways of establishing, 217–18; price for, 134; problems of, 81, 266–67; proposals for, 23–24; and protective customs, 91–92; role of men of letters in, 278; Russo-American impasse, effect on, 51–53; sector-by-sector approach, 120–21, 127, 130–31, 224; and smaller European nations, 95–96; and the sovereign state, nature of, 92–94; and Soviet imperialism, 47; spiritual basis of, 247–49; supranational, democratic control of, 222–23; supranational authority, necessity for, 219–20; term, 80, 97–98, 100, 110–11, 133, 216, 217; time element, 103–105; vertical (*see* functional approach, *supra*)

International Bank for Reconstruction and Development: 130, 256
International Economic Co-operation (In-

ternational Economic Integration) (Jan Tinbergen): 98
International law. *See under* Law
International Monetary Fund: 118–19, 130, 256, 288
International Red Cross: 274
International Refugee Organization: 236
International Telecommunications Union: 288
Internationale: 200
Interstate Commerce Commission (United States): 150
Intervention: 199, 200n.
Investment Fund ("Spaak Report"): 135
Ireland: 262, 265, 266–67, 273, 277, 282, 285
Iron Curtain: 4–5, 99, 125, 166, 167, 167n., 239–40, 245
Irredentist movement (Italy): 197
Irving, Washington: 264
Isabella of Castile: 12
Islam: 4
Israel: 1, 2, 273
Istituto per gli Studi di Politica Internazionale: 130
Isvolski, Alexander Petrovich: 200
Italy: Catholic parties in, 45; Cavour on, 163; colonies, 236; communism in, 129, 207; and European defense, 59, 61, 174; and European integration, v, 24, 38, 83, 88, 100, 106, 109, 126, 209, 221, 275; and fascism, 30, 204; and federalism, 40, 59; and France, 55, 197, 205; and free-trade area, 133; imports into, 72; interventionism and World War I, 196–97, 204; Irredentist provinces, 203; labor, 145; and Marshall Plan, 210; nationalism and the sovereign state, 22, 25, 93, 269, 270, 271; and NATO, 213; and neutralism, 30, 196–98, 198–99, 203–204, 206, 208, 212; and OEEC: 68; steel industry, 74, 141, 144–45; traditions from, 263, 277; unification of, 5–6, 17, 18, 25, 74, 197; and the Vatican, 45; *mentioned,* 14, 109, 127n., 262, 272, 276

Jacobin state: 164, 166
Jacobs, Jean: xii
James, Henry: 276
Japan: 13, 202, 250, 272
Jefferson, Thomas: 244, 262, 266, 272
Johns Hopkins University, The: v, vi, xii, xiii
Judaism, in the United States: 273
Justinian: 12

Kalevala: 264
Kant, Immanuel: 82, 263
Katholikentag: 187
Kefauver, Estes: 170
Kemal, Mustapha: 33
Khrushchev, Nikita: 165
Klopp, Onno: 271
Kohn, Hans: 24n., 26n., 87n., 227
Korean War: 58, 127, 142, 285

"La santa alleanza dei popoli" (Mazzini): 20
La Vie Intellectuelle: 207
Labor: and common market, 73, 75, 77, 140; and ECSC, 73–74, 140; as European problem, 107; and free-trade area, 134; immigrant, fear of, 91; in Italy, 74, 145; Monnet on, 73; non-European, restrictions against, in a united Europe, 153; problems of, 74; regulations, and joint market, 123; as a resource of the West, 88; on strike in Holland and Denmark, 162; transfer of, under "Spaak Report" Readaptation Fund, 135; in a united Europe, 74, 151, 152, 153, 154
Labour party. *See under* Great Britain
Lafuente, Modesto: 271
Language: 21, 22, 24, 92, 278
Lansbury, George: 199, 205
Larevellière-Lepeaux, Louis Marie: 16
Lausanne, Treaty of (1923): 13
Law: civilized processes of, and nationalism, 28; international, 15–16, 17; Roman, Europe rooted in, 248; rule of, as characteristic of modern civilization, 251; rule of, and NATO treaty, 253
Le Monde: 207, 267n.
League of Nations: 37, 38, 82, 205
Lebanon: 231, 234, 235, 236
Lebon, Pierre: 181
Leczinski, Stanislas: 15
Lee, Robert E.: 270
L'Europe en Face de Son Destin (Edouard Bonnefous): 101, 101n.
Legaret, Jean: 181
Legitimacy principle: 16
Leibnitz, Gottfried Wilhelm von: 18
Lejeune, Max: 183
Lemonosov, Michael: 21
Lend lease: 268
Lenin, Nikolai: 26, 27, 43, 161, 165, 166, 172, 283
Leopold II: 162
Letters (Hector St. John Crèvecoeur): 263
Liberalism: 5, 44, 122, 128, 164

INDEX

Liberalization Code, and OEEC: 126, 131, 144
Liberty: change in Communist view of, 240; constitutional and idealism of 1830's and 1840's, 24; English, United States as frontier of, 25; in Europe, after World War II, 30, 51; European ideas of, in Asia and Africa, 245; in France, as result of proposed union with Britain, 23; German dedication to, 238; and German rearmament, 174; of Germany, postwar, 49; joint protection of, 227; under law, of the West, 29; love of, and question of integration, 219; and market economy, 146; meaning of, as national independence, 22; and Nazi occupation in Italy, 205; new forms of, in eighteenth-century Europe, 22; right of, English historical, 26; security of, Saint-Simon and Thierry on, 23; struggle for, and creation of an executive power, 170; in unity, 48; and United States attitude toward nationalism, 168; universal concept of, 22; as Western cause, 171–72

individual: as characteristic of modern civilization, 251; in Cyprus, 33; defeat of, in Europe, 29; in eighteenth-century Europe, 21; and human rights (*see* Rights); and national sovereignty, 29; and NATO treaty, 253; in nineteenth century, 24; principle of in Atlantic Community, 244; in Saar, 34; sacrificed by fascism, 26; and self-determination, 33; in Switzerland and Belgium, 24, 32; in United States, 26; Voltaire on, 22

Lincoln, Abraham: 244, 244n.
Lippmann, Walter: 251
Little Entente: 203
Little Europe and Big Europe (*see also* Europe of the Six, Europe of the Fifteen): distinction between, 103
Livingstone, William: 264
Loftus, John: 166n.
London: 190, 193, 263, 283, 284
London Telegraph: 20
Longfellow, Henry Wadsworth: 264
Lorraine: 15, 68, 142–43
Louis XIV, *Memoirs:* 14
Louis XV: 15
Louis XVI: 163, 164
Loustanau-Lacau: 180
Louvain, University of: 266
Low Countries (*see also* Belgium, Netherlands): 14, 30, 40; and Belgian coal, 143; and steel, 141

Luxembourg (*see also* Benelux): 83, 88, 93, 121, 224, 281

McAuliffe, General: 88
Machiavelli, Niccolò: ix
Mackay, Charles: 20
MacMahon, Arthur: 268
Madison, James: 272
Mahan, Admiral Alfred Thayer: 272
Malaise: 26, 30, 31, 41–42, 43, 46, 83, 94, 162, 203
Malthusianism: 120
Manifest destiny: 22
Mann, Horace: 264
Mansfield, William Murray, first earl of: 264
March on Rome: 198
Marigny, Antoine: 18
Marshall, General George: 83, 177, 242
Marshall Plan: advent of, 55; and British government, 54; and economic integration, 53–54, 67, 98; and federalists, 59; and Germany, 58, 178; Hoffman, as administrator, 125; and neutralism of political leaders, 210–11; purpose of, 209–10; results of, 57, 210, 237, 243; Soviet rejection of, 252; and the state, 211
Martel, Charles: 12
Marx, Karl: 248
Masson, Frédéric: 271
Mazzini, Giuseppe: 7, 19, 20, 25, 37
Mediterranean Sea: 1, 232–33, 244, 283
Mein Kampf: 165
Memoirs (Louis XIV): 14
Mendès-France, Pierre: 190
Messina Conference: v, 89, 217; and atomic energy, 62, 94, 225; Committee of Government Delegates, 94; and common market, 62, 88, 90, 94, 128, 225
Michelet, Jules: 25, 271
Mickiewicz, Adam: 7, 25
Middle East: v, x, 234, 242
Militarism: 28, 270; German, 174, 178, 181, 185
Ministerial Agriculture Committee: 116
Mitrany, David: 50
Moch, Jules: 182
Monnet, Jean: 41, 51, 56, 57, 62, 73, 77–78, 78n., 85, 126–27
More, Thomas: 82
Moscow, transfer of capital to: 27
Moscow Conference: 177, 178
Moselle canal scheme: 171, 186
Motley, John Lothrop: 272
Mumford, Lewis: 277

Munich Institute of Contemporary History: 185
Mussolini, Benito: 3, 29, 30, 43, 198, 199
Myrdal, Gunnar: 262
Mythology (Edith Hamilton): 232n.

Naegelen, Marcel-Edmond: 179-80
Napoleon Bonaparte: 3, 16, 18, 22, 28, 86, 166, 215, 232, 265, 266
Napoleon III: 17
Napoleonic wars: 22, 23
Naters, Van der Goes van: 81-82, 82n.
National Defense Commission: 180, 183
National Socialism: 29, 38, 186
National sovereignty. *See* Sovereign state
Nationalism: age of, and integration, 220, 227, 266; in America, and federal system, 268-69; in Asia and Africa, 27; attempts to depart from, 61, 67; and capitalism in America, 129; and Catholics, 44, 45; colonial, in Australia and Canada, 289; and colonialism, 168-69; and communism, 26; decline of, 44-45; development of, 265, 269; and dictators, European, 29, 30; economic, 54, 66-67, 128, 134; in eighteenth-century Europe, 21; and Enlightenment, 266; European, in interwar period, 25-29; evaluation, question of, 110; and German militarism, 108; in Germany, 34, 40; in Great Britain, 42; historians, support of, 271; historic end of era, 164; and human rights, 22, 28; and liberalism, conflict of, 24; limitations of, 89; military influence on, in Europe, 270; national hatred, Goethe on, 22-23; national independence, United States respect for, 168, 169; nineteenth-century, 19, 24; origins of, 22-23; political, strengthening of, 221; as problem in integration, 32-34; rebirth of, and national states, 49-50; and religion, 273; revival, modern, 207; and rights of the state, 211; in Russia, 27; and Russian and German tyranny, 29; and self-determination, 28; standardization as product of, 276; and Turkey and Greece, 33; in United States, 267, 270, 271-72; World War I, role in, 24-26
Nationalist party (Flanders). *See* Front party
Nationality, principle of: 17, 20
NATO. *See* North Atlantic Treaty Organization

Naziism: 43, 171, 184, 200, 202, 205, 266, 276
Near East: and Europe, cultural products of, 233-34; and Europe, historical connections between, 232-33; position of, 234-36; relationship with Europe, and myth of Europa, 231-32; religious element in, 273
Nenni, Pietro: 213
Netherlands (*see also* Benelux, Low Countries): 218, 278, 282; Beyen, Foreign Minister of, 125; and Brussels Treaty, 83; coal prices in, 143; and common market, 130; development of, 102; Dutch historians, national framework, 271; free trade proposal, 130; imports, 72; and integration, 32, 88; labor, 162; Motley on, 272; as sovereign state, 93
Neutralism: analogies of, in Europe and America, 199-200; and Brussels Pact, 208-209; changes in form, 210-14; in Europe since World War II, 207-208, 208n.; in France, in interwar period, 202-203, 205; in Germany, in interwar period, 203, 206-207; in Great Britain, 204-205; in interwar period in Europe, 202-205; in Italy, 196-99, 203-204; and Marshall Plan, 209-10; modern form of, 214; professional, since World War II, 211; as reflected in attitude toward war after World War I, 200-201; as reflected in refutation of ideologies during interwar period, 201-202; successes of, causes, 211-12
New Statesman and Nation: 267n.
New York Herald Tribune: 130n.
New Zealand: 102, 281, 285
North Africa: 169, 184, 236, 258
North America: 125, 153-54, 156-57, 246, 257
North Atlantic Community (*see also* North Atlantic Treaty Organization): and common market, danger of, 259; development of, 251-53; and European integration, 257-58, 259-60, 261; and free trade, 136; and Great Britain, 282, 290; and international economic organizations, 256; origin and concept of, 250-51, 254; Preamble, 244; and spirit of compromise, 25
North Atlantic Security Pact (*see also* North Atlantic Community, North Atlantic Treaty Organization): 58, 59, 208, 209, 210, 211; and European integration, 227; and NATO and SHAPE, 173; and neutralist attitude,

INDEX

212–13; origin of, 251; and West Germany and neutralism, 212
North Atlantic Treaty Organization (NATO): activities of, 116, 256, 257; and Canada, 254–55; as defense alliance, 253, 255, 257, 258; Dulles, on common political effort, 168; and European unity, 227, 237, 241; French obligations, and United States policy in Arab world, 213; and a united Germany, 190; and Great Britain, 282, 286; and Greek nationalism, 33; members of, 285; and morale of troops, 173; Nenni on, 213; and North Atlantic Community, 244, 251; and OEEC, 256–57; and supranational staff, 93; weakness, 170
Northrop, F. S. C.: 107, 107n.
Northwest Ordinance (1787): 269
Norway, 22, 44n., 266, 269, 278
Novikor, Nikolai: 21

Obraković, Dimitrije: 21
Observer, The: 170
Oder-Neisse line: 181
Odoacer: 2
OEEC. *See* Organization for European Economic Co-operation
Olympic Games: 193
Organe des Vollkommenen Friedens (Johannes Sartorius): 19
Organization for European Economic Co-operation (OEEC): and atom, 118; benefits of, to ECSC, 117; Council, 126; development of, 126; and economic and political collaboration, 55, 67–68, 81, 125; and Germany, 178; and Great Britain, 54, 119, 283; meeting in Paris, 133n.; membership, as European economic institution, 116, 125; and Ministerial Agriculture Committee, 116; and NATO, 256–57; Preamble, 81; and trade liberalization, 73, 118; 131, 132, 144; and UNESCO, 267; as way of co-operation or association, 69, 88, 95, 96, 109, 115, 116–17, 119-20, 122, 137, 138
Ossietzky, Carl von: 199
Ottoman Empire: 12, 13, 33, 232

Pacifism (*see also* Neutralism): 211; writers, 199
Page, William: 264
Paine, Thomas: 269
Palacký, František: 28, 271
Pan-Europe movement: 38, 82, 86, 103
Pankow: 193
Panofsky, Professor: 277

Paparrhegopoulos, K.: 271
Paris: 50, 127n., 133n., 178
Paris Agreements: 178, 179, 182–83, 189–90, 192, 192n., 286
Paris Congress (1856): 17
Paris Treaty: 182
Parker, Theodore: 264
Parkman, Francis: 272
Patrie (term): 21
Patriotism (*see also Malaise*): differences in first and second world wars, 172–73
Paul I, Czar of Russia: 86
Pax Christi: 187
Penn, William: 18, 82
Peschel (author): 186
Peter the Great: 13, 27, 86
Petite Histoire de l'Idée Européenne (Bernard Voyenne): 11n., 18
Pflimlin, Pierre: 127
Philip II, King of Spain: 14, 272
Pineau, Christian: 194
Pleven, René: 180
Poincaré, Raymond: 200
Poland: 6, 13, 14, 15, 16, 29, 239, 262, 269
Political integration (*see also under* Economic integration): and Monnet, 126–27; neutralist opposition, 211
Pope Leo X: 82
Popular Front: 203
Portugal: 3, 44n., 109, 286, 286n.–287n.
Potsdam: 51
Poujade, Pierre: 164
Power: electric power community, usefulness of, 109; and sectoral integration, 146
Powers, Hiram: 264
Prescott, William Hickling: 272
"Present State of Economic Integration in Western Europe, The": 85–86, 86n., 91
"Progress Towards a New Europe as Viewed by a Dutchman" (Beyen speech): 130
Projet de Paix Perpétuelle (l'Abbé de Saint-Pierre): 19
Protestantism: 183, 188, 273
Proudhon, Pierre Joseph: 37
Prussia: 3, 6, 15, 16, 18, 264

Ranke, Leopold von: 21
Rathenau, Walther: 43
Readaptation Fund, of "Spaak Report": 135
Relance européenne: 84
Remarque, Erich Maria: 199
Renouvin, Pierre: 17, 19
Republique des lettres: 21

Resistance (World War II): 49, 50, 186–87, 205, 275
Respublica Christiana: 3
Reudel: 16
Reuter, Professor: 81
Reversal of Alliances: 15
Reynaud, Paul: 183–84
Rhine River: 16, 55, 69, 86
Rights: individual, 21, 34, 187; minorities, 24; rights of man, Voltaire on, 22; security of, and new nationalism, 22; and self-determination, 32–33, 245
Ripley, George: 264
Risorgimento: 197
Rittenhouse, David: 266
Ritter, Gerhard: 186
Roman Empire: 1, 11, 12, 98, 244
Rome: vi, 1, 2, 86, 87, 99, 199, 232, 243, 263, 264
Rome Conference (1953): 120
Romulus Augustulus: 2
Roosevelt, Franklin D.: 201–202, 202n.
Rothfels, Hans: 186
Royal Society: 265
Ruhr: 56, 57, 68, 143, 181, 183
Russia (*see also* Communism): armies, possibility of withdrawal to Russian frontiers, 240; and atomic energy, 78; autocratic regime in, and Italian attitude in World War I, 196; boundaries of, 13, 14; boundary decisions in Europe after World War II, 51; and China, 111; civilization of, 99; colonization by, 13; common market of, 102; and economic reorganization of world on racial bases, 158n.; economic strength of, 102, 153–54; Enlightenment in, 21; Europeanization of, 5, 13; expansionism, 83, 86, 87; and France, 192, 194, 203; and Germany, 48–49, 171, 190, 191, 192–94; and Great Britain, 53, 194; Hapsburg monarchy, dissolution of, 28; imperialism, force of, 46–47; integrated Europe, concept of, 239; internal disintegration, 166; Iron Curtain as line reached by Russian army in 1945–48, 167; and Jacobin mind, 47–48; under Lenin, 26–27; and Marshall Plan aid, 210; menace of, 86–87; messianic spirit of, 5, 86–87; minorities against, 171; as national state, 42; nationalism in, and Napoleonic wars, 22; North Atlantic Alliance, responsibility for, 251; orthodox faith, as keeper of, 86; and Poland, 6, 15, 16; and policy following death of Stalin, 212; policy, understanding of, 171; relaxation of, and Paris Agreements, 189; Revolution (1905), 27; and revolution, global, 166; role, in unity of Europe, 241–42; and satellites, 29, 44n., 47, 52, 99; size of, 84; steel consumption, 65; as superstate, 260–61; and United States, 51–53, 58; universal monarchy, urge for, 28; and vacuum left by destruction of German power, 251–52; value of integrated Europe to, 237; Von der Gablenz on inhabitants of, 167n.; and West Germany, rehabilitation of, 252; and Western policy toward, 166–68; as a world source of science and technology, 246; world status, Churchill on, 242, 242n.; and World War I, expansion after, 28; writers of, 87; *mentioned,* 6, 18, 21, 24, 30, 58, 85, 89, 94, 111, 250, 279, 280

Saar: 34, 141, 142–43, 171, 186, 195
Saint Augustine: 248
Saint Francis: 248
St. Laurent, Louis Stephen: 252, 254
St. Petersburg, transfer of capital from: 27
Saint-Pierre, l'Abbé de: 19, 82
Saint-Simon, Comte de: 23
Saragat, Giuseppe: 208n.
Sartorius, Johannes: 19
Scandinavia (*see also* Norway, Sweden): 30, 143, 162, 262, 268, 272; and common market, 133n., 135–36; and integration, 24, 40, 88, 106, 290
Schelling, Friedrich Wilhelm Joseph von: 5
Schneider (Germany): 186, 194
Schneiter, Pierre: 179
School, Inge: 186
Schuman, Robert: 7, 45, 56, 57, 81, 128, 129, 179, 243
Schuman Plan (*see also* European Coal and Steel Community): and British participation, 69; and European Defense Community, in France, 179–81; and federalism, 59, 68, 69; and German problem, 55–56; Heilperin, Second Schuman Plan, 128; and Hoffman "Integration Speech," 126; pessimistic forecasts at start, 145; and reconstruction, 57; and sectional (functional) arrangements, 57, 128; success of, 78; treaty, signing of, by Italian Foreign Minister Sforza, 127n.
Section Française de l'Internationale Ouvrière (SFIO): 179
Seeley, J. R.: 279
Self-determination: 15–16; of Asia and

INDEX

Africa, 245; national, since nineteenth century, 32–33; national, in Saar, 34; and national jealousies between world wars, 27–29; as a past slogan, 287; right of, 32–33, 245
Separatist movement, and Adenauer: 45
SFIO: *See* Section Française de l'Internationale Ouvrière
Sforza, Carlo: 127n.
SHAPE. *See* Supreme Headquarters Allied Powers Europe
Sharp, Granville: 264
Silone, Ignazio: 44–45
Singapore: 283, 285, 286
Slavic world: 5, 244–45
Smith, Adam: 279
Social Democrats: 182, 190
Social security: policy, in European states as opposed to America, 154; systems in Scandinavia and Benelux, 162
Socialism: 44–45, 53, 129, 164, 179–80, 198
South America: 156, 157
Southeast Asia Treaty Organization (SEATO): 286
Sovereign state: attitude toward, today, 213–14, 216, 269; authority, 163; and Belgian Social Democrats, 45; and Catholics, 44, 45; citizens of, and decline in civic consciousness, 172; creation of, struggle for, 37; as decisive unit in history, 32; decline of, 42–44, 50, 63, 89; direction of education, religion, etc., in Europe, and effect on spirit of association, 275; duty to, in Germany, 187; equilibrium, attempts at among, 3; and European army, 59; and a European Community, 220–21, 224; faith in, loss of, 198, 206–207; international obligations, and reluctance to become involved with, 208; liberals as inspiration for, 44; and Jean Monnet, 41; nationalism developing before organization of, in Europe, 269; neutralism as opposition to, 198–99; power of, and American associationism, effect on, 274; powers, and coal and steel industries, 69; powers, transfer of, to supranational body, 88; privileges, necessity of giving of, 171; restoration of, after World War II, 49; rights, and integration, 69, 92–94; rights, relinquishing of, 211; rights, and Schuman Plan, 69; rights, transfer of, 88; and Socialists, 45; and supranational bodies, 80; system of, and Marshall Plan, 211; in unionism, 103; world wars, effect on, 42, 43

sovereignty: and administrative and economic bodies, decline of, 46; of American thirteen states, 269; of Austria, 106; in British Colonial Office, 288; and common market and Spaak Commission, 62; in Commonwealth Relations Office, 288; concept of, persistence of today, 7; and co-operation, 105; as enemy of Western cause, 169; and European Coal and Steel Community, 57; European Coal and Steel Community members, renunciation by, 139; and European Defense Community Treaty, 212; and Europe of the Six, 105; existing today, 67; French Constitution, abandonment of idea in, 178; and functionalism, 51; of Germany, 48–49, 55, 56, 61, 178, 182, 190–91, 195, 212; joint exercise of, implied in European integration, 219; and nationalism, present, 169; origin of, 3; and peace and freedom, 29; pooling of, necessity for, 110; problem of, 54; relevancy, present, 287; relinquishing, in integration and co-operation, 258–59; restraint, need of, 255; revival of, 61; and Schuman, Adenauer, and De Gasperi, 45; "sovereign equality," in U.N. Charter, 95; supporters of, against supranational body in Atlantic government, 170; and supranationality, 103, 104, 105; surrender of, 134, 253; transfer of, and Churchill on European union, 53; and unification, 54, 68; and United States respect for, 169
Sovereignty. *See under* Sovereign state
Soviet Union. *See* Russia
Spaak, Paul-Henri: 7, 59, 60, 65, 84, 120, 128, 243
"Spaak Report": as basis of Brussels Conference, 71, 133n., and common market, vi, 62, 131, 135; development of, v–vi; and exchange rates, 135; and free trade, 132; future of, 134; Investment Fund, 135; Readaptation Fund for transfer of labor, 135; recommendations of, 131; and tariff system, 134; Venice Conference, 128n.
Spain: 5–6, 12, 14, 15, 22, 44n., 109, 175, 203, 206, 271, 272, 273, 276
Spengler, Oswald: 248
Spheres of influence: 51, 52
Spirit of World Politics, The (William Ernest Hocking): 235, 235n.
Staël, Madame de: 223
Stalin, Joseph: 27, 29, 47, 61, 166, 212, 241, 251

Standardization, in America: 275-76
Status of European Integration, Conference on: v
Storia della Politica Estera Italiana dal 1870 al 1896 (Federico Chabod): 197, 197n.
Story, Joseph: 264
Strauss, David Friedrich: 264
Stresemann, Gustav: 38
Suez crisis, and European integration: vi
Sully, Maximilien de Béthune, Duc de: 18, 82
Supranational authority, body, government, principle, etc. *See under* Supranationality
Supranationality: authority, and coal and steel pool, 51, 56, 127; authority, and free trade in Benelux, 135; body, and Britain, 88, 89; body, and free-trade body, 130; body, term, meaning of, 80; body, transfer to of sovereign powers, 80, 88; character, necessity for in European Community, 219; concept of, 219-20; control, and North Atlantic Treaty Organization, 170; and co-operation, 89, 100, 105; democratic control of, in an integrated Europe, 222-23; and Europe of the Six, 61, 105, 106; of Europe of the Six vs. co-operation of Europe of the Fifteen, 110; and European Coal and Steel Community, 95, 108; 127, 138-40; experience of, in World War II, 50; features, in atomic energy development, 258; and federation, uses of, 109; framework, necessity of, for European integration, 217; government, Anglo-Saxon conception, 39; idea, as Latin, 39; and individual states, 220-21; industry, integration of bodies in, 127; institutions, and Churchill on European union, 53; institutions, and European Coal and Steel Community, 70, 95, 148; institutions, necessity for, 68; institutions, and OEEC, 256; integration and atomic energy, 78; and joint market, 122; level, and European Coal and Steel Community, 68; necessity for, 89; and neutralism after World War II, 211-12; organization, and Jean Monnet, 41; power, in Europe, 51, 69; principle, introduced by European Coal and Steel Community, 224; reconstruction of Europe, 46; and sovereignty, 103, 104, 105; staff of North Atlantic Treaty Organization, 93

Supreme Headquarters Allied Powers Europe (SHAPE): 59, 170, 173
Sweden: 3, 14, 43n.-44n., 102, 109, 265, 270, 271, 275, 276
Switzerland: 24, 25-26, 32, 39, 43n., 50, 270, 275, 281; and common market, 135-36; and integration, 106, 264-65, 266
Sybel, Heinrich von: 271

Talleyrand-Périgord, Charles Maurice de: 16
Tarchiani, Alberto: 208n.
Tariffs. *See under* Trade
Temps Modernes: 207
Theogony (Hesiod): 11
Thermidor (French Revolution): 166
Thierry, Augustin: 23
Thiers, Louis Adolphe: 271
Thompson, Benjamin: 265
Tinbergen, Jan: 98
Tocqueville, Alexis de: 34, 274, 279
Totalitarianism: 30, 40, 52, 163-64, 246
Toynbee, Arnold: 83
Trade (*see also* Common market, Free trade): British and French, comparison of, 280-81; cartels, elimination of, 129; currency, and customs tariffs, 118-19, 122, 123; customs tariffs, effect of integration on, 91; customs tariffs and quotas, elimination, 73, 75 (*see also* OEEC, *infra*); customs unions, 82, 101, 108, 123, 133, 259-60; economic integration, effect on, 126; and economic integration, goal of, 139-40; exports, in a united Europe, 154-55; free-trade system and reconversion fund, 134-35; GATT, 96, 118, 250, 256, 286; high-tariff area, danger as closed shop, 96; import duties, effect of economic integration on, 91; imports, in a united Europe, 152, 155-56, 157; most-favored-nation clause, 259; OEEC, competence of, 117; OEEC, role in elimination of restrictions, 117, 126; and payments, suppression of restrictions, 107, 131; in pre-World War I period, 131-32; preferential tariffs, 134; prices, double standard, 140; protective measures in a united Europe, 152; quotas, 66, 73, 75, 118, 132, 145, 154; quantitative, 96, 117, 126, 132, 140; sterling area, 282, 283-84; tariffs, lowering of, 75; and tax frontiers, 121; transport tariffs, discriminatory, 73; United States and Britain, contrasted,

INDEX

279–80; world, expansion and liberation of, 111
Trade unions: 162, 163, 182, 183, 187, 188
Transport, European Conference of Ministers of: 84, 116
Transportation: community, usefulness of, 109; international, and European Coal and Steel Community, 140; laws, and joint market, 123; planes, construction in Europe, 65; restriction of, in a united Europe, 152; and sectoral integration, 146; tariffs, and OEEC, 73
Treitschke, Heinrich von: 271
Trieste, settlement of dispute over: 32, 47
Truman Doctrine: 253
Tucholski, Kurt: 199
Turgot, Anne Robert Jacques: 265
Turkey, and Greece: 33, 253

Unification, European (*see also* Integration): and agricultural production, 154; as answer to threat of communism, 165–66; of Britain with Europe, 41; and Churchill, 53–54; commercial relations and world co-operation, 157; concept of, and rearmament of Germany, 180; economic consequences thereof, 150–51, 157–58; eighteenth-century concept of, 21–22; and Enlightenment, 265–66; of Europe of the Six, 107, 128; and European Coal and Steel Community, 56, 57; and exports and imports, 154–56; and federal powers, 70; and federalists, 57, 61, 63, 68; and functionalism vs. federalism, 51; and Germany, 49; idea of, development, 18–20; of Italy, 74; labor, use, 74; and Monnet, 70; movement, 42, 43; and national party systems, 165; and nationalism, origins of, 22–23; and necessary internal economic policy changes, 151–52; need for, 34, 86; and North America and Europe, industrial disparity between, 153–54; in political literature of the Continent, 37; and protective measures in world trade, 152–53; and reorientation of industrial traffic, 155, 156–57; Saint-Simon and Thierry, proposal for, 23; supranational, and Catholic parties, 45; sympathy for, 44; term, 98, 137; and United States aid, 61; urgency of problem, 49

unity: and ancient traditions, 1; by conquest, 3; in diversity, ix–x, 31–32, 34, 39; feeling, lack of in Europe today, 215–18; Goethe, survival of spirit in, 22; idea of, 37; and Napoleonic wars, 22; spiritual, of Europe, 98; term, meaning of, 98; in United Kingdom, 31–32; and United States example, 26; after World War II, 42
Union Européenne des Fédéralistes: 50
United Kingdom. *See* Great Britain
United Nations: and Britain, 285–86; Churchill on world supremacy of, 242, 242n.; failures of, 252, 287–88; and France, 206; Korean War, 285; mentioned in OEEC Preamble, 81; nonpolitical functions of, 254, 289; as recent invention, 268
United Nations Charter: 95, 241, 244
United Nations Economic Commission for Europe: 142, 236
United Nations Economic and Social Council (ECOSOC): 288
United Nations Educational, Scientific and Cultural Organization (UNESCO): 267
United Nations General Assembly: 252
United Nations Relief and Rehabilitation Administration (UNRRA): 236
United States: aid to Europe, 31, 58, 61, 83, 84, 85, 120; anti-communism in, 194; and ANZUS, 285; Arab world, policy toward, 213; as associate member of OEEC, 256, 257; and Atlantic Alliance, 58, 227; and atomic energy, 78; attitude toward European integration, 82; and British role in European integration, 53; and Canadian trade, 284; capitalism in, 129; church and state, separation of, 272–73; civic consciousness in, 172; and a common market, 136; contributions to, from Europe, 263–64; 276–77; and currency convertibility, 260; deception by European statesmen, 48; economic potential, use of in European unification, 83; equalitarianism, 34; European Defense Community, support of, 127; as example of independence for Asia and Africa, 245; as example of integration, 50, 220, 262–63, 266, 277–78; as example of unity in diversity, 26; export trade, 280; federal projects and United States sovereignty, 39; first federal constitution, 39; free internal market, size of, 102; and Germany, 55, 58, 193, 194, 202, 238; government, and invention of term *economic integration*, 98; and Great Britain, contrasted, 279–80; 289–90; and imperial-

ism, 267; and industry, 65–66, 67, 260, 280; influence, force of, 87–88; Interstate Commerce Commission, 150; and Jacobin mind, 48; leadership of, and economic integration, 132; and Marshall Plan, 209–10; the military, significance in, 270; military protection, importance to Europe, 58; as nation of joiners, 274; and nationalism, 168; 169, 268–69, 271–72; and Paris Agreements, 189; political system, contrasted to British, 289, 290; problems of, in common with Europe, 81; and Saragat, 208n.; standardization in, 275–76; and strengthening Europe, 242; success of unification in, reasons for, 267–68; as super-state, 260–61; technical assistance, 157; trade, 279–80; and Truman Doctrine, 253; United Nations, dominant role in, 236; world status of, 25, 46, 174, 242
United States Congress: 253
United States Senate, and Vandenberg resolution: 252
Universal Declaration of Human Rights: 236
Universal Postal Union: 288
Universalism: 22
Ural Mountains: 1, 13, 125

Vandenberg, Arthur: 252
Van Zeeland, Paul: 7
Venice Conference: 128n., 133n.
Versailles, Treaty of: 18, 28
Vienna Congress: 16
Vierteljahrshefte für Zeitgeschichte: 185
Völkische Beobachter: 29
Voltaire, François Marie, on liberty: 22
Voyenne, Bernard: 11n., 18

Walloons: 265, 266
War of 1812: 270
War of Independence (United States): 270
Ward, Barbara: 244, 244n.
Warsaw: 16, 167n.
Washington, D. C.: 118–19, 208n., 236
Washington Foreign Ministers Conference: 242
Wehrmacht: 171, 183, 184
Weimar Republic: 185
Weisenborn, G.: 186
Welsh and Scottish Nationalism (Reginald Coupland): 31
West, Benjamin: 265
Westphalia, Peace of: 3
Western European Union: 116, 190, 212, 258
Wilberforce, William: 264
William II: 200, 203
Wilson, Woodrow: 28, 199, 200n., 201–202, 202n.
Workers' Party (Belgium): 172–73
World Health Organization (WHO): 288
World Indivisible (Konrad Adenauer): 238
World War I, humanitarian justification of, as cause of World War II: 200–201

Yalta agreements: 47, 51, 52
"Young Europe": (Giuseppe Mazzini) 19

Zeus; Homeric epithet for, 11; in myth of Europa, 231, 232, 233, 234
Zurich: 53, 83, 272